# My Country Is Literature

# My Country Is Literature

Chandrahas Choudhury

London · New York · Sydney · Toronto · New Delhi

First published in India by Simon & Schuster India, 2021


This edition published in 2021



1 3 5 7 9 10 8 6 4 2

Simon & Schuster India
818, Indraprakash Building,
21, Barakhamba Road,
New Delhi 110001

www.simonandschuster.co.in

HB ISBN: 978-93-92099-10-6
eBook ISBN: 978-93-92099-11-3

Typeset in India by SÜRYA, New Delhi

Printed and bound in India by Replika Press Pvt. Ltd.

*For Suni and Marni: you are my world*

*For my late father Rahas Bihari Choudhury (1951-2002): here is a book for all the books you bought me*

*For my teachers at Hindu College, Delhi and Trinity College, Cambridge, who showed me how to live in literature. With particular gratitude to those gone too soon: the late Dr Lalita Subbu and Sunil Dua*

*To three bookshops that were an essential part of my literary education: Galloway & Porter, Cambridge; Strand Book Stall, Mumbai; and the pavement booksellers of Flora Fountain, Mumbai.*

# CONTENTS

## PART TWO

# INTRODUCTION

## The Books of My Twenties, or, How I Became A Literary Critic

So much that grows to fruition in life begins with a stroke of luck, a door that opens at exactly the right moment. In the summer of 2002, I was a literature student at Cambridge, just finished with my undergraduate degree and with only a hazy idea of my immediate future. Partly, this was because my exam result was not good enough—something that would be hard to explain to my father—to ensure scholarship funds for another year in Cambridge's very competitive environment. And partly it was because my father himself—for whom my scholarship to Cambridge two years previously had been, by a process of parental appropriation both disarming and disturbing, the greatest achievement of his life—lay battling for his life in a hospital bed back home in Delhi. The desperate facts of his situation were not completely clear to me, for my family had decided, considerately, that full exposure to the truth would disrupt my focus on my finals. But now I knew he was much more badly off than I had suspected. One morning, as I prepared to fly home, I made the long walk to the Cambridge Student Union to buy a new phone card with which to call Delhi. It was a beautiful summer's day, but I did not have the eyes for it. I was worried about the future—my father's, and with the intense self-involvement and copious self-pity of youth, my own. I was going home. Would I ever return? I wasn't sure I was prepared for adult life in India.

As I stood in the shop waiting to be served, I espied on its noticeboard, amidst the vivid fliers for lectures, seminars and plays, a white A4 sheet of plain text:

BOOK REVIEWERS WANTED
Paid Opportunity
If interested, please email: ********@aol.com

Someone out there wanted *book reviews*?

These words sparked in me a rush of hope—even a sense that there was someone above watching out for me, dangling a straw for me to clutch at. Walking home, the email address copied out on the back of a bookshop receipt, I began to feel that, even if I were to leave my precious, newly forged life in England behind forever, I would still on the flight home have in my head a vague map for my future and a road, however tenuous, to a livelihood.

For if there was one thing that I felt capable of doing and that actually chimed with my ambitions, it was writing book reviews. I had begun taking the genre, so often synonymous with mediocrity and hackwork, low pay and backscratching, seriously only after arriving in England. There had been nothing about my teenage years in India to attract me to it. But at Cambridge, even as I spent my work hours decoding the prosody of Shakespeare's verse, wrestling with the somewhat alarming implications of the Dionysian instinct in Greek tragedy, and finding intellectually credible rather than reflexively dismissive rebuttals of Roland Barthes's idea of the death of the author (which, wanting to be a writer myself, I could not in any form or fashion endorse), I found myself more drawn to another literary world.

This was the parallel system of vivid, trenchant, 12 or 15-paragraph book reviews published in the British broadsheets, in stand-alone supplements dedicated completely to literature and thereby proclaiming its independence from—even its precedence over—other sectors of life like Food, Money and Travel.

Literary journalism seemed to me the most inviting room in the house of literature and literary study. It was a space where depth and breadth each had their place. My professors, while significant names in their field, were by and large specialists—indeed, happy to be thought of as such. No matter what their private reading tastes, professionally they had traded continents for islands. Or perhaps the very purpose of their existence was to investigate islands—the literary revolution of the Romantic poets, every detail of the novels of Trollope and their links to every detail to his life, gender-bending in Shakespeare, the tropes of postcolonial literature—in such depth that they became continents. But some of the names that popped up regularly in the pages of *The Guardian* literary review, novelists, poets and playwrights, career academics and journalists, wrote with great poise and panache about a novel one month, biography the next, history the next. Much in the same way as I worked, with an entry-level literary receptor and decidedly banal results, on tragedy one term, the modern novel the next, and American literature the third....

My new dreams and desires—the first sense of vocation that I had felt as an adult—were also closely connected with the World Wide Web, then still a new and wonderful and scarce resource in human life and not the fundamental human right and all-enveloping force, ubiquitous as the air, that it is today. The previous winter, my second in England, I had been able to afford a second-hand laptop ('refurbished,' in the parlance of the time), which allowed me to write my student essays from the comfort of my own digs instead of the student computer room.

Not only did this let me wear a holey T-shirt and pick my nose while I worked, it also, crucially, allowed me unlimited reading time at all hours of the day. (Then, as now, it was more glamorous to read online than off the grid, giving the brain little hits of news, or just hyperlink drifting.) During the Christmas vacation, when most students went home and Cambridge was cold, silent, and desolate, I stayed up all night surfing the horizonless internet, drinking cups of coppery tea made with circular and tagless Sainsbury's Kenya teabags, boiled up Indian style with milk and water in a saucepan. I found I loved to browse the archives of the book review pages of *The New York Times* by typing in the names of writers who had floated into my consciousness—Tolstoy, Henry Green, Constantine Cavafy, Gabriela Mistral—and reading everything that had been published about them over the decades. And then everything I could find by the writers who had written something interesting about one of them. Everything was something in itself and a link to something else.

This was not the mandated, dutiful reading of an academic syllabus; in this space, every writer had to earn the right to your approbation. Day by day, the literary web in my mind, a mirror of the web of which I was such an enthusiastic votary, expanded with names and notions, ideas and intellectual positions—all the nuances of expressing pleasure or disappointment with the construction of a verbal artifact, all the crisscrossing lines of connection across the centuries, across genres, and between one writer and another. The maths student Alexander Ritter, a sureshot candidate for a Cambridge First, alerted me to Arts and Letters Daily[1], a web portal recently set up by two academics in New Zealand that linked daily to three essays in the humanities published across periodicals around the world. Here were debated, at a higher voltage than in the dense tomes of literary criticism that I pored over for my student essays, the problems and possibilities of modernism and postmodernism, first and third-person narration, the hermeneutics of suspicion and the biographical fallacy, alongside powerful manifestoes, critiques and broadsides on history, politics and economics.[2]

Now this sort of reading, to me, was progress. I knew I wanted eventually to be a writer of novels. But the path to this goal lay obscured by my callowness, by the total indifference of time and fate to my desires. But while time and fate got their tardy act together, it seemed incredible that one could contemplate making a living by being a jobbing writer, applying

---

[1] www.aldaily.com, still going strong twenty years later.

[2] In all of this, I sometimes neglected the reading of books. I have been trying to make up ever since.

not so much a system as a self, a sensibility, a cup of tea and a biscuit, to the reading of books.

And so, as I prepared to go back home to India, disconsolate and full of self-pity, I had this one consolation.

Someone out there wanted book reviews and was ready to pay for them.

SUCH WERE THE circumstances, both hopeful and grim, in which I began life as a literary critic. Five years later, when I was writing 70 book reviews and literary essays a year and making a modest but spiritually fulfilling living in Mumbai entirely from piecework in literature, I had reason to be profoundly thankful to the shadowy patron who had set me off in the line with hard cash for literary analysis.

The mysterious man who replied to my email identified only as 'Khaled.' He laid out the terms (decidedly unusual) of what I was expected to do. I could pick any recently published book from a prominent press to review, although I was expected to have it approved first. The next instruction was somewhat unusual. I was expected to compose *two* reviews of the book: one an enormous one, almost *London Review of Books* length, of 3,000 words, and the other an abridged version of 1,000 words. These I was to send him on email.

For each piece that was accepted I would be paid a hundred pounds. Which was almost a hundred pounds more than anybody had paid me for anything so far in my life.[3]

But what would happen to my pieces after that? (I was, understandably, very keen to see my name in print and join the ranks of my journalistic heroes.) Here, the mystery deepened. All that Khaled would say was that they were syndicated to different international publications, mostly in the Middle East.

[3] For two months in the summer vacation after my BA in Delhi, I worked as an intern in an advertising agency on a stipend of ₹2500 a month. My contribution to the firm was so meagre that when one day I broke the news that I had got my scholarship to Cambridge and would soon be leaving, nobody was more delighted than the boss.

Certainly, I never found them online. But it was early in the Internet Age and many publications still did not have full-service websites. There could be much that appeared in print that never made it to the web. Perhaps they were even being published without my by-line. But what did it matter? It was the work that interested me—both the intellectual exercise in a time of drought, and the promised pay, which gave me a sense of control over my life. Three months later, when I did return to Cambridge for what would be a final year at university doing an M.Phil, I already had my sights set on life after the academy. I would use the year, I resolved, to set up as a literary journalist, a cross between a bibliophile and a small entrepreneur. While in India, I had already pitched a book to Khaled. Over a week I had diligently ground out 3,000 words about it, then cut and restitched my piece to 1,000 words and sent them in. Big brother, little brother. It was approved.

And my money? Payment, Khaled promised, would soon arrive in the post when I returned to England. It would be difficult for him to post a cheque all the way to India.

I returned to England with great hopes. Every day, after lunch, I went to check my 'pigeonhole': a small compartment assigned to each student in the college mail room where letters bearing your name were deposited. But there was nothing. I wrote to Khaled. He assured me the promised piece of paper was on its way.

One day, just when I was beginning to lose hope, I found the promised envelope lying in my pigeonhole like a golden egg. Inside I found a cheque, drawn on a British bank, for a hundred pounds.

It was not the first money I had ever earned, but it was worth ten times its face value. Even today, it feels like the invisible hand that opened the door of the house of literature and said, *You may come in.*

BEYOND THE STRAIGHTFORWARD truth that I was not good for anything else (except perhaps writing about cricket), there were many reasons why literary criticism suited my nature and my circumstances. Like most people who love literature, I had been bookish and introverted from my childhood. Books were a retreat from the stresses of the world and an advance into a realm of pleasure and progress. They were validated by life itself, which bestowed certain rewards and opportunities for studying them well: not just books of practical value like textbooks, but even, eventually, works of literature.

But until I went to university in Delhi I always read in a voracious, unsystematic, undiscriminating way (valuable in its own right, perhaps, as a childhood base to a succeeding superstructure). I thrilled to stories and poems without being able to explain why, and was happy to accord equal weight on the scales of literary pleasure to Hermann Hesse and James Hadley Chase. In other words, I fit the classic profile of what Orhan Pamuk describes in one of his books as the naive reader.

It was only at university that the relationship between literature and literary study, the deep past of literature and the way it flowed into the present, became clear to me, and the world of literary criticism and its possibilities opened up. Here was a new stage in the reading life, requiring the disenchantment, in a technical sense, of the naive reader.

But at the same time, I found I could go only so far in aligning myself with the values of those newly prominent readers ('critics') who broke down a text, almost like a doctor studying a blood sample, or interrogated it in the light of one or other kind of literary theory. Often, it seemed to me, they took an object of delight and clothed it from top to toe in interpretation's soporofic drone. To be sure, there were those critics who added a glow to, a pathway into, the writer's work; but more often they wrestled it down as if dealing with an excitable dog, as if literature was for them only a stop on the road and the purpose of literary criticism explicitly to disarm enchantment.

After some years of touring this world, watching and reflecting, sometimes participating in its discourse, watching and reflecting some more, I reached my own version of the middle path. It was a position that acknowledged the claims of both rigour and rapture. A certain kind of essay, taking pleasure in the texture and traditions of literary language; privileging the majesty and mystery of the creative impulse over the role of historical and material forces in the production of art; aware that if characters in a novel or poem are not real people, they nevertheless inhabit another order of reality and their decisions and dilemmas can be the source of the most sophisticated kinds of moral inquiry; and implicitly always asking on behalf of the reader, 'Is this book worth my time?' and 'Are the aesthetic decisions made in the narration convincing ?'—this was the sort of essay that I loved to read and aspired to write.

It had become apparent to me, in other words, that literary criticism was not just a response to literature. It could itself be literature. Far from being purely an expression of an analytical sensibility, literary criticism can be the expression of the creative instinct by another means—in fact, an especially generous expression of the human spirit, for it bestows close and often complimentary attention, for little or no reward, to the work of another writer. (One slanted but perfectly valid definition of a literary critic is someone who uses up his or her best sentences in the service of someone else's books.) I loved it when a literary critic testified to the literary equivalent of gooseflesh—when he or she pointed out the radiance of a metaphor, brought out the ingenuity of a juxtaposition, or highlighted the subterranean play and progression of a leitmotif. Each time I absorbed one of these points, the space inside my head for literature seemed to become more charged and my capacity for generalisation from the absorption of disparate particulars increased. Literature, after all, does not—cannot—should not—explain its own moves and methods. If it did so it would never have the intensity and ambiguity, the swiftness and the slyness, that are the primary sources of delight in literature. Writers desperately needed readers, not just in the sense in which I had understood it in the past—as buyers who created a market and a literary culture—but in the sense of adepts who, almost as lovers understand the nuances of every pause in each other's speech and every cadence of their phrases, could bring to the text a higher, almost religious sense of its force and feeling. A book reviewer was one such figure, making a mark piece by piece, coming to each book, as a scientist might do, with a provisional theory of literature and allowing it to be transformed or modified in the light of new evidence. Because of his or her amateur status and because of the nature of the profession—deadlines, precarity, the play of chance in the arrival of assignments, the wanton destruction wrought by copy editors who had their own crosses to bear—little of what he or she wrote would survive the erosive effect of time. But this at least was the aim: to become, for every half-worthy book that came your way, the sort of reader the writer had dreamt of (or, in the case of very bad books, dreaded).

Just as importantly, walking this road, one could learn to be both a reader and a writer—and not just a writer of literary criticism. Book reviewing was not only the most vital part of my present, then, it was where my past and my future lined up in a fulfilling, inspiriting way. I cherished the feeling of agency it gave me as a reader, the sense that I was doing something almost as active in making a report of my reading as the writer had done in making a book to be read. There is a world of difference between reading and reading with a pencil in hand, waiting to attack the printed page with marginalia, however callow, and thoughtful lines and arrows. There is always the suspicion of something self-indulgent about reading for pleasure. But done this way, copying out words, sentences, and paragraphs into the blank pages at the back of the book, reading was work. And if attention be seen as a form of worship, then it was worship too.

In literary criticism, then, lay for me in my early twenties the experience of pleasure and power, duty and discovery, literary apprenticeship and literary communion: the book not as a fixed artefact, written up and spoken for, but a continuously repeated and renewed event co-created by writer and reader. The book reviewer was both a reader of writers and a writing reader: his work dramatised this encounter. As I tapped out the sentences and paragraphs[4] for Khaled on the novelistic reportage of Joseph Mitchell, Karen Armstrong's life of the Buddha, and Amin Maalouf's meditations on human identity, I took great pleasure in the hum inside my head.

In fact, what I liked the most was that with every sentence I wrote that supplied a poised paraphrase or ventured a confident judgment, I felt ever further from the gauche young student floundering in the murky waters of literary study who had answered to my name as recently as three years ago, memorising entire essays, painstakingly written but entirely derivative, to be regurgitated on the thin, forgiving foolscap pages of a Delhi examination hall in the heat of April. I needed no more degrees to attest to my progress or prove to the world that I deserved employment or respect. I had been set free to travel where I pleased. My country was literature.

LIKE ALL COUNTRIES, literature makes certain demands of its working class, adjusted to their peculiar circumstances and ambitions. A manual for the aspiring book reviewer would counsel the reader to nurture all manner of disparate traits. The idealism hymned in constitutions and national anthems; the sanguinity and smarts of the street vendor; opportunism and the ability to conceal desperation. A good prose style, supported by a good style in writing unsolicited letters that are then never answered.

In my case, I had already gratefully received from literature an organising centre for my life; now I also needed from it a living. Even as I churned out an essay a month for Khaled, I became newly ambitious. (Remember, I had yet to see any of my essays in print.) I continued to study—much more closely than the poetic effusions of Walt Whitman, the subject of my MPhil dissertation—the book review pages of the great newspapers and magazines of the Anglophone world, especially America: not just the venerable *Times*, but the *Washington Post* (which had

[4] Then, as now, with two fingers—some things never progress.

two book reviewers, Jonathan Yardley and Michael Dirda, who wrote a piece every week), the *London Review of Books, The New York Review of Books*, the *New Republic*, and in particular *The New Criterion*, an American monthly whose arts pages were as full of vivid writing and lofty feeling as its political section was a catalogue of white-supremacist small-mindedness and spleen. Many of these journals had the email addresses of their books editors listed on their websites. In view of my impending break from the sanctuary of the university—which I had once feared but, I now found, I was now impatient to inaugurate—I took to writing an email every week to one such editor. I would introduce myself (saying that I was a student of literature at Cambridge, which was a help), attach some clips of my work for Khaled, and ask for a commission.

One day, I landed a break. Early in 2003, I received a reply from the books editor of the *Washington Post,* saying he'd enjoyed reading what I'd sent him. Would I be interested in reviewing a new book by the journalist Riccardo Orizio on his encounter with several dictators?

Would I indeed!

I remember the parcel from America arriving in my pigeonhole—a work assignment from across the Atlantic. Till then, I had not realised that publishers sent out not books but galleys, resembling the cheap and tatty cribs perused by Delhi University students, bound in soft covers in colours reminiscent of the folders my parents used to bring home from their jobs in the Life Insurance Corporation of India. But here was one more milestone in my upward progress in the republic of letters. While still a student, I had turned pro. When my review came out, I was able to read it on the internet: the same internet where for so long I had pored over the reviews of others, studying their openings and transitions the way a chess player might, copying out their best sentences.

Another envelope soon arrived in the post with a print copy of *Book World*, the Post's books supplement. It was the first time I could see my name in print in a major publication: a moment no writer ever forgets. And not only was this wonderful for my self-esteem, it also boosted my standing among my classmates in my MPhil in American Literature, some of whom were American. Suddenly there was a gap between me and them (although some of them had much greater ability than I). Their work was read by academics; mine by the reading public.

A few days later, another parcel arrived unannounced from the *Post*: a shining new hardback edition of the book I had reviewed. So they did give you the real book after all!

A few days later, another envelope arrived, this time with a cheque for $350: the final step in the ritual traffic of books, words, newspapers and money that go into the writing of a book review.

Three hundred and fifty dollars for reading and writing about a book! Life, often so unjust, was sometimes much too generous.

I AM KEEN to emphasise the role of money, to record the exact sums of money that trade hands in the writing life. Although there is plenty of great literature about the place of money in human affairs, the money *in* literature is so rarely discussed. Details of a writer's income rise to the surface mostly when a writer suddenly bags a big advance or a prize, thus escaping the overlapping states of quiet penury, resentment plain or disguised, or stubborn resilience in which most other writers labour over their work, knowing that they will never make a living from writing. Naturally, those writers who do are loath to reveal much about how they do it, for fear of exciting jealousy—or pity, for some of the sums involved are derisory.[5] True, literature gives its votaries a different sort of wealth: the enchantment of words and ideas, the sense of independence and agency, aesthetic rapture on tap (especially when one is young) and a defence against life's buffetings. But none of this

[5] Until one realises that even the most modest income from writing is about the same as that made by a domestic, a waiter, or a plumber. If they can live on such sums, so should a writer.

means anything without a basic income and the self-respect and security it provides, especially when all around you are telling you that you are worth so more than what you have settled for.

I had no one to turn to for advice in this matter. But many jobbing writers before me, I knew (from having read a few memoirs of the sort that I am myself now composing) had stitched together a modest living from literary journalism. And that, after a brief stint in Bombay as a cricket writer, was now my aim.

As it happened, it would be more than a decade before I wrote for the *Post* again, and several years before I made as much as $350—for long, my private benchmark of big money—for a single piece. I thought I was now in business, but I was wrong. Work from Khaled soon dried up, just as mysteriously as it had begun. One day he wrote to say that he was temporarily suspending operations, and (in the euphemism preferred by editors everywhere) would be back in touch as soon as he resumed. So, back home in Bombay, I had to turn my eyes to the domestic market.

This was a considerable comedown. The going rate in Indian newspapers for book reviews was ₹1,000 to 2,500 for a piece. Payment arrived, I discovered, many months after publication, and sometimes not at all; in chasing it down, one sometimes wrote many more words than one had done for the assignment itself. But thankfully work was—unsurprisingly, given the terms of the trade—in plentiful supply. There were great books being published all the time. I had a new education to give myself in the literature of my own country (to which I had paid scant attention in my teens). And for a few years I had a roof over my head in my mother's flat in Bombay. Here were circumstances still favourable enough for literary enterprise.

Often, the space allotted to book reviews in Indian newspapers was modest—the surest sign in journalism of a subject's marginal status. Six hundred words was seen as being quite enough room to cover all the important aspects of a work. But the restrictions of space taught concision and focus in writing, and the supply of free books compensated for the meagre pay. Besides, the sudden mushrooming of a literary subculture of personal weblogs ('blogs') also provided an escape from the constrictions of the formal book review and the mainstream media. I entered this realm under the benign supervision of one of the great influences on my life in my twenties, the Mumbai writer Amit Varma, first encountered during my two-year stint in the offices of Cricinfo, where his desk was exactly across the aisle from mine. All day long we exchanged snippets of conversation about cricket, American journalism, novels, Bombay, and the meaning of freedom both in the standard and—a Varma pet cause—libertarian sense of the word, while after 5 pm, when restrictions were lifted, we tussled with bat and rubber ball in ferocious 'Test' matches down the very same corridor, thereby spending our day across the two axes of a sort of cross. My literary weblog, The Middle Stage (http://middlestage.blogspot.com) is actually a space that he had set up, created a readership for, and then generously conceded once I had written a few guest posts on it.

From around 2005, then, for about five years I began to post essays on literature every few days (some of which are in this book), today something on Boccaccio's *Life of Dante*, tomorrow something on Chekhov, then an analysis of scene in a novel by Shirshendu Mukhopadhyay, then a comparative study of tigers in the poetry of William Blake and the Odia poet Salabaga. No commissions or permissions were required. No payment was involved. It was just an exploration of the possibilities of a form and a medium. Soon there appeared an audience for this sort of work—not huge, plateauing at about 150 visitors and 300 page views a day—but thrilling to a young writer seeking to make a mark. Blog posts were a wonderfully liberating form, linking directly to the platonic ideal of the essay.[6] Nothing stopped you from quoting a 300-word paragraph to establish a point

[6] There is much to regret in their being superseded today by pellets of Twitter-thought and the effusions of Instagram, although one might also detect their coming back into vogue from the amount of good writers trying to monetise their work on Substack.

about another writer's style, or from finding an obscure book published 50 years ago and giving it the once-over. For many years, until just after I published my first novel in 2009, The Middle Stage was the literary project dearest to my heart, my own garden in the virtual world.

Meanwhile, trickles of work kept coming in from abroad (those parcels of galleys, those promptly issued cheques that now took months to process, because they had to be sent by my bank all the way back to America). Every few weeks, I lobbed a petition into the inbox of some editor at a newspaper or magazine.

*From: Chandrahas Choudhury <chandrahas.choudhury@gmail.com>*
*Date: Mon, Jan 3, 2005 at 3:32 PM*
*Subject: A query*

*To: <erica.wagner@thetimes.co.uk>*

*Dear Ms. Wagner,*

*Would you have room on the pages of the* Times *for a reviewer of novels, especially novels in translation?*

*I'm a writer living in Mumbai, India, where I work at cricket journalism, book reviews, and my own stories. I did English at university (I graduated from Cambridge in 2003) and during my years in England I developed a great love for the novel form, and began to work at reviews of novels. My work been published so far in the* Washington Post, The Scotsman, *and the* San Francisco Chronicle, *but never, curiously, in a British newspaper, so I'd like any work you could offer me.*

*Here are some reviews I've published in the last six months: pieces on Orhan Pamuk's* Snow, *MG Vassanji's* The In-Between World of Vikram Lall, *and Sandor Marai's* Casanova in Bolzano.

*I hope to hear back from you soon,*
*Yours,*
*Chandrahas*

This particular letter was, like so many others I sent out, never answered. Perhaps the Global Network of Book-Review Editors had put out a red alert about me. Even so, it reveals I had already built up some useful contacts who kept my life going with two or three commissions a year. I was now sailing a small schooner on the seas of world literature: nothing very dramatic, but nonetheless a pleasing state of motion and emotion.

And sometimes editors did write back. There's nothing sweeter to a book reviewer, in the years of his or her apprenticeship, than a reply from an editor in some faraway land. This one letter, often no longer than a couple of sentences, activates a whole world of agency and optimism, an entire universe of past pleasures that will now once again be reprised. Days spent in an armchair or recumbent under lamplight (in literature you do your writing at a desk, your reading lying down); notes to be made and then the piece to be composed and polished; you send off your piece and wait for comments or edits, then work on it one more time; your work appears neatly laid out in a newspaper or magazine, at which point you read it again to see if it stands up to scrutiny. All these visions loom in the sights of the worker bees of literature—which every writer should at some point, I believe, endeavour to bee.

But hold on…wait a second! There's a word missing from my piece. This isn't what I said! I've got to take this up with the editor.

*From: Chandrahas Choudhury <chandrahas.choudhury@gmail.com>*
*Date: Mon, June 4, 2007 at 2:18 PM*
*Subject: Modestly!*

*To: <robert.mccrum@observer.co.uk>*

*Hi Robert,*

*Modestly!—the whole point of the piece, I think, was that the book was modestly good. With that word cut out of the last sentence, it felt as if I'd overpraised it.*

*Yours,*
*Chandrahas*

*From: Robert McCrum <robert.mccrum@observer.co.uk>*
*Date: Mon, June 4, 2007 at 2:35 PM*
*Subject: Re: Modestly!*

*To: <chandrahas.choudhury@gmail.com>*

*No, with the word cut out you made your point well, and not too pompously.*

*As published, it was a good review.*

*Thank you.*
*RMcC*

Well…what can one say? Oscar Villalon of the *San Francisco Chronicle*, Stuart Kelly at *The Scotsman*, the legendary Robert McCrum of *The Observer* (despite the above disagreement, one of the most generous and thoughtful of my employers till he left the post in 2008), Michael Prodger of the *Sunday Telegraph*: these became the presiding angels of my literary business, the ones who were in my sights as I scoured the publishers' catalogues for the new season's novels and added titles to my list of 'forthcoming books' saved as a draft in Gmail. A 'yes' from any one of them meant that the cowries I was earning from the Indian side of my work could be topped up with a little splash, a warming tinkle, of dollars or pounds; $165 was the going rate at the *Chronicle*, £100 at *The Scotsman*, perhaps £150 at *The Observer*. Sometimes I wrote to all of them in a row about the same soon-to-be-published book, beginning with the highest-paying journalistic market and then going down the list. Once you have agreed, in choosing a life in literature, that money is not the most important thing in life, money is thereon of the greatest importance.

These small sums, erratically forthcoming, did very little for my worldly prospects, including my romantic ones. Had they constituted my salary at a newspaper or magazine, I would have been greatly despondent and resentful. But being the pearls of self-employment, they were worth much more than could be calculated by a narrowly economistic measure. They underwrote my freedom and independence, my sense of self-worth and mission, my mornings wandering around on buses and trains, my afternoon naps. They protected me as much from indulgence in bars and restaurants and other sites of conspicuous consumption[7] as they did from the horror—the deepest, most dispiriting note of my life for the two years that I worked for a cricket magazine—of being a drudge in an office, a servant of clock and contract. And they allowed me to sleep soundly at night—often after a long stint of reading—and to wake up late in the morning. Surely that was as much as one could reasonably ask from a trade and wage? Between the age of 25 to 30, when most young people seek to rise swiftly in worldly post and station, I never submitted my CV anywhere, making almost a fetish of my independence. I rarely left Bombay. I lived as frugally as possible. From the books arriving at my door from different parts of the world and the life of the city around me, I tried to keep myself going on the book-review–literary-criticism axis and—what was much more challenging and often frustrating—to learn in parallel how to be an artist in my own right.[8] I kept my nose to the wheel. There were few other prospects for a satisfying life in literature other than the path I had taken. Of course, there were other prospects and jobs available in journalism. But the cost would be too great. Taking them up would mean accepting that literature was not the most important thing in my life, but merely a pleasurable sideshow, a hobby, a road followed halfway and then abandoned. The best way to evade these difficult questions was to always have an assignment in hand, a deadline to meet,

---

[7] For a few years the generous households of Amit Varma and his wife Jasmine, and the writer Sonia Faleiro and her partner Ulrik and their dog Zoey, were my principal source of alcoholic refreshment, garnished with trade gossip and commentary on each other's most recent blog posts. A big thank you to you all. More about them and the place of alcohol in the literary life can be found in my essay, not reprinted here, 'The Drinking Companions of My Twenties.'

[8] In art as in life, the time lag between right realization and right action is often considerable.

a paragraph to compose, a question to ask oneself about form, linguistic register, narrative structure, or whether to get up or continue lying down a bit longer.

(So consumed with books were my twenties that for the longest time I thought of calling this book *The Books of My Twenties.* For that is usually the most formative decade in the life of any writer or reader: shaping one's taste and aesthetic values, giving pleasure and insight beyond measure, a touchstone on the path to true selfhood, opening out a course that then often leaves literature behind as it swerves towards life.)

LATE IN 2006, word reached me that the Hindustan Times group was starting a new business newspaper, *Mint.* It would have a weekend edition, *Lounge,* with TWO WHOLE PAGES devoted to books. Here was my chance to rise up a couple of notches. I wrote to the editor of *Lounge*—the veteran journalist and to this day arguably the most readable columnist in India, Priya Ramani—not with the usual request to review books, but asking to be appointed the paper's weekly book reviewer, turning in a piece for publication every Saturday. I think the letter was met with some bemusement. But my reputation was in good shape, and to an editor the prospect of seeing a tricky slot filled up in an entire edition of feature writing must have had some appeal. And so I was appointed: not given a job or a contract, exactly, but told that I would be paid ₹15,000 for four pieces a month—or five in the four months that had five Saturdays. Minus tax deducted at source, my salary came to ₹13,500—the first time my Indian work would pay more than my subterranean trade in world literature.

The new work did more than just provide financial security. It gave me a focus. For the first time, I had a position in and a responsibility to *Indian* literature: the work in fiction, reportage, biography, and history being produced by my countrymen, including new translations of novelists who had worked in Indian languages other than English in the past century. Now my *country* was literature, in a different sense than before. And

I had new perks. For the first time, I could choose, rather than merely propose, what books I thought worth reviewing (with a little oversight from Priya and her cheerful deputy Sanjukta Sharma, who had a much stronger sense of the pulse of the audience i.e., I would not be allowed to write pieces about obscure novelists from the erstwhile Soviet Union more than once a year). As and when the new Rushdie or the new Naipaul, or a new book on Gandhi or Nehru, came out, writing about them smartly and readably, sometimes by reading 400 pages a day if a deadline was tight, was my responsibility. Leaving out science and economics, I was responsible for all major new releases. This meant that I needed to brush up bigtime and rapidly on my South Asian history and politics—a delightful prospect, legitimising large new consignments of book purchases from the pavement bookstalls of Flora Fountain, the real finishing school of every Bombay writer.

Just as pleasant were the new rituals of my book-reviewing life. Once a week, I would take the train from distant Borivali (from late 2009 onwards, when I moved into the first rented apartment of my own, a bus from nearby Prabhadevi) to Dadar. A walk across the long overbridge brought me almost directly to the doorstep of the *Mint* office in Dadar East, where all the new books from the publishers would have arrived and be piled up on Sanjukta's desk, pleading to be reviewed. Between us, we would settle on a winner of the week's affections. I would throw the new title into my shoulder bag, and several others as well—a book reviewer's perk, and one that should never be denied them.

Later that evening, after seeing my girlfriend—like me a struggling artist, who lived on the other side of town from me in south Bombay; ours was, in Bombay terms, a long-distance relationship—I would commence work for the week at the window or door of the train back to Borivali, marking up the pages to the beat of the train totting up the stations. The titles of many of the books I read in those years immediately evoke not their own contents but the humming and clacking of the train cleaving through the city, the white lights in the windows of the shoebox apartment buildings on either side of the tracks, the blank or beaten gazes of people going home after the day's work, run down from year after year of the daily grind. Books had spared me a similar fate.

Sometimes, I would feel the eyes of a co-passenger on me, watching with curiosity and amusement as I made little notes at the back. I would look up; our eyes would meet.

'Preparing for competitive exams?'

'Uh…kind of.'

How could I explain? *I'm hard at work on a book review!*

A BOOK IS only one text, but it is many books. It is a different book for each of its readers. My *Anna Karenina* is not your *Anna Karenina*. Your *Arzee the Dwarf* is not the *Arzee the Dwarf* that I wrote. When we think of a favourite book, we recall not only the shape of the story, the characters who touched our hearts, the texture of the sentences. We recall our own circumstances when we read it: where we bought it (and for how much), what kind of joy or solace it provided, how scenes from the text began to intermingle with scenes from our life,. How it roused us to anger or indignation, or allowed us to make our peace with some great private discord. This is the second life of the book: its life in our life.

In this way a reader comes to *own* a book, in a much deeper sense than mere purchase or possession. When you are a writer, you produce an original work; it is then published in a few thousand copies. But when you are a reader, it is the copy that you possess, bought in a favourite bookshop or in a distant city, marked up, in your handwriting, with the little murmurs of your mind, the pages stained with coffee, ink, or tears, that is the true original of the work, singular and irreplaceable.[9]

---

[9] In 2011, I had the happy privilege of being in conversation with Orhan Pamuk at Jaipur Literature Festival. When we met the day before the event, Pamuk only had copies of the Turkish editions of his novels. Could I bring along my English editions, he asked, so he could read out a few passages from them? This I did. As soon as we finished, there was a small stampede in

This explains the immense charismatic and salvific power of libraries to their owners: a bookcase, a room, a house full of books each with some deep personal association, some already read and representing the pleasures of the past, others yet to be read and symbolising the possibilities of the future. The bibliophile always throws up his hands in astonishment when he brings home a new stash of books and hears, 'But why? You already have so many books you haven't read!' The relationship between the reading of books and their possession, my dear XYZ, is not a functional one. In any case, what the more casual, uncommitted kind of reader never understands is that even a single book—having some relationship to hundreds of books that have come before it, and effecting the germination of hundreds of books to come—is actually already a library.

And just as every book is in a certain sense a library, so too does every library, even one full of the most disparate works, the most diverse genres, have a kind of unity. For any serious reader demands to be judged not by the book currently on the nightstand, but the quality of his or her library, which is in effect his or her autobiography. To own 3,000 books that one is yet to read is a sign of ambition, of taste, a tribute to the one thousand books that one *has* read.

And let's not forget, living is hard work. We desire so much to be our best selves, yet so often fail. We need all the help we can get to work out how to play our hand: some extended experience of the shrewd sagacity of Adam Smith, the moral cussedness of Gandhi, the ecstatic soul force of Gopinath Mohanty, the lapidary worldliness of Irene Nemirovsky, the mystical reveries of Lal Ded and Kabir, the lyrical rationalism of Nehru, the biting sarcasm of Arundhati Roy, the honeyed sensuality of Jorge Amado, the wisdom and long-range

---

the crowd to get to him, whereupon, not without justification, he panicked and took flight. Carrying with him, sadly, my heavily marked-up copy of *My Name Is Red.* When we met the next day, I demanded my Pamuk from Pamuk. He said he couldn't remember what had happened to it. It was lost. I have never been able to buy another copy.

perspective of Lin Yutang and Colin Tudge, the models of self-cultivation in Ngugi Wa Thiong'o and Manoranjan Byapari...I could go on with my impersonation of a library catalogue for another three days. Suffice it to say, the company of books is the company of some of the greatest people who have walked this earth over the last 2,000 years.

Even so, it is a mistake to privilege books over people. But it can take some readers a long time to learn this.

OVER THE SPAN of my 20s, then, literary criticism became both home and the world for me, a place where I could achieve self-definition while also absorbing other truths, other trades. In particular, literary criticism became a site where I could fuse and further my two great loves among literary forms. The essay, and the novel. I want to say something about each of these.

Of course, the jobbing book-reviewer should take pause before he claims the status of either literary critic or essayist (and I claim both in this book). These are overlapping categories, and the nuances of the differences between them can reveal a great deal about what is at stake in the act of literary response (which after all is something that is going on in the mind of every reader, not just those readers who write about their reading).

Any book review is, by the loosest definition, an essay: that is, a piece of discursive prose about a certain subject, in this case a book. But book reviews are highly perishable—written in haste to deadlines, published in periodicals which are in a few days carted off by the *kabadiwala*, and, by virtue of having always to focus on what is newly published, often forced to engage with works that are themselves ephemeral and mediocre. Ideally a good book review is a thoughtful report on a book, supplying evidence to support its claims about the author's worldview and style, and arriving at an evaluation, spelled out or implied, of the work in question.

A book review rises to the status of literary criticism when it shows itself to be historically and technically informed on various literary and moral aspects of the work it addresses and the genre in which it is written. It also qualifies as literary criticism, in the academic sense (which is where, with the professionalisation of literature, the great bulk of literary criticism is today generated) when it shows the rigour of a certain literary-critical method or theory of literature, even if it sometimes thereby recuses itself from the realm of the lay reader, or, just as problematically, jettisons questions of aesthetic value in favour of social or political questions, or subsumes literary creation to theoretical superstructures.

Even higher on this scale, therefore, is the book review or work of literary criticism that aspires to the status—it is the reader who must judge whether it achieves it—of an essay: that is, a distinctive combination of objective and subjective perceptions, written up in an unmistakably individual voice; possessing and proposing nuances of thought, perception and style that enact the pleasures of thinking, feeling and reasoning about art; and seeking to recreate the drama of literary engagement in a language that itself incarnates those qualities that make literature the most elevated site of that universal human currency and connector, language. Then a book review can become all of these things: literary criticism, essay, literature.

To me the literary commentary of many writers—some book-reviewers and some not—reaches this level of intensity: VS Pritchett, Alberto Manguel, James Wood, Pico Iyer, Andre Maurois, Pankaj Mishra, William Pritchard, Chaturvedi Badrinath, Shama Futehally, Algis Valiunas, Clive James, Robert Dessaix, Arshia Sattar, Eric Ormsby, Meenakshi Mukherjee, Kenneth Rexroth, Michael Schmidt, DR Nagaraj, Adam Kirsch, Paul Theroux, Mario Vargas Llosa, Milan Kundera and Jorge Luis Borges.

AND NOW TO the novel—my favourite subject of all. (i.e., This will take some time.) The novel is an astonishing literary invention, raised over three centuries to ever-new heights by hundreds of ardent and questing exponents. It is a very capacious, amiable form; it participates in both the quotidian and the ethereal. From my early twenties onwards, I began to feel that, although I loved all kinds of literature, it was novels that had first claim on my allegiance. Individual novels can be highly partial to certain moods and subjects, but the novel in general leans towards large-heartedness, complexity, contrast, self-awareness, scepticism, a dissembling sophistication and a shambling grace.[10] The passions and sentiments of characters are balanced by the commentary and rumination of narrators; scenes of solitude and private life are set in counterpoint to the world of the street and of society; magisterial language and highly polished sentences are combined with naturalistic speech and street slang. Meaning is made at the level of human drama and also by the form in which the story is cast, by who is doing the telling. The novel is also a sophisticated time machine. In a good novel the flow of life, highly contingent and unstable, can be experienced on the page; the experience of time is intensified and all the banal moments and longueurs of real life are ruthlessly weeded out.

Here was life, I thought to myself as I marked up and knocked back a novel every few days, seen in the round with a thrilling—sometimes terrifying—intensity of perception. The flow of artfully constructed verbal pictures in novelistic narration was rapid and vivifying; the precisely tuned sentences

---

[10] At 29, having just published my first novel, I moved into a small apartment in Prabhadevi in Bombay and met Rupesh Pai, the proprietor of Quick Bite restaurant based in the building next to mine. A remarkable character: seemingly always at work and yet never too fussed, interested in everything and surprised by nothing, able to find a line of connection to just about anybody and even a line of credit for some souls reluctant or unable to pay, conversant to different degrees in six languages, a great raconteur with a highly developed awareness of dramatic pauses and inflections, possessing a great store of proverbs and maxims, extremely worldly but occasionally so touchingly naive that I, who was ten times as naive as he was, wanted to burst out laughing. I soon came to think of him as a personification of the Novel. (It seemed completely apt that he had never read a novel in his life.) Naturally, such a character deserved his own novel. The protagonist of my novel *Days of My China Dragon* is based on him. This was then the first novel that he read. I've never seen anyone read a book so fast.

quickened the pulse, stung the conscience, created a thirst for experience. The more novels I read, the hungrier I became to read more—to live life, or at least a couple of hours of every day, with the heightened sense of intensity and significance that they conjured up. The sense of reassurance provided by novels was amazing, like that given to a country by a strong central bank. No matter how long one lived, one would never run out of great novels to read.

Even better, novels could provide, for acutely self-conscious souls such as myself, a liberating escape from the self. In novels you could get into the minds of other human beings and stay there until you could see reality as much through their eyes as your own; in effect you became a compound human being, both yourself and someone else. The last page of a novel often felt to me like a devastating farewell from one or all—sometimes you had to really think to work out which one—of the protagonist, narrator, or writer.

And just like in life, reality in novels did not easily give away its secrets. To pierce the veil of reality of novels was to gain confidence in doing the same at some point for life. You had to work out the code of the book, tune your own receptors to the pitch of the writing, piece together the narrator's worldview from the shards of observation about characters, be alive to the play of irony, the meanings of certain juxtapositions, cuts, and switches of perspective. Novels were written to be read, but novels were themselves readers: they read and interpreted the people within their narrative field, and they also supplied the means to read entire cultures, the lives of distant countries that one might never visit.

The novel, literary history tells us, had its beginnings in the birth of modernity in the west. In societies like India and Egypt, Brazil and Korea, it was a transplant. But wherever the novel went it merged with that world's indigenous storytelling traditions and reappeared with a new face and form, a new way of being. It was the literary version of the traveller who makes himself at home anywhere he goes. (I narrate the story of its rebirth in India in two essays in this book, the one on Fakir Mohan Senapati and the one called 'The Indian Novel as an Agent of History'.)

And, fired by my position as chief book reviewer of a newspaper, the more novels I read by Indian writers past and present—Amitav Ghosh and Bibhutibhushan Bandyopadhyay, Senapati and Nayantara Sahgal, Salma and Yashpal, Anjum Hasan and Vikram Chandra—the more I wanted to persuade every countryman of mine, every reader everywhere in the world who loved novels, to read these writers. Even better, in reading them I was convinced I had chosen the right profession—that there were few instruments so well suited to the depiction and interpretation of Indian life as the novel—that there was a lifetime's worth of reading and writing, thinking and travelling, for me in this realm alone.

Having been formed by reading novels as much as the contours of my own biography and the conflicts of my psyche, I have in middle age come to see novels also as an unusual kind of wisdom literature, a place where a young person, acutely conscious of callowness and malformation, may be exposed to the nuances of human nature, social life, romantic love, and history, to the subtle workings of cause and effect. And also, a sort of imaginative safe space, where rage, violence, grief, and trauma can be vicariously and cathartically experienced and one's own psychic wounds healed. I don't doubt that this was one of the main reasons for my attraction to novels in my youth. A novel can be a refuge for those who are thrown off by life, for the action of understanding what is going in a text can serve as a sort of substitute for the challenges of action in the world.

And so I find this double aura of poise and perplexity hanging over all the books of my twenties. I could be very adult on the page. But those who met me after having read me often sensed, I felt, a great disjuncture between writer and person. I could speak in my writing voice with a poise and confidence that was worlds removed from my ability to direct my own selfhood outside of literature: my sense of myself as a young man alienated from his society both by his upbringing in a fractured and frightening home with its doors barred against the world, and then by his marginal status as a drifter and a writer in a society that might set great store by learning but not necessarily by books or novels. In my relationships, I was a prisoner of my own history, diffident and reactive, pliant and conflicted, reconciled to the feeling that I might never escape this burdensome selfhood in this life.

There was another realm, however, in which I might speak my love and spend my passion without the sense of social and psychic barricades. That was literature, and I was enormously grateful to it. The 60 or so essays in this book are about diverse writers and subjects, but they are all an expression of that gratitude, of life lived and work done under the sheltering sky of literature. The fires of art create the means for all manner of transcendence. Writing book reviews and living entirely by literature gave me the time and space, the models and the means, to become a novelist. And becoming a novelist, being able to escape into the imagined worlds of characters I had myself created, gave me the means to remake myself a person.

In retrospect, looking back at my twenties, this explains why it took me much longer to become a novelist than a literary critic. For literary criticism can be composed from a point and station within the field of literature. But novels are made half from life, half from literature.

And I had a lot of ground to make up on one of those fronts.

LITERARY CRITICISM IS a practice that can be carried on all through adult life. Often, the literary critic's perspective deepens and matures with age. But book-reviewing, it seems to me, is very much a young person's profession, a wonderful calling for a time where energy and a hunger for aesthetic experience and education, the desire to give something to literature before you drink at its fountain, is at its strongest.

After about three years of being the weekly book reviewer for *Mint*, all the while also trying to write another review a month to top up my income and to keep up my relationship with novels from around the world, I found that the taste of literature, ingested in such enormous quantities, pursued with such relentlessness, dependent on just-published books of uncertain quality, was beginning to turn sour. Sometimes, it is those who read for a living who are most likely to lose touch with the experience of reading to feel alive.

Other things also happened to move me on in life from such a tight round of reading and response. I published my first novel, *Arzee the Dwarf*, in 2009, and entered the field of Indian literature in a more noticeable and pleasurable way. I was now present in all the bookshops, and it was my own book that was being reviewed in the newspapers. I now wrote my essays from the combined position of literary critic and novelist.

But this also generated new problems. Where I had once reviewed Indian and South Asian novelists from a near-anonymity that was liberating, now my opinions were seen as coming from a peer, and while my approbation became more warming, as coming from a fellow practitioner, any dispraise was resented to an even greater degree, as an attack in bad faith from a competitor. My literary life now had a greatly expanded social element, again very enjoyable and educative; I met other writers at book launches and literary festivals, with the complications of affection and avoidance that can occur when such relationships are moved onto the page.

So once again a new season. I began to focus again on reviewing non-fiction (where there was less prospect of a conflict of interest), on novels and novelists from other countries (the ones on Saramago, Herta Muller, Hrabal, and Edna O'Brien in this book all come from this phase), and on great Indian novelists who were dead. (There were so many, although I hope it was not writing novels that killed them.)

And when my request for a raise of two thousand rupees from *Mint* was rejected (I was now earning, by dint of previous such requests being gratified, ₹25,000 a month), I realised that I had perhaps hit the glass ceiling in the profession that had sustained me all through my lopsided and idealistic twenties. It was time to teach myself other tricks. The wake-up call was on point. With the growing crisis in the world of print journalism and the rise of social media sucking up readerly attention and energies that previously might have directed towards literature, many of the spaces where I had previously published work were fading or entirely folding. I had been fortunate to enjoy the last decade of a golden age of book-reviewing.

And so literary criticism became a smaller part of my portfolio of work. I wrote perhaps an essay a month, picking my subjects carefully, asking for larger amounts of space in which to construct an argument, and refusing low-paid work. I released myself from the ephemeral and the inessential, and began to read again with the same ardour of old, nursing and mulling over the great novels of world literature for weeks, reading five or six books simultaneously so that I could combine and contrast their voices in my head, and directing my reading to the needs of my writing. Even my work for The Middle Stage faded away, despite periodic attempts to resuscitate it. It was a much calmer life, a progression to another stage.

And I began to look for other countries to live in. It wasn't so much that I left literature behind; just that, instead of making it the centre of my life, I tried to make it part of a centred life. For so many years, I had made it bear every demand of my life and every burden of my soul: the spiritual sustenance of work, the torments of unrequited love, consolation in times of crisis, dreams for the future to fire the present, money to pay my bills, a reputation to prop up my long 19-letter name. For so many years of my youth, I had felt a greater closeness to and complicity with characters and books over people.

But sooner or later I would have to face up the truth that if books show us how to love and understand people, as I believe they do, then it would be tragic—a refutation of the very power and grace that we ascribe to literature—if they did not lead us to a renewed engagement with people.

And so I launched a new ship from the harbour of literature...perhaps later than I should have given my privileges and education, but thankfully not too late. I found love again in my thirties, several times, on terms very different from the romantic relationships of my twenties. I moved cities and found a little apartment in Kalkaji in South Delhi to live in. It was for 'one person only,' my landlady said (the official reason was that the water tank, which was common to the building, would not bear the demands of a second resident or visitor). And I agreed wholeheartedly. I wanted all rights over my space. Of course, hundreds of other writers lived there with me. But I was the only one who needed to shower.

Nor did I stay home much. Novels and the indigence of my twenties had fired in me a great hunger for travel. Suddenly fate waved a magic wand. I had the luck to see distant parts of the world on residencies and fellowships. Sometimes I came home, put down my suitcase for a day or two, unpacked all the books I had picked up from the great second-hand bookshops of the world—Strand in New York, Skoob and Henry Pordes in London, Halper's in Tel Aviv, Blossoms in Bangalore—and then set out again on a journey of my own fashioning and funding. For a few years, work of all kinds poured in. Much of it had very little to do with books, but having spent so much of my twenties importuning people for work, I rarely said no. I began work on a new novel, *Clouds*, that would take me seven years to write. For the first time, I realised that sometimes, in order to write a book, you must let the book write you first, to take you to places where you can change and grow. I began to cook with great interest and commitment, and to invite people home to dinner parties once a week. I took to heart Adam Smith's thought—part observation, part exhortation—in *The Theory of Moral Sentiments* that 'Man was made for action, and to promote by the exertion of his faculties such changes in the external circumstances both of himself and of others, as may seem most favourable to the happiness of all.' I liked the peace and solitude of my one-room apartment, the company of my beloved books and my closest friends. And then the rush of novelty, of high spirits and deep conversations, of people mixing in my space, browsing my books (I even allowed them to borrow one, on two occasions) and leaving behind memories. So long resistant to being drawn out, as reticent and impassive as a closed book, made nervous and even jealous by people more at ease with life than I, I now took pleasure and even pride in reaching out to people. I tried to leave people in no doubt that I loved them, both by concrete action and exertion and sometimes by discreet inaction, such as by never judging them by their reading (difficult, spiritually ennobling work when someone's favourite novel is *The Alchemist, The Fountainhead,* or *One Night at the Call Centre*).

I began to ruminate on the relationship of laughter to hope and healing. I had always loved the play of the comic spirit in literature: the cackling, bantering narrators in the novels of Bohumil Hrabal, the warm mockery of Jorge Amado, the fantastic set-ups and boisterous hijinks of Cervantes and Sterne, the salty chirruping of Senapati, the impish tenderness of Isaac Bashevis Singer. Increasingly, I found myself living my own life as a comedy, laughing at my past trials and tribulations; acknowledging the quirks, hang-ups, and illusions that made me such a challenging romantic partner and even friend; plunging headfirst into the past or plotting my glorious future in certain exquisite hours of reminiscence and reverie in bed or under the boughs of the peepal tree, an arboreal cafe full of tweeting birds and scrambling squirrels, that shielded my apartment from the harsh Delhi sun and snoopy neighbours.

Sometimes I just sat there in the centre of my room looking at my books, absorbing their vibrations like some sort of New Age guru, taking them in not as language but as a wordless love, a silent communion of kindred spirits.

Yes...what a country is literature.

THE PAST IS a strange country, too. It is now decades since I last saw my father in the flesh, although I hear him in my head quite often. We never got to say goodbye. He passed away that long summer when I first began my adventures in literature.

And for many years afterward, I dreaded remembering my father. For to remember a loved one who has passed away so young is to be overwhelmed once again by the trauma of their departure, the pain and suffering of their last years, the maddening questions *could I have done something differently* and *what did I not see*? I restricted myself to observing my father's memory through pitrupaksha, the annual day of rituals to remember one's ancestors, and to wearing one of his old shirts from time to time. That was as much as I could take. When my first novel was published in 2009, I was not even able to place his name on the dedications page.

So my father did not live to see my winding, often tumultuous journey in literature. But of course, I couldn't have done it without him. His memory interleaves my every feeling for the universe of books, for my own journey is, more properly, the second episode of a journey of father and son. A village boy, born and raised far from the world of English and books, my father rose far above what was expected of him. He became the only one of five siblings to go to university. In Cuttack's Ravenshaw College, for the first time he gained access to more books than he could read. Somewhere in my family home are stored the works of English literature and Political Science that he received as prizes for outstanding results, with his name and the mid-70s date proudly inscribed on them in his dashing hand. He loved to copy out quotes and witticisms in notebooks, and to write letters to newspapers. He admired a certain kind of iconoclastic individual: Arun Shourie, Khushwant Singh, Mahesh Bhatt, Dom Moraes. He had a very loud, slightly metallic laugh, like the sound of a car stalling. When he started laughing it took him a long time to stop.

My father had great dreams for himself, many of them seeded by education. And in turn he had great dreams for his children too. I owe my early facility in English to the long evenings of reading and spelling overseen by him after returning from work; he wanted me to rise above our middle-class life in the same proportion as he had risen into it. As I grew into books and bibliophilia, he took even more pleasure in acquiring books for me than he had done for himself. (In fact, his own reading rather fell away, becoming confined to newspapers and magazines.) Despite growing up in a world without luxuries, or perhaps because of it, he had a great love for grand gestures, whether emotional or material, often carried out without any consultation with those towards whom they might be directed. One day when I was 12, and we were living in a one-bedroom apartment in Santa Cruz in Bombay, he came home with a thousand books, tied up with string in bundles of 70 or 80 each. He'd seen a library disposing of its old stock; instead of bothering to sift through them, he just decided to bring the entire consignment home.

No parent could have taken greater joy in a child's juvenilia than my father, who saw in every sentence and paragraph signs of world-shaking genius, unfortunately also managing to convince me that this was true. Possessed and indefatigable, he roamed the streets of Bombay on Saturday afternoons, knocking on the doors of newspaper offices with my manuscripts, trying to get through to well-known writers who might give me some words of advice or encouragement. After a point, Project Son/Literature became an obsession for him, for which he received a great deal of affectionate ribbing by his colleagues at work and occasionally a few admonishments. There was a sort of contract between us. In return for all the books I could read, I was to honour my talent by writing every day. Talent, after all, was nothing without hard work and dedication. Success was 1 per cent inspiration, 99 per cent perspiration. Your father will always love you, but you must also earn his respect. The model writer, to my father's mind, was Behram Contractor or 'Busybee,' the elfin editor of the Bombay tabloid *The Afternoon Despatch & Courier.* Come rain or sunshine, the 700 words of Busybee's column 'Round and About' appeared every weekday on the last page of *The Afternoon,* and were read by thousands of office-goers in cafes and restaurants or on their journey home from work. Did Busybee ever get held up by the flu? No. Did he ever wait for inspiration to descend from the heavens? No. His job was to write, and he wrote.

Strong stuff to digest when you're a teenager. But now that I am a professional, I practise it like a peach.

So I couldn't have become a writer without my father. The strange thing is, I'm not sure I could have become a writer with him either.

At least, not the sort of writer I chose to become, steeped in literature through and through. Not the sort of writer who might proclaim with a touch of grandiosity, after the manner of VS Naipaul's book-jacket bio, 'After three years at Trinity College, Cambridge, he began to write, and since then has followed no other profession.' I look back now at the life I led in my twenties, and I say to myself, *he just wouldn't have allowed it*. He would have never tolerated such insubordination under his roof, such a reckless, self-indulgent plunge into literature. He would never have accepted the insult of my ignoring completely the master plan he had already hatched for me, with some choices already built in—become a Cambridge don, or else aim for the Indian Foreign Service and failing that, the Indian Administrative Service—which I needed only to put my head down and execute. He would have contested me morning, noon, and night. Literature was a wonderful calling card, but in his view, shaped by his own experience of rising up in the world, it was not in itself a profession unless it linked to secure employment. Whatever the calling of one's soul, it was important to do something that the world—or at least your father—respected.

And so, bereaved at the onset of adulthood in a way that would take me all of my twenties to process, I also found myself, as I was becoming a man, released of the duty to please, to obey, to convince, and inevitably to confront an older man on highly unequal and unfavourable terms. For my father's rage was as volcanic as his love, and was delivered with the same intensity and conviction. When someone opposed what he, whether after much rumination or through spontaneous perception, had proposed, he opposed the opposition until it collapsed, buckled, pleaded for mercy. Already, in my teens, we had clashed ferociously on a number of occasions; as his health failed, his dealings with me took on a sorrowful, wounded air, as though he had experienced a great betrayal, while in the experience of being able to stand up to him I had my first sense of a growing power, undermined by a nagging guilt at having wounded the person who loved me the most in the world. When I won my scholarship to Cambridge, I was secretly as delighted to be able to escape his authoritarian house as he was that his rigorous training had culminated in the perfect result.

It was only later, as I grew to a fuller awareness of what goes on in the minds of men and women, that I began to wonder whether he was not more lost and lonely than I would ever know, or ever be. I remembered the evenings late in his life when, his body beginning to abandon him, he sat all alone in his room in a rocking chair, the lights turned off, adrift on a sea of rage and recrimination, as if already living in a different world—a terrifying vortex that one approached with dread, and could never tell anyone about. Even so, so caught up was I in my own burgeoning life and in how to navigate his challenging currents that it never occurred to me that I might come home one day and not find him there. Then he was gone.

So, with my father's passing away, I was suddenly both desolated, and free. Not a bad combination, in retrospect. And I also knew something else: all the work I had done in literature so far would have no cachet in the unfatherly world; I would have to start all over again from scratch, as if I had just decided to become a writer. Perhaps that is why I was so happy to repudiate his influence entirely and to set out on my own quest—because in doing so I was expressing a deep need to assert myself, which was more important than money and security. Had he been alive to annotate my progress, my father, I know, would for many years have thought me a vagabond, a wastrel, a scapegrace (while probably greatly enjoying reading my essays in newspapers and magazines and commenting on that paragraph, this phrase, soon thereafter to leap back into his position in the trenches). Instead, captain of my own ship, I made decisions broadly in line with the spirit of my father, while being spared his immensely wounding disapproval, his scorching mockery. He would not have let me go so easily, for to do so would be to admit to his own failure, to the dissolution of his own authority, to the validity of disobedience and provocation as a path to progress and independence. And, having brought me so far down the road of literature, he would not have let me grow.

And that's okay. Every adult must in time confront this abiding problem in human relationships: it is very difficult not to want to control those that you love. Twenty years later, my father and I have made our peace across the worlds. In fact, I know I am very close to the writer and man he would have wanted me to be. A few years ago, one night in Bhubaneswar, I even opened an old box and read all the letters he had written to me during those years when I left him for Cambridge. They were gentle, fond, affectionate, proud, a little plaintive and troubled. It felt as though we were ready to talk again…in the same life, for all of life.

THE 60 OR so essays in this book are selected from the many pieces written across all the years and situations that I describe here. I have not put them in any kind of order, except a basic progression from essays on fiction to those on non-fiction. Read *My Country Is Literature* exactly as you please. Every essay is self-standing; there are connections across them that you will pick up no matter what order you read them in.

Literature is a free, freeing country. In our century, even more so than any past, it is ever more important that we read widely and deeply, overleaping the confines of fashion, nation and canon—that we make of the shelves of our library a picture that Literature, if it were a person, could look at and say, yes, this is all of my music in microcosm. It is my endeavour in this book to share the map and mood of my journey, in the hope that it will be of some help to you on your own.

You are what you read, declare the parents of the world, the bibliophiles, the professors, the publishers. I don't quite agree. But God, it has certainly taken me a long time to explain why not. And I am very willing to change my mind. Perhaps one day I will.

*Bhubaneswar, July 2021*

# PART ONE

# 1. Perumal Murugan's Portia Tree

*One Part Woman* by Perumal Murugan, translated by Aniruddhan Vasudevan (Penguin, 2010)

*Trial by Silence* by Perumal Murugan, translated by Aniruddhan Vasudevan (Penguin, 2018)

*A Lonely Harvest* (by Perumal Murugan, translated by Aniruddhan Vasudevan (Penguin, 2018)

One reason why we read fiction is for the pleasure of entering imaginatively into a highly worked-up moral field that is not our own. Fiction reveals to us the plasticity of our own consciousness: after only a few paragraphs or pages, we are able to bind ourselves with the point of view of one or several characters. Even if they themselves seem bound by a situation, a city, their own natures, in living vicariously through them we experience the space between our own imaginative life and theirs as freedom. They bestow on us an enlargement and deepening of our own sense of life, our awareness of cause and effect. No reader deeply stirred by a novel ever quite relinquishes the trace it leaves behind: having once made the story the focus of our reading life, we now sense that it is a part of our reading of life itself. This experience of permeation is perhaps the greatest compliment we can pay a writer.

Some years ago, the writer Perumal Murugan proved himself worthy of just such respect and reverberation with his novel *One Part Woman* (in Tamil, *Maadhurbaagan*). Set in a village in western Tamil Nadu in the early years of the 20th century, the book narrated in a torrent of exquisite, empathetic detail the predicament of a peasant couple, Kali and Ponnayi, deeply (and for those around them, often provokingly) in love with one another. But they have a problem: they are unable, even after twelve years of marriage, to conceive a child.

Although Kali and Ponna are utterly rapt in one another, the norms of the world and the tongues of people always remind them of what is missing from their lives. The child-shaped hole in their lives is brought up in nearly every social encounter and eventually in their own dealings with each other, although never to the point of breaking the bond between them. If anything, Kali is repeatedly counselled to take a second wife, but refuses to do so. Instead, he grows ever more reclusive, spending all his hours in the barnyard that lies a little distance from his home, tending his fields and his animals. Meanwhile, Ponna, compulsively scratching the wound, turns every subject to the question of children: 'The plant that we plant grows; the seed that we sow blooms; is it only me who is the wasted land here?'

When all patience and propitiation has been exhausted, one final option, albeit very extreme, presents itself. At the popular annual chariot festival of the half-male, half-female god, Ardhanareeswara—in his mingling of both sexes into one whole, the very emblem of the interplay of the male and female principle in every human being and, by extension, of conjugal felicity—there opens up on the final night an abandonment of all norms, the erasure of identities. Then, any man and woman may consort with one another in the dark, and children born of such encounters are held to be bestowed by the god himself. It is suggested to both Kali and Ponna by her own brother, Muthu, that she journey to the festival all alone to find a man on this night, hopefully to be impregnated by him. It is very hard for her to contemplate this act of tawdry yet potentially life-changing adultery, but she wonders if she would do it if her husband gave his permission.

The tension between the present and the future, the individual and the couple, between sexual fidelity and the need for children, is thus strung by Murugan to the highest pitch. In the end, as the result of a misunderstanding orchestrated by

Muthu for what he believes to be a good cause, we see Ponna going to the festival and being seduced by a man believing her husband has discreetly consented to it. Meanwhile, Kali belatedly discovers what he then takes to be the greatest of all betrayals. *One Part Woman* ends with an image of Kali, drunk and devastated, in the very barnyard where he and his wife had spent so many happy hours, and looking up at the portia tree that he himself had planted many years ago—the most prominent motif in the book: a symbol of pleasure in the natural world, of Kali's own capacity for creation and nurture, of the passing of time. What would happen next? Would he take his own life? We could not say.

It is clear Murugan himself was exhilarated by his own story in *One Part Woman* and unwilling to take leave of his characters. In fact, he had generated such a harvest of possibilities that in the years that followed, he came up with not one but two sequels, now ably translated by Aniruddhan Vasudevan as *Trial By Silence* and *A Lonely Harvest*. What is thrilling about this follow-up is that the books are not continuous. Instead, they audaciously take advantage of the freedom that fiction allows and life does not, and generate two versions of events arising from the same narrative crux: Kali and Ponna sundered by a single night's happenings at the chariot festival.

In *Trial By Silence*, we see Kali where we left him, now attempting to kill himself by hanging from a noose on the portia tree. But his mother arrives just in time and saves him. Shortly afterwards Ponna arrives home from her night at the chariot festival, and is shocked both by his brush with death and by her discovery that he had never given his consent. She is branded a whore by her husband, who refuses to touch her or converse with her and retreats into a private universe, stewing and suffering silently in his barnyard with his animals and becoming even more estranged when it turns out she is pregnant. Ponna herself cuts off all her ties with her own family for having plotted the destruction of her marriage. In this way an entire web of connections is broken up; the world of the family becomes a set of solitudes.

And in *A Lonely Harvest*, we find that Kali succeeds in killing himself. The grotesque details of his grimace at point of death and his cadaver are no less unsettling in light of the knowledge that he continues to live in another book (which experience leads to the insight that the 'reality' of fiction is of a different order than that of life). Ponna is left a widow with a small farm, an aged mother-in-law, and (soon) a child in the womb. But she refuses to leave the barnyard where Kali spent all his days and in fact moves house there, seeing his presence in every small detail, especially in the portia tree.

We are thus made spectators to two kinds of tragedy. In one, we see how lonely and riven two partners in love and domesticity may become while keeping up a kind of perfunctory life in the world together. In the other, the desire to perpetuate life results instead in the snuffing out of a life, and in the desperate efforts, pervaded by regret and yearning, of those left behind to patch together an existence that will never redeem the past.

These are exquisite formal patterns, and they are realised in writing of great involvement and fidelity to point of view. Nowhere is Murugan's command of his material more evident than in his depiction of space as a extension of human personality, and in his intricate braiding of the human and natural world. In a seemingly artless, low-key 'village prose' that is nevertheless limpid and expressive, he makes us partners in the peasant's endless round of chores, showing how in his imagination the possibilities of trees and soil, bird and beast, water and stone, sun and season, are channelled into mutually supportive combinations. Raising livestock and working his fields in *One Part Woman*, Kali is a master of creation who is yet mocked by the world for being impotent; then in *Trial By Silence*, his decision to abandon his crops and cattle and let everything decay around him in his beloved barnyard becomes a metaphor for the blighting of his mind by the plague of cuckoldry; then in *A Lonely Harvest*, he kills himself in the very same haunt, and the control of the space passes over to the two women of his house, who in taking it over and adapting it to their own needs and capabilities discover its pleasures all over again while finding in it disturbing hints of his presence.

There is much to admire also about the equity of empathy distributed by Murugan between his male and female protagonist—sometimes expressed in the very shape of the story, in the form of chapters alternating between their respective viewpoints. And, given his own starting position, his extraordinarily layered and lucent exposition of female subjectivity and agency in the characters of both Ponna and her mother-in-law Seerayi give the lie to what has regrettably become an axiom of modern gender politics and of some strands of feminist literary criticism: that male writers inevitably produce stunted or distorted depictions of female characters. (If the only identities we could depict truthfully were our own, there would no point in writing fiction in the first place.)

If anything, the most powerful emotional effect of the book is the sense that in their long years of mutual adoration and affectionate mockery (of which many lovely scenes fleck all three books) both Kali and Ponna have become, like Ardhanareeswara, half-man and half-woman, able to treat sexual difference as a bridge to the other and not as an island. Here is one such passage:

> Kali was intimately familiar with every inch of Ponna's body. He did not even know his own body that well. There was one little lash on Ponna's eyelids that was thick and slanting away from the other eyelashes. He sometimes held it between his lips and tugged at it. She once said to him, 'Let me know if you want to remove it.' But he replied, 'It is my most favourite piece of hair, let me tell you.'
>
> He also liked to play with her tongue by keeping his finger on it. She would pull it in at his touch, and he would ask her to bring it out again. 'If feels soft, like touching a snail,' he said once. 'See, now the snail's going into its shell!' she said, and closed her mouth.
>
> He loved the fine lines on her lips. He once counted them and said, 'Fourteen.' She said, 'You are crazy.' And he agreed. 'Yes, indeed I am.'

And, as an extension of the same depth of feeling for one another, when they are sundered, both parties are able to marshal imagination and memory as an antidote to pain—and even as a substitute for embodied presence. 'She pervaded his thoughts,' we read in *One Part Woman*. 'She came to occupy them so much that he could tell her every movement and gesture.' In a startling scene in *A Lonely Harvest*, we see Ponna going into the fields after Kali's death and finding a brinjal patch that had been lovingly planted by him.

> Ponna caressed the bristly stem of the brinjal plant. It felt like she was caressing his arms. She held the stem against her cheek. Definitely his hand....She kept walking through the plants. How many hands did he have!

The effect gradually metamorphoses into the cause; creation back into the creator. And simultaneously we feel on our skin the caress of fiction, reminding us of all that we can be, all those we can be, should we relinquish our tight grip on ourselves.

## 2. Everywhere and Nowhere: Bibhutibhushan Bandyopadhyay

*A Strange Attachment and Other Stories* by Bibhutibhushan Bandyopadhyay, translated by Phyllis Granoff (Rupa, 2005)

Most writers of fiction remain a presence within their stories, and the reader is palpably aware of their voice interpreting the world of their characters, or their worldview suffusing the story like sunlight upon a street. But a few have the gift of being able to dissolve themselves into their creations so that, after guiding the reader by the hand for a little while, they suddenly appear to have vanished into thin air. Where have they gone? Their characters have taken over the story: the unfolding of the story's events is presented as if filtered through

their consciousness, not that of an observer from outside the frame of action. The total communion with the world of a character that this provides is one of the greatest satisfactions that a reader of fiction can experience.

This capacity for narrative empathy, for depicting a scene the way a character might see it, is everywhere apparent in Bibhutibhushan Bandyopadhyay's *A Strange Attachment and Other Stories*. And this, combined with Bandyopadhyay's many other qualities and his translator Phyllis Granoff's fine ear for speech rhythms, make this volume one of the essential works of Indian fiction in English translation—a kind of late gift, like a misplaced parcel arriving in the post many years after it was sent, from the venerable author of *Pather Panchali*. Bibhutibhushan died at the age of 56 in 1950; many aspects of the Bengal of which he wrote are still part of its lived reality, and in Granoff's rendering his voice, too, is astonishingly sprightly, vivid, and contemporary.

Bandyopadhyay allows his narrative voice to be coloured by his characters' point of view most clearly in his stories about children (whose way of looking at the world, as those who remember the scenes of Apu and Durga in *Pather Panchali* will know, he could reproduce with remarkable fidelity). In the story 'Dalu Gets Into Trouble', a huge lumber boat drops anchor at the village of a small boy, Dalu, and his younger brother Santu. Spellbound by the boat, the two brothers spend hours every day gazing at it. One day one of the sailors invites them aboard the boat, but much as he wants to go Dalu demurs, worried that someone will see them in broad daylight and tell their mother. He decides that they will come back after sunset, under cover of dark. But what about his younger brother?

> Santu wasn't overjoyed at this new plan. How could anyone dare to go down to the river's edge after dark? What about the witch living in the tamarind tree on Cinte the Bagdi's land? She pounced on little boys and dragged them to the very tip-top of the tree. No, sunset was a bad time of day. Santu told his brother his fears.

Bandyopadhyay's courtesy towards his character here lies in the way he imports Santu's concerns into the narrative without any indication that these are specifically Santu's thoughts. The questions troubling Santu are pressed upon the reader as if they are of vital importance, which of course they are to the boys. And later, when the two boys ask the sailors what kinds of things they have seen on their travels and are told of 'sharks, crocodiles, two-headed snakes, even red-faced monkeys and double-crowned palm trees,' we share their wonder because we have become so accustomed to seeing things from their perspective. Here we see fiction authentically carrying out its pledge to the reader, which is to give us new eyes.

Bandyopadhyay had a marvellous sense of the piquant and the absurd, and he could write a very swift, light-footed prose that beautifully expresses this sense of comedy in human affairs. In the story 'Haridas, Released Soul', the schoolteacher Haridas is sorely plagued by the cares of worldly life—an inadequate salary, a family pestering him with their wants, a headmaster dissatisfied with his work—but cannot see how he can free himself of these bonds. But, the narrator tells us, 'The Lord heard Haridas's prayer.' Every sentence in this passage gives off comic sparks:

> One day Haridas caught the third grader Shripati Kundu reading a book under his desk. Twice Haridas called him to order. 'Hey, what's going on there? None of that. Do your sums. Here, add this.'
>
> But why should Shripati do his arithmetic, when on that very day he had been sent by the Lord as a messenger to the poor Haridas, beleaguered by the trials of earthly existence? [...] Shripati paid no attention to Haridas; he went right on reading the book under his desk. Haridas did not scold him a third time. He got up from his chair and snatched the book away, not forgetting to give Shripati's ears a good twist on his way back to his desk. Curious, he opened the book. He was expecting a drama or a novel, or at least a good ghost story. But that was not to be. The name of the book was *The*

> *Hero's Voice*; its author was Swami Vivekananda. Haridas had never paid much attention to religion, but he did know about Vivekananda. He kept the book, thinking he might have a look at it some time later.
>
> The next day was Sunday. Haridas didn't have to go out and give private lessons. He relaxed with a cup of tea and then picked up the book. The more he read the more interested he became. What was all this? I am He. I am the Lord. I am Brahma. I am the Great One.
>
> What noble, majestic words! What exalted thoughts, reaching into the heavens like the lofty mountain Himalaya! Slowly, very slowly, the school master Haridas began to change. His head stretched up until thud, it bumped right into the vast empyrean! His heart and mind glowed with the light of an ineffable intuition, known only to Haridas himself. Haridas had become the ageless, deathless, eternal soul! The Lord and he had been walking hand in hand through countless aeons. Haridas was He; Haridas was the Omniscient One, Haridas was the Divine Lover; Haridas was the Great Hero.

Consider how skilfully the narrative communicates first Haridas's dashed expectations ('He was expecting a drama or a novel, or at least a good ghost story. But that was not to be') and then the rapid swell of his thoughts as his mind is engulfed by the message of *The Hero's Voice*. Just as it is the new convert who preaches with the greatest zeal, so here we have the comic spectacle of the initiate ascending up to the pinnacle of spiritual elevation in a fervent fast-forward.

Bandyopadhyay had roots in both the village and the city. The stories of *A Strange Attachment* picture the beauty of village landscapes and the variety of nature's bounties with a prayerful attention matched only by a pleasure in the world fashioned almost entirely by man, in the excitement of bustling crowds and the talk of shops and streets. His characters, in their variety, reflect Bandyopadhyay's open-mindedness and liberalism. That is to say, they do not suffer from that failing that sometimes affects the created beings of short-story writers: of being too similar, of having the same kinds of motivations and wanting the same kinds of things and therefore coming to seem familiar even at first glimpse.

For instance, the protagonist of 'Uncle Bhandul's House' lives all his life in rented accommodation in the city, and invests all his savings in constructing a house in his native village, the place he loves most. So slow and laborious is this process that the narrator of the story moves from boyhood to manhood in that time. Yet Uncle Bhandul carries on doggedly, intent on returning one day to his own house in his own village, and we feel we can identify completely with his dream. In contrast, Canvasser Krishnalal, the hero of a story by that name, has spent all his life as a travelling salesman in Calcutta and loves the city ardently. When he loses his job, his condition becomes so wretched that he is thrown out of his boarding house and has to return to the scrap of land his family owned in the village. He quickly grows disgusted by village life: 'Krishnalal had never spent much time in the village before. The people were all uneducated; they didn't even know how to talk to each other politely. They didn't drink tea; in Calcutta even the beggars all drank tea. Everywhere you looked was mud and jungle.' Here we see Bandyopadhyay talking in his character's voice about the same village life that, in another story, he would describe with such affection. Finally, Krishnalal flees back to the city: 'If he was going to starve to death, it might as well be in his beloved Calcutta.'

Probably the best reader that Bandyopadhyay ever had—would that every writer of fiction has such luck—was Satyajit Ray, who fashioned from Bandyopadhyay's novels *Pather Panchali* and *Aparajito* the films now known as *The Apu Trilogy*. Ray's book *Speaking of Films* contains several paragraphs of acute commentary on Bandyopadhyay's work. At one point, Ray advises aspiring scriptwriters to read Bandyopadhyay and note his wonderful ear for lifelike speech: 'His lines fit the characters so well, they are so revealing that even when the author provides no physical description, every character seems to present itself before us simply through the words it speaks.' And as an illustration of the 'gold mine of cinematic observation' to be found in Bandyopadhyay's work Ray cites the story 'Puinmacha' (which appears in *A Strange Attachment* under the title 'The Basella Trellis'). Ray writes:

> Annapurna's daughter Khenti has just got married, and it is now time for the bride to depart. The palki is resting on the ground with the bride and the groom in it. Annapurna, whose heart is torn by anguish, glances at the palki and notices—I translate—'that the end of Khenti's modest red baluchari has trailed out of the palki, and is nestling against a drooping cluster of medi flowers by the bamboo fencing.'
>
> In its context, this is a heart-rending detail, and a perfect film close-up of the kind described by Eisenstein as 'pars pro toto', part standing for the whole.

Indeed, Bibhutibhushan's empathy is so vast that each person touched by the roving lens of his narration seems momentarily to turn into the protagonist of the story. The work of many great fiction writers seems somehow self-consciously literary, but not so with Bibhutibhushan, who prizes and produces a clear flowing stream of narrativeness: that mysterious quality of constant motion and confident verisimilitude that makes a reader forget he or she is reading a story.

When we read a paragraph of Bibhutibhushan, we suddenly know exactly why we read fiction.

# 3. Fakir Mohan Senapati's Roundabout Fictions

*Colonialism, Modernity and Literature*, ed. Satya P. Mohanty, (Orient Longman, 2011)

*Six Acres and a Third,* Fakir Mohan Senapati, translated by Rabi Shankar Mishra, Satya Mohanty, Jatindra K. Nayak and Paul St. Pierre (Penguin, 2006)

In a famous essay published in 1990, the poet and literary scholar AK Ramanujan asks the provocative question, 'Is there an Indian way of thinking?' In the closing years of the nineteenth century, the Odia writer Fakir Mohan Senapati appears to have asked himself that question in another form: 'Is there an Indian way of writing a novel?'

Senapati's brilliant answer took the form of *Chha Mana Atha Guntha*, published in serial form in an Odiya magazine from 1895–97, then as a book in 1902, and at long last in an English translation equal to its linguistic energy and narrative agility as late as 2006. Upon publication of *Six Acres and a Third*, as the English translation was called, it instantly became apparent that the book was one of the greatest novels of the Indian pantheon, as revelatory and powerful today as in its own time.

What did Senapati do that was so remarkable? His novel tells the story of the rise and fall of a greedy zamindar, Ramachandra Mangaraj, as he plots to capture the verdant landholding—the eponymous six acres and a third—of a pair of humble weavers in his village in Odisha. This in itself was not revolutionary. All over India at this point of time, a generation of writers across a swathe of Indian languages was discovering the power of the novel as a tool to depict and interrogate the structures and injustices of the world around them.

The crux of Senapati's achievement lies not so much in what he said, but in his narrative method. From the very beginning, Senapati's narrator like a village storyteller conversing with an audience of familiars by a lantern under a tree at night, uses a plural 'we' to bind himself and the reader up with the world of the story. At one point, the narrator, who often addresses the reader directly, remarks that 'unpleasant truths are better left unspoken; in other words, we are forced to forget half the truth and tell you the other half.'

These words might serve as a loose definition of satire, which tells the truth by denying the truth. When the narrator describes the greedy ways of his protagonist, the venal zamindar Ramachandra Mangaraj, all the while insisting that he is really a 'kind and pious man,' Mangaraj is exposed more effectively than a simple and uninflected chronicle of his evils could have managed. The narrator is, in effect, repaying Mangaraj with the same duplicity that Mangaraj himself practices on those around him—he has a friendly hand on Mangaraj's shoulder while simultaneously winking at the reader, confident that 'for intelligent people, hints usually suffice.'

This jaunty line of attack is Senapati's way of describing a cruel, exploitative order in a way that gives the reader pleasure and a sense of participation. His work reveals not just a profoundly sceptical and germinal vision of Indian life and society, but also a sophisticated understanding of how fiction has an autonomous existence—that a novel is both a serious representation of some outward reality and also a kind of game.

'We're not absolutely sure what was meant by this,' says the narrator in the novel's opening paragraph, 'but our guess is that these men were slandering Mangaraj.' Reporting every story and slander that comes its way from multiple sources; making his own pronouncements on good and evil, human nature and history; and always keeping an entire field of meanings and implications in play with that ingenious 'we're not absolutely sure,' Senapati's narrator produces a fine weave of observation of character, family, village, society, and colonial government. The reader finds in the book fascinating interludes on the place of the temple and the pond in village life, brilliant single-chapter character portraits (such as the one of Mangaraj's

shrewish maid Champa), and meditations upon human nature and Indian history.

The energy of Senapati's narration also owes much to its love of metaphorical grandstanding, which yokes the natural world to the social order. Water lilies fold themselves up and hide during the day 'like young Hindu daughters-in-law.' Cows chew their cud 'like baishnavas, moving their mouths as if they were repeating the divine name'—who can ever forget that image? Grand meanings suddenly emerge from metaphorical juxtapositions. At one point, speaking of the birds found near the village pond, the narrator notes how the cranes churn the mud 'like lowly farmhands' looking for fish all day long, while kingfishers appear suddenly, conduct swift raids, and gorge themselves on the stolen pickings. 'Oh, stupid Hindu cranes,' the narrator laments, 'look at these English kingfishers…'

Sly and salty, riddling and chirruping, the narrator of *Six Acres* appears not to inhabit a stable world of truth retailed to the reader from on high, in the manner of the classic nineteenth-century English novel. Rather, we see him being shunted between competing knowledge systems and ways of making meaning: the traditional village order, colonial modernity, and the flickers of his own nonconformist intelligence. There is no one stable target, whether person or system, for the novelist's satire. The narrator casts a searching ironic light upon the injustices of the zamindari system, the depredations of British colonialism, the hierarchies and prejudices of caste, and more generally, on man's capacity for inhumanity to others.

The truth is—and this is what is most charming about Senapati—that the author was really an incorrigible ironist. His work is not dependent on the gross folly of the wicked, but on the naturally piquant and perverse make-up of humanity. In fact, if his novel persuades us about anything, it is the ubiquity of human vanity and frailty. The tone of his narrative is that of the village gossip—garrulous and conspiratorial, brimming with hints and winks and insinuations. At one point, the narrator describes the village priest, a respected man who runs the shrine of the village goddess, Budhi Mangala. 'The priest was very highly regarded in the village, particularly by the women,' says the narrator. 'The goddess frequently appeared to him in his dreams and talked to him about everything.' That 'about everything'—as if the goddess personally confides in the priest—undermines both the priest and the public who presumably believe such stories and keep the priest in position.

Elsewhere, the narrator makes fun of the assumptions of civilisational advancement held by the British. 'Today, in the 19th century, the sciences enjoy great prestige, for they form the basis of all progress,' he declares. 'See, the British are white-skinned, whereas Oriyas are dark in complexion. This is because the former have studied the sciences, whereas the latter have no knowledge of these.' Senapati, with a finely judged sense of the absurd, is here equating scientific advancement with skin colour, thereby managing to justify with a false but provocative syllogism the easy British assumption of racial superiority. At another juncture, the narrator mocks the slavish veneration of British culture by the newly emerging class of English-educated Indian intellectuals. 'Ask a new babu his grandfather's father's name,' he sniffs, 'and he will hem and haw, but the names of the ancestors of England's Charles the Third will readily roll off his tongue.'

In the years after the publication in English of *Six Acres And A Third*, the novel's place as a kind of foundation stone for the Indian novel has become ever more clear. The contributors to *Colonialism, Modernity and Literature,* a recent book of essays on Senapati, demonstrate how Senapati Indianised the novel by seeding it with the communal intimacy and the savour of Indian oral storytelling traditions, creating in place of the 'descriptive realism' of contemporaries like Bankimchandra Chatterji a narrative voice as murky and as fertile as the village pond to which Senapati devotes one of his chapters.

For instance, in one essay, the critic Himansu Mohapatra explains how Senapati's 'complex and polyphonic realism' produces a more powerfully analytical world-picture than even that of a novelist as socially conscious as Premchand, because Senapati works in such a way as to reveal the 'causal joints' of the world. Simultaneously, the 'links, nudges and dodges' of the narrator produce 'an active reader,' one who divines the sceptical and critical awareness required of him as a political subject. In another, the scholar of Telugu literature Velcheru Narayana Rao compares *Six Acres* with another late nineteenth-century work, Gurajada Apparao's play *Girls for Sale*, to show how both writers deserve to be seen as creators of an indigenous modernity that could see the faults and failings of the traditional Indian order without assenting wholesale to the values of Western modernity. Even more interestingly, the critic Jennifer Harford Vargas links the magical realism of Gabriel Garcia Marquez not to Salman Rushdie but instead to Senapati. Both *One Hundred Years of Solitude* and *Six Acres* try to shake off the burden of the colonial gaze, Vargas notes, by employing 'underground types of storytelling—mainly oral, ironic, dialogic, and parodic ones—developed by those on the underside of power.'

Without raising the subject directly, Mohanty's anthology has something to say to the contemporary Indian novel in English. The great mass of novels in this domain today, whether popular novels written in an undemanding style or literary novels seeking a more complex awareness of language and character, remain aesthetically inert and formally unambitious, unthinkingly applying dozens of large and small narrative conventions to the act of storytelling.

Through the independence and energy of his example, Senapati serves as a rebuke to complacent, even consumerist, storytelling and its caricature of formal innovation in storytelling as something self-indulgent or pretentious. As *Six Acres and a Third* demonstrates, when someone works on the scale that Senapati did to imagine the novel anew, that book always remains new.

# 4. Gopinath Mohanty's Immortal Indians

*The Dynasty of the Immortals*, by Gopinath Mohanty (Sahitya Akademi, 2016)

*Paraja,* by Gopinath Mohanty (Faber & Faber, 1987)

Is there another Indian novelist whose books contain not just so many beautiful sentences, but so many different *kinds* of beautiful sentences, as those of Gopinath Mohanty (1914–1991)? No Indian novelist is as consistently and meaningfully melodious as him, and with no one else's material does the reader feel such a strong sense—very hard to achieve in novelistic prose—of the concentration and economy of music. Most thrillingly, when one reads Mohanty's great novels of tribal life in Odisha, one realises that the notes he summons derive not just from his own feeling, cherishing sensibility, but from his material: the pleasures and dangers of the forest, the proximity and capriciousness of the gods, the elemental beat and spark of the life-force in all of creation.

Thankfully, the impact of Mohanty's stylistic dexterity and felicity in Odia shine through even in translation—or have been made to do so by some very painstaking and adept translators. *Amrutara Santana*, published by Sahitya Akademi in a translation by the Odia scholars and professors of English literature, (the late) Bidhubhusan Das and Prabhat Nalini Das, as *The Dynasty of the Immortals*, is one of two great novels about Odia tribal life written by Mohanty in his youth. The other is *Paraja*, which appeared almost thirty years ago in a translation by Bikram Das.

Mohanty's engagement with the tribals of Odisha began fairly early in life. As a young bureaucrat enlisted in the Odisha Administrative Service in the years just before independence, he lived in distant outposts in the district of Koraput, then, as now, one of India's poorest regions. But when the young city boy with an MA in English Literature came into contact

with people whom those of his own social class thought of as primitive, simple-minded hillmen, he found in them a beauty and integrity, a generosity of spirit and a animistic empathy, a love of song and story, that cried out to be enshrined in words.

But the tribals were also the 'other' of mainstream Indian civilisation, relentlessly patronised and exploited, destined to be on the wrong side of history even when India rid itself of its colonial masters. ('The Kandha,' Mohanty writes presciently, 'is to be found wherever the forest is. However, once the forest is opened up, the Kandha is evicted from his land.') Like his contemporary Bibhutibhushan Bandyopadhyay in Bengal with his forest novel *Aranyak*, Mohanty set out to describe both the rapture and the tragedy of this other way of life. But unlike Bandyopadhyay, he chose to do so from the point of view of the forest-dwellers themselves.

Readers of *Paraja*, about the tribe by that name, will immediately recognise the feel and force of the limber, capacious, almost centreless point of view in *Dynasty of Immortals*, about a group of Kandha tribals in a group of isolated, impoverished villages in the Eastern Ghats. ('Here, humankind did not get anything from nature without a struggle.') The narration swerves constantly from the intimate and the domestic to the wide-angle and the cosmic, from the narrator's almost ethnographic observations about the Kandhas to a tracking of the thoughts of diverse characters that unspools for us the same worldview from the inside. Mohanty's translators find short and long, shapely and broken, sentences that capture the many shades of light and dark, the many subtleties, that he conjures up.

Mohanty's distinctive narrative method adds to the feeling of extreme intensity and compression. In tightly sculpted and focussed chapters no more than five or six pages long, written almost as short stories, we are hit by wave after wave of powerful feeling. But the jolt in this case is not just aesthetic, but—in Mohanty's time and in our own—political. Mohanty's ecstatic style is an instrument precisely designed to reveal the beauties of the way of life of his forest-dwelling protagonists.

Out here in the forest, distinctions between the human and the animal realm, the world of human artifacts and that of nature, the living and the dead, seem to be much more indistinct than in modern industrial society. We sense this right from the opening chapters of *Dynasty*, when the man who appears to be the protagonist of the story, the elderly village headman Sarabu Saonta, collapses and dies. Nevertheless, his presence echoes across the 600 pages that follow. 'Sarabu Saonta loved this earth,' we read. 'He did not know how to love with discrimination. Life was truth, beauty; let the old body be destroyed, he would be reborn in this beautiful land.'

After Sarabu dies, his son Diudu, daughter Pubuli, and daughter-in-law Puyu are left to carry on all the rituals and reveries of their realm: the forbidding and enchanting forest. In one scene, reminiscent of the story of the killing of the male krauncha bird and the grieving sounds of its mate that inspired Valmiki to invent the shloka meter of the *Ramayana*, Diudu kills a bird on a hunt and, reaching it as it lies thrashing on the ground, thinks he sees a cloud rising in the pupils of its eyes as it expires—an astonishing image. There are other thrilling hunting scenes, in which the contrasting energies of violence towards beasts and human social dynamics are mingled as expertly as Tolstoy did in *Anna Karenina*. (Mohanty was a voracious and cosmopolitan reader and even translated *War and Peace* into Odia.)

In choosing characters who approach the business of living with such rapture and intensity, Mohanty reminds one of other 20th-century artists and philosophers who, in an age of totalising intellectual constructs, have resisted the reduction of life to any system—people like the French film-maker Jacques Becker, who declared, 'In my work I don't want to prove anything except that life is stronger than everything else,' or the Iranian philosopher Ramin Jahanbegloo, who after being incarcerated in prison, comes to the paradoxical realisation that 'the meaning of life is life itself.'

The forest is the realm not just of food-gathering, of the

hunt, but also of love, the place where human beings succumb to 'the instinct of eternal nature.' In other words, it is the place—and this is where Mohanty's focus on a very particular social world at a particular historical moment acquires a universal resonance—where man and woman become Man and Woman, carrying on the eternal dance of life and creation.

Repeatedly in Mohanty's novels, we are given this sense of what one might call deep time, the sense of an archetype playing itself out repeatedly across the centuries. The young people falling in love for the first time thrill to this new emotion; the storyteller, meanwhile, thrills to the sense of the very same figures becoming indistinct, bringing the past to life within the folds of the present. 'Then the dialogue of Kandha courtship through question and answer ensued, the exchange of words from time immemorial; thousands of years had rolled by in the formulation of such exchanges.' For his characters the link to the past is not a matter of the historical record but rather an imaginative one rooted in a feeling for nature and the cosmos. It is in this sense that the tribals, with their short lifespans and many hardships, are nonetheless 'the dynasty of the immortals.'

In 1953, a letter of complaint arrived at the office of Prime Minister Jawaharlal Nehru, sent to him by the landowners and moneylenders who comprised the elite of Koraput. The letter said (I borrow this quote from an essay about Mohanty written by the critic JM Mohanty)—'To our great calamity and disaster Sri Gopinath Mohanty is posted here as the special assistant agent at Rayagada. He is always fond of hillmen and behaves like hillmen himself. He very little respects other classes of people before them. He behaves as if only born for Adivasis.'

Perhaps the letter had an unintended effect. When the Sahitya Akademi was founded in 1954 to award literary achievement in the 24 major languages of India, *Amrutara Santana* was judged the first-ever winner of the Sahitya Akademi Award for Odia literature. It has taken 60 years to produce a worthy translation in English (marred, sadly, by the terrible layout and copy-editing that has unfortunately come to be the general standard for Akademi publications). The wait, though, has not been in vain. Mohanty's ecstatic vision, shot through with light and dark, sings here on every page. In time, the world will grant that this contemporary of Garcia Marquez and Vasily Grossman had a vision of life no less original and enduring than them. But for now, let at least us Indian readers ignore no more this marvellous hillman standing at our very own doorstep.

## 5. Anjum Hasan and the Indian Shakespeare

*Lunatic In My Head,* by Anjum Hasan (Penguin, 2007)

In a beautiful section midway through Anjum Hasan's novel *Lunatic In My Head*, we see the middle-aged college lecturer in English literature Firdaus Ansari, one of Hasan's three protagonists in the book, going to class in Shillong to teach William Shakespeare's *As You Like It* to her students.

Firdaus, we know by this point, is still a spinster, lives with her grandfather, feels herself slightly over the hill, has a much younger Manipuri boyfriend called Ibomcha, is still a virgin and slightly squeamish about sex, and has been struggling for several years to complete her MPhil on marriage in the novels of Jane Austen. She feels profoundly alienated from her life's circumstances: at the beginning of the chapter, we find her looking at herself in the mirror and thinking: 'There was no connection between her and her image; if she got up and walked away, this woman whose eyes were boring into hers would remain.'

Firdaus is not looking forward to teaching *As You Like It* to a bunch of uncomprehending and disinterested students. And even though she has some ancient notes on the play, handed down from teacher to teacher over the years, she trembles before the immense authority of Shakespeare, the demands he makes on those who serve as mediators and interpreters for him. The double-edged words of Jacques the fool, we are told, 'could still jangle Firdaus's nerves.'

Time for class. We see Firdaus begin to read out a passage from the play to a group 'of whispering backbenchers, cautiously gum-chewing middle-benchers, and girls with looks of blank sincerity up front':

> 'He that a fool doth very wisely hit, Doth very foolishly, although he smart, Not to seem senseless of the bob: if not, The wise man's folly is anatomised, Even by the squandering glances of the fool,' she read out [...].'
>
> She began to haltingly explain Jacques' twisted lines. 'The idea here, girls, is that Jacques feels that by being a fool, being given the charter, the freedom to be foolish, is liberating. Why is it liberating?...Any ideas?'

No one responds, so:

> Firdaus read out impatiently from her fading notes. 'Jacques says to Duke Senior that his only suit or requirement is that he be allowed to wear a motley coat, one that will signal to the world that he is a fool. In addition, that is withal, he must have freedom as large as the wind to quote blow on whom I please unquote, that is, direct his foolish wit or witty folly towards whomever he chooses. Those who are most provoked by his folly, Jacques goes on to say, are those who must laugh the hardest. Why is this so...? That's what I was asking you,' she broke off to say, '...if you have any clue about this, but you obviously don't. Anyway...why is this so?' She continued reading. 'Jacques explains that this should be obvious to people, as obvious to them as the way to the church is. The fact is that the person who hits a fool, which can be taken to mean hit not in a literal sense, but figuratively, that is he who criticises or berates a fool, might appear smart but is actually very foolish. [...] For if he criticises a fool he exposes himself. He exposes himself and his folly is laid bare within brackets anatomised. Even the squandering glances, that is, the casual fun that a fool might poke at a man...'

It is by any standard an incoherent, fumbling explanation: there is much dross amidst scraps of sense. But just as Jacques's chatter is wise foolishness, so Hasan's portrayal of her protagonist is one of clarity routed through incoherence. By not punctuating Firdaus's talk as Firdaus herself directs it ('...quote blow on whom I please unquote', '...which can be taken to mean hit not in a literal sense, but figuratively'), Hasan gives us a sense of how Firdaus's students are hearing her lecture, and how puzzling it must seem to them.

And by showing how Firdaus, while feeling frustration at the sluggishness of her students, is herself not willing to walk with Shakespeare without the crutch of her notes, Hasan has the courage and the confidence to present us with an indictment of her protagonist, whose reproaches to her students mask the fact that she, too, is—to borrow a phrase from *Othello*—'perplex'd in the extreme.' The most meaningful words in Hasan's passage are not those that make some sense of what Jacques is saying, but precisely the most superfluous ones: phrases like 'In addition, that is withal' and 'within brackets anatomised', which show that Firdaus is actually on the same side of the fence as her students. It is a genuinely novelistic passage, teeming with crisscrossing meanings: as a result of the author's artful layering, the words point out towards Shakespeare and back towards Firdaus at the same time, and we understand not just the place of the fool in Shakespearean comedy but the feelings of inadequacy felt by Firdaus.

Firdaus knows that her students must grapple with Shakespeare, 'simply because he was standing in the way, he was unavoidable.' She is quite right: in the castle of English literature, the biggest suite of rooms belongs to Shakespeare. But why? Firdaus's reverence for Shakespeare, and the incongruity of this fairly representative classroom scene narrated by Hasan, help crystallise a peculiarly Indian attitude towards Shakespeare, which is to see him as the gold standard of sophisticated 'high' English, as a dealer in proverbs and precepts, and, finally, as some kind of transcendent genius, a god who never put a foot wrong. Shakespeare is standing in the way, and we bow before him: we have not broken free of a relationship with him that resembles the one between the coloniser and the colonised.

Even when we do not comprehend Shakespeare, or faintly comprehend him, we are sure that he was great: the very fact that we do not understand what he is saying proves it. Shakespeare is supposed to be good for us, as green vegetables are. I remember how, in school, my seventh standard textbook had a passage from Hamlet which excerpted Polonius's immensely tedious words of advice to his departing son Laertes. The councillors of education who chose it presumably thought that it was an edifying passage that would be good for students, and by presenting Polonius's speech out of context, chose to totally ignore the fact that we are at some point supposed to laugh at Polonius's long-windedness. The dramatic situation counts for nothing; the high-flown words for everything.

This bardolatry, perversely, has the effect of diminishing our enjoyment and appreciation of Shakespeare, because it predefines the terms of our engagement with him, instead of giving us the chance to apply our all faculties to Shakespeare's enormously knotty and complicated language in an open field, as it were. Shakespeare's language is certainly extraordinary, but what is extraordinary about it is that it is not necessarily 'good', or grammatically correct, or coherent in its syntax: it is a language of both beauty and craziness, of thrilling energy and yawning stasis.

Indeed, I have on occasion heard some grizzled Indian Shakespeareans declare that they cannot bear to read anything but Shakespeare because the language of 'modern literature,' so readily intelligible and flecked with slang and cuss words, seems debased by comparison. (There used to be a figure like this in many English departments in India, and their eclipse is in its own way rather sad, because in many cases they have been replaced by figures who, waving the flags of new critical theories, are convinced that Shakespeare's reputation is a conspiracy of British imperialism, or that he represents not artistic genius but a coalescence and personification of the social and ideological energies of his time.) But actually Shakespeare himself is full of curses, scurrility, ribaldry, and slang, now given a patina of respectability by the passage of four centuries.

Shakespeare (but not the Indian Shakespeare) is as rude as anybody in the canon, for the exigencies of his dramatic and intensely practical art, which thrived or withered according to gate receipts, required that he write for groundlings as much as sophisticates. A line like 'Now is he total gules' (*Hamlet*, II, ii, meaning 'now he is totally red with blood') sits uneasily with our view of Shakespeare as representative of high culture: it could belong just as easily to a rap song.

In fact, it is essential that we read Shakespeare without rose-tinted glasses, and note (alongside his wondrous density and compression of sense; his startling nominalisations and verbalisations, compound words and neologisms; the knotty texture of his thought; the marvellous and supple rhythms of his lines) his often gratuitous wordplay, his shambling and over-long metaphors, his immense sententiousness, and his tendency to say in ten lines what he might have done in two. 'There is a way of treating Shakespeare,' writes Frank Kermode in an essay called 'Writing About Shakespeare,' 'as a very good but sometimes not so good poet, as sometimes but not always clearly a writer of genius—as always, indeed, a writer and to be considered as such.' Just as Firdaus is all the more sympathetic for her weakness, so too the richest Shakespeare, the most intriguing Shakespeare, is one whom we discern as being both grand and grandiloquent, both majestic and fallible, a wizard with words whose trade also forced him into hackwork, and whom we might imagine sitting in his room after a long day at the playhouse, sometimes short of inspiration, and saying to himself, like Richard II, 'I cannot do it; yet I'll hammer it out.'

At the close of that passage in *Lunatic in my Head*, we see Firdaus back home after an eventful day. Once again, the ghost of Shakespeare insinuates itself into her consciousness, stands in the way:

> In bed at night, listening to her grandfather coughing his chronic cough, Firdaus, still in complete possession of her new-found clarity, realised—with the shock one might feel when an old ache suddenly vanishes—that all self-confidence was connected to language. If she could clearly articulate what she felt, if she could find the right words, if she could speak them forcefully into the world, she would be able to make an impress on reality. [...]
>
> She felt calm and drowsy. Her nose hurt less now. At the very border of sleep, Jacques' lines came back to her: 'Invest me in my motley; give me leave to speak my mind, and I will through and through cleanse the foul body of the infected world', and she knew that in some roundabout way he was speaking about the power of language too, about the power of the tongue, its wit and cunning, its ability to make men reveal their deepest selves.

'Invest me in my motley; give me leave to speak my mind, and I will through and through cleanse the foul body of the infected world'—these ringing words might be read as Shakespeare's coded appeal to his audience, and indeed as the appeal of every writer to their imagined reader.

## 6. A Distracted Love: Salman Rushdie's Academic Admirers

*Midnight's Diaspora: Critical Encounters with Salman Rushdie* (Penguin, 2009)

It may seem outrageous to allege that a book claiming to be about Salman Rushdie never really lays hands upon the declared object of its attentions. But this is precisely the objection invited by *Midnight's Diaspora*: *Critical Encounters with Salman Rushdie*. This set of responses to Rushdie by a group of political scientists, anthropologists, and literary critics—all career academics except for one, Shashi Tharoor—conducts its business, for the most part, in a language far too clotted and abstract to give any enjoyment to the lay reader. But even on its own terms, the scholarship on display in this book barely passes muster because it is either too narrow, tendentious, reductive, or self-absorbed.

*Midnight's Diaspora* begins with the transcripts of two plodding interviews with Rushdie held at an event in his honour at the University of Michigan in 2003. The subject of the first, conducted by the political scientist Ashutosh Varshney, is 'The Political Rushdie'; that of the second, pursued by the literary scholar Gauri Viswanathan, is 'The Literary Rushdie.' One might ask: why this division of labour? The novelist is after all one being, both literary and political at the same time, and in Rushdie's case particularly so.

A plausible answer might be that both interviewers are playing to their respective strengths, the better to illuminate the literary and political facets of Rushdie's oeuvre. But this is to presume that a person with a PhD is incapable of a stimulating conversation on a general subject with Rushdie—and that in itself would say something depressing about the nature of higher education. All that this Rushdie-chopping seems to do, actually, is betray the anxiety of academics about certificates of authority and specialisation. Despite this allotment of territory, the questions are mostly superficial, revealing a mental universe as cramped as Rushdie's is capacious. Viswanathan declares in advance that hers 'will be the great rambling interview—very much like the great rambling Indian novel'—a grandiose remark that inspires more dread than excitement.

Varshney, meanwhile, asserts that Rushdie's work is highly political: 'He seems to be singularly incapable of telling a story without political sharpness, without political courage.' It follows, then, that we should not 'entirely abandon Salman Rushdie to the literary scholars and critics.' So far so good. But the limitations of Varshney's perspective immediately become apparent when, in the first sentence of his essay about Rushdie's novel *Shame*, he calls that book 'a political commentary on Pakistan scripted as a novel.' Isn't it strange that a book that self-identifies as a novel should be called a political commentary that is 'scripted'—the verb is so ugly and distorting it demands that anyone quoting it should introduce a pause—as a novel? And shouldn't we be suspicious when it is a political scientist making this peculiar claim? Scores of readers—or should we say non-readers—of Rushdie made a similar mistake over 1988–89 when they decided that *The Satanic Verses* was actually a scurrilous attack on the Prophet scripted as a novel. This is not to suggest that Varshney is an intellectual confrere of Ayatollah Khomeini. But the two *are* making the same kind of category mistake.

The simple truth is that the novel is a flexible prose instrument that encodes through storytelling, at different levels and even there on multiple registers, ideas not just about character and causality but also history, politics, religion, ideology, class, and gender relations. To frogmarch it into the narrower corridor of one's preset categories is to un-novelise it. Unsurprisingly, given the nature of his expertise, Varshney's engagement with Rushdie and *Shame* lasts for only a page. The rest of his essay is about the problems inherent in the political self-conception of Pakistan. It is a very good essay, and there is much to be learnt from it about Pakistan. One might even say it is a short story about Pakistan, scripted as scholarship.

And even on his own ground, because Varshney is so sure that Rushdie is at heart a political animal, it does not occur to him to ask the question that Jack Livings does in his excellent *Paris Review* interview of 2005, 'Could you possibly write an apolitical book?', to which Rushdie gives a very interesting answer. Livings's interview is part of the series called 'The Art of Fiction' and, surprising though this may seem, this is indeed the proper category through which to explore the work of a writer of fiction. Consider, for instance, the illumination of novelistic practice, and how it offers a complex view of a society through its own, specific ways of working, offered by Rushdie in this answer to Livings:

> I read less contemporary fiction than I used to and more of the classics. It seems they've hung around for a reason. When I wrote *Fury*, for instance, I read Balzac, in particular *Eugénie Grandet*. If you look at the opening of *Eugénie Grandet*, it uses a technique like a slow cinematic zoom. It starts with a very wide focus—here is this town, these are its buildings, this is its economic situation—and gradually it focuses in on this neighborhood, and inside the neighborhood on this rather grand house, and inside this house a room, and inside this room, a woman sitting on a chair. By the time you find out her name, she's already imprisoned in her class and her social situation and her community and her city. By the time her own story begins to unfold, you realize it's going to smash into all these things. She is like a bird in this cage. I thought, That's good. That's such a clear way of doing it.

Indeed, it is a fault of the entire anthology that there is very little serious textual engagement in it: Rushdie is more springboard than subject. Elsewhere in *Midnight's Diaspora*, there is a ponderous defence offered by Akeel Bilgrami of Rushdie's critique of Islam in *The Satanic Verses*. The paraphrase of Bilgrami's idea—that we should defend Rushdie not merely on free-speech principles, but on the larger case that the novel is actually the ally of moderate Muslims against fundamentalist conceptions of their religion—is more interesting than its laboured and digressive execution. Thomas Blom Hansen's subject—the changing picture of Bombay in Rushdie's novels—initially seems promising. But even Hansen's exploration quickly slides away into the area of his own research, which is violence and Hindu nationalism as embodied by the Shiv Sena, and then further to even more arcane matters. Hansen's long, obtuse digression about 'Alexander Kojeve's reading of Hegel's master-slave dialectic' and how this applies to the Sena seemed to me one of the low points of the book, puzzling on its own terms and twice-removed from the subject of Rushdie.

The suspicion that this book may be no more than a group exercise in self-advertisement under the bright and attention-attracting flag of the Republic of Rushdie is confirmed by Shashi

Tharoor's concluding essay on Rushdie and Indianness. Tharoor is a more literary and readable writer than the others in this book. But so often his prose mingles regard and self-regard, real subject and disguised subject. Here he allows himself exactly one genuinely insightful paragraph about Rushdie before he wanders off into a consideration of the main emphasis of Rushdie's work. '[A]s I have written in my book *India: From Midnight to the Millennium*,' he declares, 'the singular thing about India is that you can only speak of it in the plural.'

The suggestion seems to be that Rushdie and Tharoor have been working on parallel lines all their lives, celebrating India's teeming pluralism and excoriating chauvinists of all stripes. 'My India, like Salman Rushdie's, has room enough for everyone,' declares Tharoor. Good to know, sir. But does it have room for Rushdie?

These 'encounters' with Rushdie appear, in sum, about as genuine as those of Mumbai's cops with gangsters. Although the book concludes with a short afterword by Rushdie himself in which he expresses his gratitude for 'the intensive, close, spirited readings offered in this collection,' my guess is that perhaps he is being more polite than truthful, especially from sentences in the same piece like: 'As time passes, however, I admit to having more and more difficulty with this whole business of being Explained, rather than merely—happily—read.' If you have ₹399 to spare—and we live in hard times—spend it instead on Rushdie's exuberant early-career collection of essays *Imaginary Homelands*, which will tell you far more about his work than does *Midnight's Diaspora*.

# 7. Life Winding Down in Willa Cather and Saratchandra

*The Professor's House*, by Willa Cather (Alfred A. Knopf, 1925)

*Srikanta*, by Saratchandra Chattopadhyay (1917–1933), translated by Aruna Chakravarti (Penguin, 1993)

Many people are familiar with a wrenching experience associated with the reading of novels: that of coming towards the close, to a realisation that the sheaf of pages in our right hand is so much thinner than the one in our left, and that our fortnight or month-long involvement with a set of characters in a vividly imagined landscape and timescape will soon abruptly come to an end, and that we have no control over this termination of contract and relationship. Surely this feeling is more painful than, say, the news of the death of a distant relative or acquaintance. To postpone closure, we try to read more slowly, linger over every sentence, close the book for a while and drift into the past—the past of the story, not that of our own life.

Often novels also enact this mood with respect to their protagonists. Many novels that portray aged characters, or people who have endured some great struggle, attain closure on a kind of diminuendo—a term from music meaning a diminishment of force or loudness, and in the case of novels a flickering and weakening of energies animating the work.

In the third and final section of Willa Cather's great novel *The Professor's House* (1925) we find the protagonist, the professor of history Godfrey St Peter, a man in his 50s with a large family, suddenly feeling an immense weariness after having completed a project lasting several months, which is to write down whatever he remembers of the life story of a very dear, and now dead, student of his, Tom Outland. (That story forms the second section of the book, simply titled 'Tom Outland's Story', and its effect is quite the opposite: it is of such force as to make the blood of every reader throb.) Alone at home while his family is away on vacation, St Peter begins to behave in a highly unusual way:

> All those summer days, while the Professor was sending cheerful accounts of his activities to his family in France, he was really doing very little. [...] All his life his mind had behaved in a positive fashion. When he was not at work, or being actively amused, he went to sleep. He had no twilight stage. But now he enjoyed this half-awake loafing with his brain as if it were a new sense, arriving late, like wisdom teeth. He found he could lie on his sand-spit by the lake for hours and watch the seven motionless pines drink up the sun. In the evening, after dinner, he could sit idle and watch the stars, with the same immobility.

He begins to feel the imminent close of his life as an instinctive conviction, 'such as we have when we waken in the dark and know at once that it is near morning; or when we are walking across the country and suddenly know that we are near the sea.' (What perfectly chosen examples.) A few days later he goes off to sleep in a room with a gas stove. A freak accident fills the room with gas fumes. Awoken by the smell, he feels strangely loath to switch the stove off, and drifts into sleep or unconsciousness again. Luckily he is saved by the family's maid.

And towards the end of Saratchandra Chattopadhyay's *Srikanta* (published in four parts from 1917 to 1933, eight years to either side of *The Professor's House*), Srikanta, the weak and sickly protagonist and narrator of the novel, is told by an astrologer that he is shortly about to go through a very bad time, a matter of life and death. His wife Rajlakshmi takes him away from the city to their village, hoping his health will improve. There, Srikanta sees out the days in the same dreamy and desultory state as St Peter:

> I passed my days in reading and gazing out of the window at the hard blue sky and dun-coloured fields. Sometimes, I wandered about by the side of the canal or stood for a

> moment on the rickety bridge. But, more often, I sat at my table and put down on paper the strange and varied events of my life. I knew myself. I had little drive and less ambition. [...] It was enough for me to be allowed to live. Sometimes, shamed by the energy and enthusiasm of the others, I would try to rouse myself, to break out of the inertia that had settled on me like a cloud. But, before I knew it, I was back again within its enveloping folds and was my weary, half-conscious, half-dying self again.

A little later the news arrives that Srikanta's childhood friend, the Muslim poet Gahar, is seriously ill, allowing Saratchandra to extend this meditation on passing away. Even though he is ailing himself, Srikanta immediately sets out for Gahar's village, only to find when he arrives that Gahar has already passed away and been buried. Gahar was a great lover of nature; now, walking through his courtyard and the rooms of his house, Srikanta remembers the last time he came to visit this house:

> It had been spring then and the vines newly in bud. Now, nurtured by the new falling rain, they were laden with clusters of flowers. So many had been swept away by the wind, so many had fallen to the ground. I remembered Gahar's desire to give me some flowers and his frustration at the sight of the wood ants that crawled all over the trunk. I bent down and picked up a handful and felt it was my friend's last gift [...] I had eaten and slept here so often in my childhood; I had played within these walls. I had fought and sparred with Gahar and heard stories from his mother. No one was left to share those memories. My roots were being cut away from me...

'My roots were being cut away from me...'—that is a very powerful encapsulation of the experience of old age. One feels that, although their behaviour is received with incomprehension by those around them, St Peter and Srikanta would have been able to understand one another perfectly. As readers, we may find Cather deepens the meaning of Saratchandra and vice versa. And—to return to where we started out—I would venture that we feel distress at the state of characters like Srikanta and St Peter so deeply because, subliminally, we tangle this sense of human life ebbing away with the extinguishing of another kind of light: that of the novel itself, and the break with a world in which we have invested a great deal of our lives and in fact partly helped create.

## 8. Rage and Love in Manu Joseph's *Serious Men*

*Serious Men*, by Manu Joseph (HarperCollins, 2010)

'If you want to understand India, don't talk to Indians who speak English,' says Salman Rushdie—or at least he does so in Manu Joseph's novel about race, caste, sex, and power in India, *Serious Men*. This citation of what appears to be a characteristically provocative remark by Rushdie appears in the novel in the form of a 'quote of the day' on an organisation's chalkboard. The fabricator of these ingenious quotes is Ayyan Mani, a middle-aged Dalit who works as a secretary to the director of a fictional institute of physics in Mumbai called the Institute of Theory and Research.

Ayyan—the narrator always refers to him by his first name—deeply resents the power structures that continue to privilege the high-born both within the institute and more widely in society, while ceding a few concessions here and there to men like him. It is only under an alias—in this case, Rushdie—that Ayyan can make himself heard, since in this environment the name matters as much as the thought. The remarks left by Ayyan on a noticeboard of the institute (and attributed to a mysterious 'Administration') constitute one of the ways in which he carries on a sardonic commentary, much of it within his own head, on the affairs of the institute and its elite, self-absorbed class of scientists, most of them Brahmins.

As if fulfilling the ancient duties of their caste, the Brahmins spend most of their time thinking 'deep, expensive thoughts' on abstruse scientific subjects, or else plotting a way forward for themselves, in little cliques and cabals. Ayyan loves these machinations that run in parallel to 'the search for the truth' that seems to him such a charade, and does everything he can to stoke them, hoping to set off a 'war of the Brahmins' that will provide plenty of viewing pleasure from his ringside seat.

Joseph's novel opens with Ayyan sitting on a Mumbai seafront at twilight, ogling at attractive young women with their 'tired high-caste faces' as they walk past. It stays with him as we see his envy of all the things around him that he cannot have, and goes home with him to the dilapidated room in a congested chawl where he lives with his wife and son. Ayyan is 'something of a legend' in the chawl, having risen up to a white-collar job. But although he would like to cut himself off from his roots and take his family someplace better, more middle-class, there is nowhere for him to go, and he perfunctorily keeps up the old social connections. Here is Joseph's reading of why Ayyan behaves the way he does in the neighbourhood he should think of as home:

> Even though the men here loved Ayyan through the memories of a common childhood, he had long ago cut himself off from them. He laughed with them always, lent money and on humid nights chatted on the black-coated tar terrace about who exactly was the best batsman in the world, or about the builders who were interested in buying up the chawl, or about how Aishwarya Rai was not very beautiful if she were observed closely. But in his mind he did not accept these men. He had to abolish the world he grew up in to be able to plot new ways of escaping from it. Sometimes he saw bitterness in the eyes of his old friends who thought he had gone too far in life, leaving them all behind. That bitterness reassured him. The secret rage in their downcast eyes also reminded him of a truth which was dearer to him than anything else. That men, in reality, did not have

> friends in other men. That the fellowship of men, despite its joyous banter, old memories of exaggerated mischief and the altruism of sharing pornography, was actually a farcical fellowship. Because what a man really wanted was to be bigger than his friends.

Nor can Ayyan, even though he wishes to, forsake the burdens of his religion. As a gesture of rebellion against the disabilities and racial suffocation visited by Hinduism on the lowest castes for millennia, Ayyan has converted to Buddhism. But his wife Oja still retains her belief in Hindu gods, and ascribes the part-deafness of her son Adiya to their wrath. 'Buddha's eternal smile, she had always interpreted as the peace of a cosmically powerless man,' we are told (and what is striking about this sentence is not just the scathing thought but the odd syntax, which gives us Buddha's smile on its own for a half-second, as Ayyan might see it, before Oja arrives to scythe it down with her contempt). 'It was the other gods, the Hindu gods, who had all the magic.'

Even if Joseph's novel was only a depiction of this densely imagined subaltern resentment and gloom (far more complex and convincing than the treatment of the same theme in Aravind Adiga's *The White Tiger*), it would be a striking achievement. But as it turns out, Ayyan is merely one half of the field of consciousness sympathetically explored by the novel through a focus on particular characters. The other half is that of a representative of all that Ayyan mocks about caste, class, and science: Arvind Acharya, the aging director of the Institute, and one of the 'them' of Ayyan's bitter binary worldview.

Like most Brahmins, Acharya is not greatly concerned by caste issues—his place in the caste order makes him oblivious to the privileges and constrictions of caste. Nor is he greatly interested, as his secretary is, in love or sex. These drives are to him sublimated in the practicalities of marriage, and his body is more the shell for his mind than an agent or object of desire. What possesses him is science, and a search for the truth, even if that truth is only a new step into the abyss of all that is unknown, soon to itself fall away and be replaced by a new consensus. He seeks, and has always sought, 'A moment in time—a rare moment in time—when man was about to learn something more about his little world.'

What is more, Joseph has the confidence to not merely assert these things about his protagonist, but to explore in great depth what the life of the mind of a man of science may be like. This makes his book stand out in the field of contemporary Indian novels. He works up a memorable picture of Acharya's big, shambling figure, his bald head, his beautiful face that has something of an infant's innocence, his impatience and irritability, and the iron hand with which he runs the institute. But he also explores, dramatically and persuasively, Acharya's pet theory: that life on earth was seeded by alien microbes, and that the search for extraterrestrial intelligence is taking the wrong form by imagining aliens as intelligent beings not very different from humans.

Acharya's dream project is to send up a balloon 41 kilometres above the earth, where no life is thought to exist, to return with samples of the air there. If any traces of life are discovered in this vicinity, 'it would mean that it was coming down, not going up.' But Joseph thickens our sense of Acharya's flaming mind by relaying to us his speculations not just about alien life, but on all kinds of conundrums. 'Through life,' we hear Acharya say, in a moment of reverie, 'the universe saves itself the trouble of making whole star systems by concentrating vast amounts of energy as consciousness.'

Nor is the auditor of that remark insignificant, for she herself represents a consciousness and an energy to which Acharya, despite himself, finds himself powerfully attracted. Oparna Goshmaulik, an attractive young collaborator on Acharya's Balloon Mission and the only woman of stature at the institute, falls for Acharya's unique charms. In attempting to seduce and possess him, she visits upon him all those agonies of body and mind, painful and pleasurable at the same time, that are commonly the torments of youth. Yet Acharya feels a loyalty to Lavanya, his wife of several decades, and walks away from Oparna's first invitation to a tryst in her basement laboratory. Their short-lived affair (spied upon by the all-seeing Ayyan) and its disastrous repercussions are described by Joseph with a fine awareness of all that passes between two adults who have shared, and now regret, intimacies. What is most unexpected and pleasing about *Serious Men* is that its microbe-loving protagonist is one of the most unusual lovers in Indian fiction. Acharya seeks to ferret out aliens, but instead finds something almost as strange and wonderful in the basement of his own institute.

Among the dozens of finely judged vignettes in the book, here is one. It has nothing to do with any of what we might consider the novel's primary themes, and so is all the more pleasing for the care with which it has been brought off. Acharya has promised to return early from the institute to drive Lavanya to the hospital for a check-up. Both husband and wife are now something of a mystery to one another; neither can quite believe how old the other has become, so different from the Acharya and Lavanya called up by their decades of memories. Here they are, driving to hospital in 'an ancient sky-blue Fiat.' The long sentence in the opening paragraph is one of the few in the book that sound off-key, excessive, but nevertheless the scene is striking:

> Acharya did not say anything to her. That was not unusual. They got into the car and drove in silence. Taxis broke lanes and crossed his path, singing cyclists almost died under his tyres and gave him self-righteous glares before resuming their songs, buses were at his bumper and pedestrians stood in the middle of the road waiting to cross the other half, but Acharya's blood pressure did not rise.
>
> 'This country has become a video game,' he said. He did not speak for the rest of the journey.
>
> When they reached Breach Candy Hospital, he got out of the car, locked the doors and went into the porch. At the reception, he realized he had left something in the car. He

went back, muttering to himself. Lavanya was sitting inside the car with a calm expression on her face.

'You can open it from inside,' he told her.

'I know,' she said, as she struggled out of the vehicle.

'Then why didn't you do it?' he asked angrily. 'Why are you being dramatic?'

'I am being dramatic?'

'I know I forgot you in the car. So?'

'So nothing. It happens. Did I say anything?'

'At the reception, he realized he had left something in the car.' That 'something' is not used (although on second reading it might seem so) just because if the narrator said 'Lavanya,' the pay-off of the next few sentences would be destroyed. It also accurately describes the interim stage of discordance by which Acharya arrives at a perception that his wife is missing. And then—although Acharya himself accuses his wife of being dramatic for her passive resistance—what is striking is the undramatic nature of the conversation that follows, which nevertheless moves us, because we are allowed to fill in the gaps, to imagine what the faces of Acharya and Lavanya might be like as they stand next to each other, perhaps not looking one another in the eye.

If there is a fault in Joseph's novel, it is that the complexities and many layers of caste tensions in India are reduced, in the novel's scheme, to a face-off between Dalits and Brahmins, with no other groups in between. This was almost inevitable, one sees, if the material had to be brought down to manageable limits and the other aspects of the story nurtured. But Joseph's writing has an unmistakable assurance and intelligence, and he steers almost completely clear of the contrivances of plot, infelicities of style, stereotypical narrative arcs, and oddly ingratiating manner found in so many contemporary Indian novels in English. Ayyan and Acharya, comprehending their fraught positions in great depth, are shown to be, in their own distinctive ways, extremely serious men.

# 9. Saadat Hasan Manto's Bombay

*Bombay Stories*, by Saadat Hasan Manto, translated by Matt Reeck and Aftab Ahmed (Random House India, 2012)

Saadat Hasan Manto (1912–1955) might be thought of as the patron saint of modern South Asian fiction for at least three reasons.

First, Manto was personally and artistically impacted, in a way that he transformed into enduring narrative prose, by the massive cataclysm of history that was the partition of colonial India in 1947 into two nation states, Hindu-majority India, and Muslim-majority Pakistan. The decision sparked off the largest two-way migration in modern history, with millions of Hindus and Sikhs in what was suddenly Pakistan crossing into India, and millions of Muslims in what was now a broken-up India attempting to flee to Pakistan. Both sides leapt at each other's throats on the long, strife-torn route. What Manto wrote then in the light of what he had known, heard or witnessed—and what he did with this material artistically, within the four walls of his own independence as a writer of fiction—make him an eerie and thrilling writer to this day.

Second, Manto's daring and iconoclastic writing served as a kind of declaration of independence from the main narrative tenets and orthodoxies of his times, which was that fiction should be 'socially relevant' and 'progressive' in its content, that it locate the personal within the larger realm of the public sphere, and that it deal coyly and euphemistically—or at best metaphorically—with the subject of bodily functions and desires. Manto was in his lifetime repeatedly charged by his critics (many of them writers themselves) with obscenity, and was even taken to court for what was seen as the outrageous licentiousness depicted in his work.

But what his critics saw as a prurient emphasis on the bawdy, Manto merely understood to be a determined emphasis on the

body—as a site for pleasure and violence, trust and treachery, a house for yearnings of mind and spirit as well as its own longings. The world of the prostitutes, pimps, waifs, wastrels and debauchees that he wrote about in story after story was a universe that existed in reality—as much a centre of Bombay (now Mumbai) as the film world or the world of polite society—and was stratified and scored by religion, politics, ideology, migration and economics as interestingly as any middle-class or radical world. The current of defiance embodied by Manto is one of literature's most necessary currents; its spirit is given voice by the writer Tahar Ben Jelloun when he remarks, bitingly, of censorship, 'What bothers censorship is the representation of reality and not reality itself.'

To Manto, the writer must think through every sphere of human life, public, private, or secret. If he is the frankest sensualist in Indian literature, it is because he knows that sensuality is not without its own rules or ethical codes. For this reason, he speaks as powerfully to the 21st century as he did to his own.

Third, Manto stands implicitly for a certain progressive ideal of civilisation—and then, just as instructively, for a tragic rejection of that very ideal. His conflicts are even more telling than his choices.

Although partition found him living on in his beloved city of Bombay (where he had made a living and forged a reputation working as a screenwriter in films and an editor for journals), Manto felt insecure in the city in the poisoned years after partition and suddenly decided—to his everlasting regret—to move with his family to the new state of Pakistan. There, he struggled to find work, was prosecuted for obscenity, and drove himself to drink. He became a wreck, passing away soon after.

What makes Manto so readable, and so symbolic of the fault lines of his time, is this artistic partition that he went through a few years after the actual historical event by the same name. Manto discovers that the ideological certitude and censoriousness of a new nation-state was thin gruel compared to art's invitation to freedom, doubt, linguistic and sensual pleasure, and dissent. He discovers, that is, what he already knew, and submits to suffering as he once thrilled to freedom.

In Manto's own biography, as much as in his stories, the human being is a whirlpool of conflicting impulses, often most deluded precisely when most sure of himself. Human beings also appear constricted or enabled not just by nature (their class, or gender) but also by culture—in the world of Manto's stories, by the tangled history, cosmopolitan culture, and worldly, laissez-faire philosophy of Bombay, so infrequently seen in the history of the subcontinent and so valuable for precisely that reason. It is a superficial criticism of Manto's stories to see them as titillating tableaux of the whims and deceits of pimps and bawds. What we are also supposed to appreciate is the polyglot tongues, toppled hierarchies, fantastic metaphors, and moral reverses and sacrifices of this universe.

That is why it is surprising to note that none of Manto's many previous translators have done what Matt Reeck and Aftab Ahmed do in their new collection of Manto translations, and titled their collection *Bombay Stories*. Bombay is not just the place where Manto's stories are set, but that world's primal word, the two syllables of which generate all else in the geographical and narrative field it encompasses. Colloquial and frank where too many previous translations of Manto have been euphemistic and censorious, Reeck and Ahmed give us a Manto who walks with us in time, instead of receding from us in the vehicle of the archaic English and slightly appalled, sanitising gaze of many previous translators.

'If you haven't been to Bombay, you might not believe that no one takes any interest in anyone else,' writes the narrator in Manto's story 'Mammad Bhai.' But it is just not the sights and sounds and moral universe and freedoms of Bombay that are common to Manto's stories, but also a narrator. Almost without exception, the stories are told by a character who shares much of the real Manto's biography and is referred to by the characters in the stories as 'Manto saab.'

The more we see this figure, the more mysterious he becomes, particularly since he keeps watching men fall in love with women without ever falling into the net himself. When at one point he confesses to a great admiration for a certain woman's beauty and intelligence, he protests immediately, 'For God's sake, please don't think I was enamoured!' It is as if his men and women can get together only when Manto saab agrees to keep watch.

Love in Manto may sometimes be transcendent. But it is always physical. '"Love." What a beautiful word!' the prostitute Saugandhi is shown thinking in a story called 'The Insult.' 'She wanted to smear it all over her body and massage it into her pores.' Here Manto, in a characteristically ingenious invention, makes love not something that emanates from the heart and soul and irradiates the body, but something like an ointment or balm that is rubbed into the body from without. Manto's romance is often deliberately anti-romantic—one woman, the Jewish girl Mozelle, carelessly smears on lipstick in such a way that her lips 'seemed as fat and as red as chunks of buffalo meat.'

Over and over again in Manto's stories, as in the fiction of Isaac Bashevis Singer, men and women come face to face in private and confront one another with their dreams and discords, their histories of guilt and pain. Readers of these stories who know Bombay today as Mumbai might find the city's spirit a pale shadow of the mid-century Bombay that Manto describes. But that world lives on forever in Manto's stories, and in these new translations, Manto is himself reborn as our contemporary.

## 10. When Night Begins to Grow Old: The Fiction of Raj Kamal Jha

*Fireproof*, by Raj Kamal Jha (Picador, 2007)

The goodness or badness of a work of fiction lies, among other things, in the choice of details that the writer chooses to present to us. And the test of those details is their relevance, the way in which each thing noted seems to become an essential part of a larger picture. When a reader commits to a novel, he or she signs an implicit covenant with the writer. Irrelevant detail in fiction is a breach of that contract: when description seems gratuitous or self-indulgent, we have a right to complain about why our time is being wasted and the story being drowned. I thought of these things while reading Raj Kamal Jha's new novel *Fireproof*, a book which somehow manages to be both tedious and profound.

*Fireproof* is a novel about the tragedy and the horror of the communal violence of Gujarat in 2002. A reasonable question to ask here is what a novel can tell us about this cataclysm that all the newspaper reports, journal articles, and books on the subject have not. To this Jha's very good, very striking answer is: non-fiction and reportage cannot present the voices of the dead. But fiction can. Of the many narrators in *Fireproof*, most speak to us from the afterlife, where they have 'discovered gifts we never knew we had.' Many of these voices speak for no more than the length of a page: they are admirably concise and powerful. The plot itself turns on the interventions made by the departed in the world of the living.

One of these interventions involves the protagonist, Mr Jay, who, even as people are being massacred by the dozen, waits in the hospital for the birth of his first child. In this way Jha juxtaposes the 'newborn' and the 'newdead.' The baby turns out to be grotesquely deformed. Jay is appalled, but is forced to take it home, and slowly he begins to feel for it what every parent feels for a child. Much of the novel is told from Jay's perspective. Like the narrator of Jha's first novel, *The Blue Bedspread* (whom we also find in the company of a newborn child), Jay has some guilty secrets which the action of the novel slowly reveals.

But now we come to the writing. Jha's has a liking for lushness that is often not far off from cliché: 'Outside, the sky was beginning to stain the colour of ink, the purple blue that forms *when night begins to grow old*, a colour that *softens the edges of this hard city*, washes the washed-out yellows and the whites and the greys of the houses (my italics).' Or, 'He sees her mouth move, as if she were gulping the night down, chewing it, drinking it, as if she had been emptied and needs the darkness to fill her up once again.'

Jha loves what his narrator in one place calls 'adjectival neons.' Some of his descriptions sound like he is preparing a chart of the universe for the colour-blind. His two favourite adjectives are 'soft' and 'smooth': 'This time I began peeling her skin off, pink skin, soft skin, smooth skin.' Or, 'I feel her hair against my hands, between my fingers, I can feel its soft, smooth rustle.' This kind of detail sometimes borders on the pointless, and sometimes it clearly crosses that border: 'There are always flies on the bananas. Buzzing, flying in circles, triangles, straight lines, ellipses.' Jha's tendency to belabour the obvious brought to my mind JK Stephen's very funny sonnet about Wordsworth, in which he chides the poet for that aspect of his work 'Which bleats articulate monotony,/And indicates that two and one are three,/That grass is green, lakes damp, and mountains steep.'

At the opposite end of the spectrum, Jha also likes the urgent sound, the sense of great significance, intimated by laconic one-sentence paragraphs. This is a perfectly legitimate way of working, but Jha employs this device without discretion. His work has many bits which go like this:

The telephone rang.
Once.
Twice.

Or,

> Ithim was with me now, his father.
> Father and son.

*The Blue Bedspread* had some of these faults, but at least it was an admirably spare book. Some of its sections are no more than a paragraph long, and by virtue of this discipline they move the story forward very swiftly. In *Fireproof*, by contrast, great swathes of Jay's narration are bogged down by the most excruciating point-by-point, sensation-by-sensation, moment-by-moment detail. An egregious instance appears at the close of one chapter, when at the end of a long day Jay receives a puzzling phone call from a woman he only seen once in mysterious circumstances:

> But before I could think through what she had said and what I had heard, before I could try to look beyond those walls around her, I knew I was fighting another battle, this one more immediate: a battle with sleep that came like water rising, rushing upwards, in a wave. Beginning with my feet, rippling in and out between my toes, rising to my ankles, then to my chest, lapping against my shoulders, climbing over my jacket, gurgling as I breathed through my nose, reaching my eyes, filling them both.
>
> I slept.

Is this account at all faithful to the experience of sleep that comes 'came like water rising, rushing upwards, in a wave'? Doesn't that kind of sleep overwhelm conscious thought in an instant, and make impossible exactly the kind of slow, hyperconscious tracking which the narrator presents us? Which reader can imagine what it is like to feel sleep 'rippling in and out between my toes'?

Indeed, the body is Jha's most favoured subject: in general, he never passes up the chance to go over it in slow motion whenever he can. Here the narrator is watching over his mother, who has just suffered a scorpion bite:

> Even the slightest wavering and Mother might die. For if I am not careful, the poison will spread from her wrist, run into her veins and her arteries, travel along her arms, her shoulders, her neck, then down again, to her heart and her stomach to her legs to her face to her head her fingers and her toes—the pus and the black blue yellow green.

Leaving the city with Ithim on the instructions of the mysterious woman, Jay is received at the station by a midget in outlandish attire. The narrator begins to describe his shirt:

> And what a shirt it was. A profusion of not only fabric, a fabric that shone like silk and velvet, but also of wild colour and twisted asymmetry: blue and red and green and yellow and white and black, stripes, checks, triangles, circles, swirls, ellipses, straight lines, curls.

*Fireproof* has an interesting storyline, and it builds up to a conclusion of genuine grace and moral force, in which we witness the workings of a justice that avoids the senseless path of 'fire and hate.' But it is also an unbearably prolix book, and this dulls its power. Jay may hold many secrets, but Jha's unpleasantly overwritten sentences mostly do not. They seem rather like a literary instance of disguised unemployment: present, countable, but doing no useful work.

## 11. Poetry as Medicine in Ashvaghosha's *Handsome Nanda*

*Handsome Nanda*, by Ashvaghosha, translated by Linda Covill (Clay Sanskrit Library, 2009)

Very few texts in Indian literature have such a paradoxical charge as *Saundarananda (Handsome Nanda)*, written in the second century CE by the Buddhist monk Ashvaghosha. This vivid and beautiful 'conversion narrative' is both a story and a sermon; both a paean to sensual pleasure and a bitter denunciation of the deceptions of sense experience. Like Plato's *Republic*, it is both a work of literature—rich in metaphor, poetic language, and dramatic counterpoint—and yet an attack on literature from within.

The protagonist of the story, Nanda, is a handsome and pleasure-loving prince, a scion of the king of the Shakyas. Handsome Nanda has an equally beautiful wife, Sundari; he is also a half-brother of the Buddha, 'the Realised One,' who is creating a tumult across India with his revelatory perception of the nature of human suffering. An entire chapter of Ashvaghosha's story is devoted to a recapitulation of the life of the Buddha. In one of the hundreds of metaphors with which this precept-heavy text is strewn, we are told that the Buddha is the seer who had 'passed over the fathomless sea of faults—which is watered by conditioned existence, which has anxious thoughts for fish, and which is disturbed by waves of anger, desire and fear.'

Sundari and the Buddha represent, respectively, the two poles of extreme sensuality and spiritual ambition that war over Nanda. This conflict is realised in the story's most dramatic scene, in which we see Nanda at home, sporting with his wife even though his brother has arrived in the town of his birth to teach the dhamma. The two lovers are so rapt in each other's presence that, we are told, 'they rubbed off their cosmetics through caressing each other.' (Like St Augustine in the Christian tradition, Ashvaghosha seems to have clearly drunk deeply of the well of pleasure before abandoning it for the cave of austerity.)

When the Buddha comes home to visit Nanda, he finds all the housemaids enlisted in this carnival of sensual pleasure: 'one woman was grinding body-unguents, another was perfuming clothes, one was preparing a bath, and others were weaving fragrant garlands.' He sees the time is not right for him and leaves. But word of his appearance and abrupt departure reaches Nanda and disturbs him, and he seeks his wife's permission to seek out his brother. Sundari, tantalising as ever, lets him go on the condition that he return before her make-up has dried. As Nanda makes himself presentable and leaves, we are given this matchless description of a man giddy with indecision and another who has conquered his own self:

> Reverence for the Buddha drew him on, love for his wife drew him back again. He hesitated, neither going nor staying, like a king-goose pushing forwards against the waves. However, once she was no longer in his sight, he came briskly out of the palace, only to hang back again, his heart contracting, at the sound of her anklets. Kept back by his passion for love, and drawn forward by his attachment to *dharma*, he proceeded with difficulty; being turned around like a boat going upstream on a river.
>
> Then setting out with long strides, he thought 'The guru can't possibly not be gone by now!' and 'Perhaps I'll be able to hug my darling girl, whose love is so special, while her *visheshaka* is still wet.'
>
> Then on the road he saw him of the ten powers, free from pride even in his father's city, and with all arrogance similarly gone, stopping everywhere and being worshipped like Indra's banner in a procession.

Indeed, Nanda's unfulfilled hope that the guru has disappeared from sight might be seen as a foreboding of what lies in store for him, for in fact this is the last time he is to see his *wife*. The Buddha, when approached, seeks to rescue his brother from slavery to the senses, and after a brief sermon asks his monks to ordain Nanda 'so that he may find peace.'

Weeping copiously, writhing in agony, sighing and grieving at the memory of his wife, Nanda enters the realm of monkhood with his glorious locks shorn from his head and his fine clothes taken away. Ashvaghosha memorably describes his gloom in cosmic terms: 'Wearing a faded garment of tree-bark and depressed as a newly-captured elephant, Nanda resembled the full moon moving into the dark half of the month, at the end of the night, daubed with the light of the early morning sun.'

That Nanda is a monk only in shell and not in spirit works to the advantage of Ashvaghosha, for the rest of the text is devoted to the depiction of his conversion in slow, shuffling stages. Burning with sensuality and worldliness, the reprobate Nanda is given the most elaborate working-over by the Buddha and his monks. First he is led forward by false inducements and promises that appeal to his pleasure-seeking nature, then gradually his hopes are disappointed and his illusions stripped away, and he is driven on until he learns to see the truth of the dhamma for himself. This dramatic situation allows Ashvaghosha to present an elaborate exposition of the Buddhist view of the self and of suffering, of the cycle of rebirth and the route to liberation, of the tyranny of the senses and the necessity of mindfulness. And of course, it is not just Nanda who is being persuaded of the duplicitous nature of 'conditioned existence,' but also the reader.

Indeed, the distinctive feature of the text is the intensity of its attack on 'the six roving senses' and 'the glittering show of sense objects'—the very foundation of our experience of the world. 'The village of the senses never has enough of sensory experience, just as the ocean, though rivers perpetually fill it, never has enough water,' preaches the Buddha. 'As fluidity inheres in water, solidity in earth, motion in wind, and constant heat in fire, so does suffering inhere in the mind and body. [. . .] Who could sleep without worry in the world of humankind, ablaze with the fires of death, sickness and aging, any more than in a burning house?'

And the emphasis of Buddhism not on an external deity, law, or commandment, but on personal agency, practical action, and self-sufficiency is sounded in the Buddha's revelatory assertion that 'the reason for this suffering during one's active life in the world is not a God, not nature, not time, not the inherent nature of things, not predestination, not accident, but the host of faults such as desire.' The antidote to this suffering is mindfulness: 'The mind unguarded by mindfulness can be regarded as defenseless, like a blind man stumbling over rough ground without a guide. [...] Whatever it is that a person continually thinks about, his mind, through habit, will develop a leaning towards it. Therefore, you must give up what is unwholesome and concentrate on the wholesome...'

A spiritual novice to begin with, even a rebel, Nanda gradually becomes an initiate, then an adept, and finally a realised being himself, a self-conqueror. Dramatically, this is the least interesting section of the text, but Ashvaghosha partially compensates for this by showing Nanda rooting out the essential truths of existence, ascending to revelation through his own journey of striving and discovery. What the Buddha has already said once, Nanda confirms through his own means and in his own language.

Nanda's story has a curious double conclusion. One is sounded by the Buddha, who marvels at his accomplishments and asks him to go out into the world and carry his 'lantern of learning' among the ignorant. The other is voiced by Ashvaghosha himself. Ashvaghosha declares, in the last two paragraphs of the text, that, knowing the predilections of his audience, he has deliberately made use of a questionable means to achieve a worthy end, and drawn upon the sweetness of literary form and poetic language to make palatable the austerity of his message. 'This composition on the subject of liberation is for calming the reader, not for his pleasure,' he announces:

> It is fashioned out of the medicine of poetry with the intention of capturing an audience whose minds are on other things. Thinking how it could be made pleasant, I have handled in it things other than liberation, things introduced due to the character of poetry, as bitter medicine is mixed with honey when it is drunk.
>
> Seeing that the world generally holds the pleasure of sensory experience uppermost and is resistant to liberation, I, holding liberation to be paramount, have described the truth in the guise of poetry. Knowing this, that part which relates to peace should be carefully extracted from it, not the entertaining part; serviceable gold necessarily comes from ore-born dust.

But which kind of reader is the real object of this moralising message? Is it the lay reader with his mind 'on other things,' as claimed by Ashvaghosha? Or could it be that this passage is meant to disarm the Buddhist monks and teachers who were Ashvaghosha's contemporaries and who may have frowned upon his elaborate depictions of sensuality and indeed his apparent love of language, rhetoric, and metaphor as ends in themselves?

The material character of Ashvaghosha's text suggests an approach towards worldly and sensory experience more ambiguous than its explicit message, and while Ashvaghosha himself acknowledges and rationalises this, there is something expedient about his logic. Poetry, in this marvellous but apparently reluctant poet's description, is a kind of addiction and corruption, just like sense experience, yet knowledge of the weakness of human nature has prompted him to take recourse to it to convert the masses. But in doing so, Ashvaghosha seems to have supplied an escape clause not just for himself but for others. Why should the reader, even if converted to peace by the narrative, not claim the same immunity as Ashvaghosha, and steep himself in poetry with the intention of extracting the worthy part from it?

And isn't poetry, heightened language, itself an antidote to conditioned existence and to idle sensory dalliance? Is poetry only a glittering wrapper for the truth, and not a form of truth in itself? Might we not be changed or redeemed by poetry as we might by faith or by right action? Poetry may be cited in *Saundarananda* as only a vehicle for an answer to the problem of suffering, but form and content are not as easily separated as Ashvaghosha seems to suggest, and there is one condition, then, that his 'medicine of poetry' cannot cure and in fact furthers, which is the love of such sweet-tasting medicine.

## 12. The First Novel of Indian Democracy: Yashpal's *Jhootha Sach*

*This Is Not That Dawn: Jhootha Sach*, by Yashpal, translated by Anand (Penguin Books, 2010)

Any reader who has a feeling for the rigours of novelistic composition is especially likely to be transported by the awesome narrative freedom and strength of the great long novels of world literature. Having broken through the walls of artistic and formal finitude over hundreds of pages of scene-setting, plot-threading, and character tracking, such novels, or novel sequences—Isaac Bashevis Singer's *The Family Moskat*, Proust's *In Search of Lost Time*, Naguib Mahfouz's *The Cairo Trilogy*, Orhan Pamuk's *The Museum of Innocence*—seem almost to write themselves, continuously unspooling and ramifying in the same way as life. Indeed, it seems a diminution of life to have to break with their company, for what we also get from such novels is the extended experience of another mind, of an encounter with not just a world but a subtle, disembodied intelligence—the narrator—observing and annotating its ferment. To observe a story-world for weeks, even months, in concert with a novelistic narrator is to return to the world outside the book only to find something strangely absent, or limited, or silent about it. Sometimes when we find ourselves missing the characters of a novel, what we are actually missing is the narrator.

This is the experience we take away from Yashpal's novel *Jhootha Sach*, first published in Hindi in two volumes in 1958 and 1960, and now translated into English for the first time as *This Is Not That Dawn*. The novel is over 1,100 pages long. But it is not long relative to the dozens of characters it describes, the ideas it explores, and the narrative time (and indeed geographical space) it traverses.

Following a family from their roots in a gali in the great city of Lahore (now in Pakistan) to a new life in the cities of north India in the 1940s and 1950s, Yashpal's novel takes as its central, world-changing event the partition in 1947 of colonial India into the nation-states of India and Pakistan. The novel's central characters are two siblings, Jaidev and Tara Puri, who live in a small, tightly knit Hindu community in a lane called Bhola Pandhe's Gali in the old walled city of Lahore.

Yashpal's novel links the lives of its middle-class characters to the great churning in the public sphere of Lahore and Delhi in the 1940s by setting them within the overlapping worlds of journalism, literature, and education in Lahore. (No other Indian novel is so much in love with the idea of the newspaper, and the newspaper's power as a voice of reason in the public sphere.) Puri is an idealistic young writer and journalist who has already served a prison sentence for the cause of the freedom movement. Tara is a college student excited by the intellectual freedom of the university—one that is not available in the world of the gali, with its family and gender hierarchies—and troubled by her engagement to a man she hardly knows.

In the novel's opening movement, we see Puri (as he is called by the narrator) frustrated by his inability to find a job and the social obstacles in the way of his marrying Kanak, the daughter of a prosperous publisher. Tara, meanwhile, feels that her world will come to an end if she is made to marry Somraj Sahni, her loutish fiancé. But these problems pale into insignificance compared to the crisis that suddenly appears, as the British prepare to leave India, like a dark cloud over Lahore. The Hindus of Bhola Pandhe's Gali fear that Lahore might be ceded, as part of the two-nation theory that has gained currency in undivided India, to the new, primarily Muslim nation-state of Pakistan.

'What if there's a Pakistan or there's a Hindustan? We're Lahorites, neighbours of Doongi Gali,' declares one of the family's optimistic friends. But as the book shows, this cosmopolitan, or merely benign, vision of history and community has little chance against the drumroll of nationalism and the combustible fear of the other lying just beneath the surface of the subcontinent's social life. The novel also shows us that, at the time, Partition was not imagined to be a complete sealing-off of two geographically and culturally contiguous territories from each other, as turned out to be the case. People left behind their homes, families, cities, and countries imagining that they would soon be back once things had settled. But usually they never returned—or returned to find that everything they owned had been taken.

The paradox most strikingly explored by the novel is that the very (allegedly foundational) categories of Hinduism and Islam that were the basis of Partition proved powerless, despite their scriptural emphasis on peace and justice, to stop the cataclysms of violence visited by each side upon the other. People of both sides looted, killed, and raped, 'all in the name of God,' as one character sorrowfully observes. Repeatedly in *This Is Not That Dawn*, characters are shown jettisoning their private moral compasses because they are convinced that blood must be spilled to avenge the spilling of blood. Yashpal's novel, on a scale equal to the complexity of the matter at hand, shows us how the question of justice is rarely contemplated by human beings in the abstract, or outside the pressures of time or frames of history—and that in a crisis, this tendency can produce the most bloodcurdling violence while continuing to believe itself moral. These conceptions of 'comparative justice' are still doing the rounds of the subcontinent in our time.

If *This Is Not That Dawn* is nevertheless a deeply pleasurable book, it is because it offers a world so vividly imagined that the quotidian acquires the same significance as the apocalyptic. The novel is steeped in meaningful details that reveal the networks and pressures of space, gender ('the afternoons in the galis belonged to the women … If a male had to come back to the gali for some reason, he would clear his throat loudly to warn the women'), family, and tradition in the small, hermetic world of Bhola Pandhe's Gali in Lahore, and then out across the fields of city and nation.

As both Puri and Tara are propelled out into the world—

Puri when he leaves Lahore in search of a job; Tara when she is abducted by a Muslim man after escaping from Sahni's house on the night of her wedding—they are forced to bear the violence and derangement of Partition upon their bodies. Then, finding themselves still alive, they must decide what to make of their battered selves. Although it appears for the longest time that Puri, with his idealism, his love of language, his political vision, and his diligence, is the book's hero, in the novel's concluding movement we see him gradually sinking under the weight of his own worldly power in the new Indian republic and somewhat insecure masculinity—an unforgettable narrative arc. Revealingly, it is his involvement with the Indian National Congress that gradually leaches the idealism from Puri.

Instead, it is Tara, the apparently helpless, brutalised victim, who slowly gathers strength and makes an independent life for herself in the Indian capital, Delhi, watching out not just for herself but for other women in trouble. The storyline reveals not just Yashpal's feminism, but also his emphasis on the individual's right to dissent from the collective. Once she has a modicum of power and agency, Tara repeatedly resists any attempts to return her to a normative world of female deference and duty. She has many male admirers, but refuses to contemplate marriage.

*This Is Not That Dawn* was written just a few years after the Indian constitution offered a new vision of rights, responsibilities, and secular freedom to Indian citizens—a vision of a political order more egalitarian and enabling than any previously held in the history of the subcontinent. It might be thought to be the narrative and novelistic companion to that document, all the more compelling because its worldview is implied—parcelled out into the experiences and reflections of dozens of characters across the novelistic timespan of nearly two decades—and not spelt out from above. Ten years into the life of the new nation, Yashpal sat down to compose an epic story, scrubbed free of nationalist cant, about the passion and tragedy that attended its birth. In doing so, he produced the first great novel about the ideals and implications of a new view of Indianness, a novel whose mingled vision of realism and idealism rings true to this day.

## 13. Bankimchandra Chatterji's Novelistic Hindu Nationalism

*Debi Chaudhurani*, by Bankimchandra Chatterji, translated by Julius Lipner (Oxford University Press, 2009)

Hindu nationalism today has a considerable presence in Indian politics: at the core of the agenda of the Bharatiya Janata Party, the Sangh Parivar, and smaller state-level organisations; support in sympathetic publications and TV channels; even celebrity endorsement. But one realm that has been persistently indifferent to the allure of Hindu nationalism, whether in its benign or militant incarnations, is the Indian novel, particularly the Indian novel in English.

Hindu nationalism believes that Hinduism is the real engine of Indian history, and asserts the equivalence, at the level of culture if not always of religion, of the terms 'Indian' and 'Hindu.' It believes that Hinduism in India has been for centuries under siege: first from Muslim invaders from the north-west who converted swathes of Indian society to Islam, then the British, and finally, the new Indian nation-state. It holds that modern Hinduism (which it often views as a cohesive entity) continues to move towards marginalisation because of the encroachment of proselytising religions, the neglect or limitations of the secular Indian state, and the lack of religious consciousness and embarrassment about religious assertion exhibited by Hindus themselves.

Yet the story of India's past and present narrated by the

Hindu right rarely makes it into fiction, except within an ironic frame. The political rise of Hindu nationalism over the last three decades has generated many persuasive ideologues, but the movement does not, in English at any rate, have a house novelist, someone to turn ideas and abstractions into characters and plots.

This is a shame. Firstly, it allows Indian novelists of a certain ideological disposition a free run of the land. The result is often a facile secularism, a kind of reflexive celebration of India's diversity that borrows its vocabulary and its tropes from well-worn ideas, and thus has no intellectual heft. Tellingly, when Hindu nationalists appear in such novels, they are condemned from first sight by the narrator as zealots, driven by anger, hate, and lust (Arya in Manil Suri's *The Age of Shiva*, or the cartoonish Minister Prasad in Siddharth Dhanvant Shanghvi's *The Lost Flamingoes of Bombay*).

Secondly, it would appear that there is a want of serious engagement in the Indian novel in English not just with Hindu nationalism, but with the immense weight of Hinduism itself. Not only is Hindu nationalism artistically unfashionable, except as a convenient source of villainy and conflict, its absence also points to a deeper failing that, ironically, might be seen as lending credence to the Hindu nationalists' complaint about the falling away of Hinduism from the wellsprings of culture.

This suggests a narrative orientation in the Indian novel in English that is not just politically centrist or left-of-centre, but also presents religion more at the level of observation and backdrop than of sympathetic immersion or experience. Hinduism's massive repository of ideas, fables, images, exemplars, proverbs, aphorisms, and narrative structures have left an impression on the Indian novel in English far smaller than the one it exerts on public and private life in India. One might say that, while Hinduism should be part of the Indian novelist's wealth, the challenges of realising the Hindu worldview persuasively in English are such that it is usually treated as a tax.

This state of affairs makes all the more significant the appearance of an English translation of *Debi Chaudhurani*, a late work by Bankimchandra Chatterji (1838–1894), India's first major novelist. One of the earliest recruits of the Indian Civil Service established in the middle of the nineteenth century by the British, Bankim—so familiar a name in Indian letters across linguistic traditions that he is usually referred to by his first name—spent his working life as a deputy magistrate in the colonial administration.

But even though he represented the vanguard of a new class of anglicised Indians, going so far as to write his first novel, *Rajmohan's Wife*, in a strained but sonorous English, Bankim's ear remained close to the ground. His novels, particularly those of his late 'nationalist' phase, are preoccupied with contemplating the future (and reprising, and sometimes reimagining, the past) of a predominantly Hindu Bengali society hobbled, from without, by the martial superiority first of Muslim rulers and then the British, and from within, by a stagnation of thought, social structure, and gender roles. *Debi Chaudhurani* (1884), loosely based on the story of a real-life female bandit in 18th-century Bengal, offers the reader a deeply felt vision of 'the Hindu way of life'—one that celebrates but also interrogates Hindu tradition. If one were to imagine contemporary Hindu nationalism at its best and most intellectually coherent (not easy), this might be the kind of reading of Hinduism it would offer.

Like many 19th-century realists—Hardy, Balzac, Zola—Bankim was fond of female protagonists, the better to portray the constraints and iniquities of the patriarchal society that was, as much as the individual, the subject of his enquiry. When we first see his heroine, a young woman called Prafulla, it is as the victim of the neglect of society and 'the pinchings of poverty' (this is one of Bankim's lovely phrases from his one and only English novel).

Although married into a prosperous Brahmin family, Prafulla has been thrown out by her father-in-law, Haraballabh (a representative, in Bankim's view, of many of the malignant tendencies of upper-caste Hindu society) because of allegations made against her by members of her village. Even though he loves her, her young husband, Brajesvar, is powerless to defend her. Although Brajesvar forsakes Prafulla at Haraballabh's command, we find that the narrator provides only a muted critique of this decision, setting against it Brajesvar's memory of a verse from the *Mahabharata* that emphasises duty to one's father. This is one of several instances where the reader finds their long-settled assumptions about duty and family upended by Bankim, whose vision of an ordered Hindu society leads him to privilege, or at least defend, the right of parents to filial obedience.

Left on her own, Prafulla is kidnapped by a local goon, and then abandoned in the forest after the venture goes awry. Here she finds herself at the mercy of a bandit called Bhabani Pathak. But Pathak, a Brahmin, also turns out to be a scholar of Hinduism. Impressed with Prafulla's native intelligence, he sets out to train her for five years in a syllabus that aggregates the great texts of Sanskrit grammar, logic, literature, and philosophy. The last text to which Prafulla is exposed is the *Bhagavad Gita*, 'the best of all works.'

One might think of this reading list as a nationalist's reply to the policy of English as a medium of higher education advocated by Macaulay's Minute in 1834, and imposed by the British in India thereafter. Even more unusually, Prafulla is shown receiving a physical education. She learns, in tussles with a female adept, to wrestle. The implication is that Brahmins, hitherto the intellectual elite of Hindu society, must learn, in a time of crisis, to fight. Once Prafulla's education is complete, she becomes the revered leader and moral compass—hence the honorific 'Debi Chaudhurani'—of a band of skilled vigilantes who apply their private vision of justice to a lawless realm. 'Each [fighter] had a staff tied to his back—the weapon typical of Bengal,' remarks the narrator. 'The Bengali once knew its proper use; it was when he abandoned the staff that he lost his spirit.' Versions of this lament about the pusillanimity of modern Hindu society are widely echoed in contemporary Hindu nationalist tracts.

Yet Prafulla's major victories in the text are achieved not by force, but by love and ethical action. Elevated by her education, she becomes an exemplar of the ideal of *nishkama karma* or selfless and detached action advocated by the Gita, and that of dharma. All along she remains steadfastly faithful not just to Brajesvar, but even to the well-being of the patriarch who cast her out (even as the reader roots for his downfall). It becomes hard to believe in her as a character, but the reader is curious to see where Bankim takes her—whether or not Prafulla still engages our interest, the novel has certainly made us very interested in Bankim.

The final chapter of *Debi Chaudhurani* shows Prafulla renouncing banditry and returning, under an alias deciphered only by her husband, to her bridal home to take charge not just of the household but, in due course, of the entire estate. Something very interesting happens here. Breaking down the walls of the European realist novel to make room for his ideological project, Bankim, in his closing chapter, makes his protagonist, elevated by the best that Hinduism has to offer, not just the idealised wife of Hindu tradition but indeed an avatar of the gods. Memorably, he claims Prafulla as an incarnation of the Krishna of the Gita who declares: 'To protect the good, to destroy the wicked, and to establish right order, I take birth in every age.' These are the closing words of the novel—words that would have, in the unfamiliar context of a novel and as applied to a female protagonist, amazed and roused the book's original readers, and also words that suggestively replace a Western idea of linear time with a Hindu one of cyclical time. No Indian novel is as steeped in the glories of Hinduism, and so self-consciously preoccupied with a vision of the rejuvenation of Hindu society, as *Debi Chaudhurani*.

# 14. English and Hindi in Vikram Chandra's *Sacred Games*

*Sacred Games,* by Vikram Chandra (Penguin, 2008)

Vikram Chandra's novel *Sacred Games* is written, like all Indian novels in English, in English. But it is an English with a particular character, a specific principle of composition—it is a narrator's linguistic dare to match the verbal energy of the men in the book. It is an English that does not envelop its characters, but rather borrows small sums from them—we find in it a sediment of the Hindi in which they 'really' think and speak. As Indian readers we take this quite calmly, almost without noticing the art in it, and think of it as a judicious and even necessary blend—the language allows us through to the characters by appropriating some of their speech in the original. By annexing a part, Chandra suggests the whole: we can readily imagine how the characters might sound in Hindi.

Here, for example, is inspector Sartaj Singh threatening a man: 'Don't argue with me, gaandu. You want me to take your izzat in front of your family? In front of your daughter?' This is the gangster Ganesh Gaitonde: 'Under the grey sky they walked up and down, counting, and while this ginti was going, I discussed my plan with my two controllers.' Even the narrator in the Sartaj sections (the Gaitonde sections are narrated in the first person) often makes this move across tongues. Here is Sartaj at Katekar's funeral: 'A man, another constable, carried a matka full of water. Sartaj could hear the rhythmic gulp of the water as he walked. The thali full of flowers and gulal was carried by another constable, close behind… They entered the shamshan through a tall black metal gate.' The Hindi is always unitalicised, not marked out as foreign.

Further, Chandra's characters are themselves attracted by the allure and promise of English. In one of the book's most charming passages, revelatory of the struggle of millions of

Indians 'born far from English,' Gaitonde speaks of how his inadequacy in English stings him, and recounts his agonising struggles with the language:

> I closed my door when I studied English because I didn't want anyone seeing me squatting on the floor, one uncertain and slow finger on the letters....It was humiliating, but necessary. I knew that much of the real business of the country was done in English. People like me, my boys, we used English, there were certain words we used with fluency in our sentences, without hesitation, 'Bole to voh ekdum danger aadmi hai!' and 'Yaar, abhi ek matter ko settle karna hai' and 'Us side se wire de, chutiya.' But unless you could rattle off whole sentences without having to stop and struggle and go back and build them bit by bitter bit, unless you could make jokes, there were whole parts of your own life that were invisible to you yourself, gone from you. You could live in a Marathi world, or a Hindi colony, or a Tamil lane, but what were those hoardings speaking...?...What were they laughing about, the people who skimmed by smoothly in their cushiony Pajeros? There were many like me, born far from English, who were content to live in ignorance. Most were too lazy, too afraid to ask how, why, what. But I had to know. So I took English, I wrestled it and made it give itself to me, piece by piece.

Like Gaitonde's boys, Chandra has created a serviceable alloy of two languages, in which the smallest dabs of Hindi keep the language close to the ground, and allow Chandra to take off on the most lyrical flights of English and not sound as if he is talking above the characters. This is Gaitonde taking his bride back home during the Bombay riots to the colony he has built, Gopalmath, which he finds ravaged by conflict. Of the two words of Hindi in this passage, one is the resonant 'vatan':

> Then I looked about, at the homes of Gopalmath. During a lull in my own war I had left my home, and came back to find my home the battleground for a larger conflict. They, somebody, had drawn borders through my vatan. Here was

> my Gopalmath, the habitation of my heart, the town that I had caused to be built, brick by brick, where I had walked with my friends, arms on shoulders, with the smell of gajras and falling water in the air, where I had found my manhood, my life. Here was the bright quilt of its roofs, stretching from the bowl of the valley up the hill, this vibrant spread of brown and blue and red knit together by the arcing threadlike lanes, here were the numerous angular reachings of the television antennas, catching their fierce glints from the hovering sun. All of it lay desolate. And at the very edge of the horizon, to the south, a smudge of smoke. Under that unbearably bright sky I took my bride home.

Here the 'gajras' and the 'vatan' with which the English is flavoured might be seen as transforming our reading of such phrases as 'the arcing threadlike lanes' or 'the numerous angular reachings of the television antennas.' The apotheosis of this method, in which the burnished lyricism of the English is steadied and domesticated by deposits from the vocabulary of the character, appears in the chapter in which Gaitonde is arrested for the first time. In one long, long sentence, which proceeds as if miming the slow progression of the hours, he describes the routine of life in jail:

> In three weeks I was able to execute my plan. And in those three weeks, I learnt the rhythms of this new life: the whistle at five in the morning; the drowsy rows outside for the ginti; the rattling of alumunium plates and bowls and the crackling of the tari on the dal, for which tari you paid extra; the long hours of the morning, and then the smell of cooking from the bissi where they kneaded the atta with their feet and threw rotting vegetables into huge bowls; after lunch at ten, the murmur of conversation and the snores and the smell of hundreds of men sweating; the smokers with their precious little balls of charas and their long rituals of burning and crumbling and rolling; the shifting games of chess, and teen-patti, and Ludo, and the curses and the laughter over the rattle of the dice; my boys ranged around the only two carromboards in the barracks, feeding their

> passionate following of the championship league they had set up, complete with blackboards for singles and doubles ladders; the tussles and sudden enmities that flared between men packed together, that spread like winding fire through the rows of beds; the shouting and threats as two men faced each other under the eyes of a hundred, each too afraid of shame to back down; the brawny kalias from Nigeria selling tiny fifty-rupee packets of brown sugar in the yard; and their clients, hunched knee to knee in tight little circles over their chaser-pannis, breathing in the smoke with the devout expression of men who had seen another, better world. And the long wait for five o'clock and the dinner of the same watery dal, and the lumpy coarse rice, and the rubbery chappatis, and then sleep at eight.

There are two kinds of narrative art at work here: the density of the detail, and the particularity and intense commitment of the novel's linguistic method. Each leavens the other, and together they make for a style that stands as a touchstone in Indian fiction.

## 15. Jhumpa Lahiri's Emotion Management

*Unaccustomed Earth*, by Jhumpa Lahiri (Bloomsbury, 2008)

Fiction is nothing but a narrator's intelligent attention to the play of human feelings, but in the stories of Jhumpa Lahiri that attention takes a very distinctive, hyper-refined form. Her characters, genteel Bengalis now resident in suburban America, are themselves acutely conscious of the management of their emotions, of not behaving in an unseemly manner, of keeping their regrets and resentments to themselves. They not only speak without exclamation marks, but also think without them.

And on another level, their creator is similarly reticent, steering well clear—the metaphor seems appropriate because in many of Lahiri's stories characters are seen talking or thinking as they drive—of pathos or melodrama or anarchic laughter, always choosing a murmur over a shout. Both the writer and the characters, for their own particular reasons, want to put a fence around emotion, and the reader moves into the space they have left open. A sentence from the title story of Lahiri's first book, *Interpreter of Maladies,* exemplifies Lahiri's method. A woman, Mrs Das, argues with her husband over who is to take their daughter to the rest room on a journey, and loses her. All we are told about her response is that she 'did not hold the little girl's hand as they walked to the rest room.'

The stories in Lahiri's new book, *Unaccustomed Earth*, although they wander over familiar material in a familiar manner, are decidedly longer, slower, and better than those of the earlier set: they might be said to represent the perfection of a method that was at last glimpse only simmering. These are Very Serious stories, stories that take storytelling seriously, and everything in them works together to let us know they are so: the slow, even sluggish, openings, patiently building up a scene and, behind it, a situation; the precise, serene sentences, accumulating weight and meaning clause by clause; the unvarying gravitas of the narrators, whether third person or first person—a mood and meaning that are gestured at even by the statuesque author photograph on the inside cover.

The shadow of death hovers over many of them, and humour or happiness seem remote. On one of the few occasions that a character makes a joke, he finds that 'No one laughed.' A peripatetic widower sends a postcard to his daughter and her family that says 'Be happy, love Baba'—'as if the attainment of happiness were as simple as that,' the sentence continues. And although we guess this is the daughter's response, it might just as well be the narrator's.

Even so, the stories succeed on their own terms: many of them are exceptionally fine. In the title story, the widower mentioned above comes to spend a week with his daughter, Ruma, and her little son, Akash. Lahiri's achievement here is to capture all the registers of the encounter between three generations, and evoke the ghosts that drift alongside. Ruma and her father have never been particularly close, and indeed she suspects that he does not really miss her mother. He is never named, as if to emphasise that he is only a visitor. This is very subtle.

But Ruma's father and Akash take to each other immediately, and Ruma is 'briefly envious of her own son.' Her father takes to working on her garden, as he used to in their old home—his home—and in an insight characteristic of Lahiri, we learn that 'when he thought about his garden was when he missed his wife the most.' He is now seeing another woman, but cannot bring himself to reveal this to Ruma: the positions of father and child have been reversed. Both are on unaccustomed earth, and Lahiri beautifully draws their situation out to something like a close.

And in the book's best story, 'Year's End,' a teenager, Kaushik, is told by his father, also a widower, that he has remarried: that Kaushik now has a stepmother and two stepsisters. Kaushik loved his late mother dearly, so his father is prepared for outrage and staunch resistance. But Kaushik, although taken by surprise, reports that 'no turbulent emotion passed through me as he spoke.' He is both his father's child, and in a literary sense, Lahiri's.

When Kaushik arrives home after his exams, he is received by his father, and notes how the decor of the house has been changed by a hand with a different taste in interiors. But the house itself seems eerily silent, 'as if Chitra and her daughters were discreetly hidden in one of the many cupboards.'

'Where are they?' he asks finally, and in those three words are contained all the uncertainty and pathos of one of the many orphans in Dickens. We hear Kaushik's plaintive question almost as a cry: in the same instant the boundaries between the author, the character, and the reader are erased, and Lahiri's fiction, usually so assiduous in its damping down of emotion, suddenly lets go.

# 16. Vijaydan Detha: Between the Folktale and the Short Story

*Chouboli and Other Stories, Vols 1 and 2,* by Vijaydan Detha, translated by Christi Merrill (Katha Books, 2011)

Every reader of imaginative literature makes a conceptual distinction between a folktale and a short story. Folktales have protagonists who are often generic, distinguished by their birth (a prince) or their profession (a potter). In the world of the folktale, creatures change form or come back to life from the dead, the characters are buoyed by boons or buffeted by curses, and good usually wins over evil in a way that is narratively satisfying.

The short story is a more modern form and can be seen both as a response and a rebuke to the folktale. It privileges psychology and interiority, believing that the drama of the human mind is just as striking as that of worldly action. It also disdains magic, although it frequently invents fantastical and imaginative premises of its own. Morally, the short story is not committed to upholding virtue or goodness; narratively, it is not committed to always finding a clear resolution. A folktale is something that can be repeated and retooled; a short story, if its essence is to be kept, can only be read, privately or aloud, because it is the linguistic creation of an individual imagination.

Can a piece of narrative prose then be both a folktale and a short story? To have done so seems to be one of the achievements of the Rajasthani writer Vijaydan Detha. As Detha's splendid translator, Christi Merrill (who works on Detha in tandem with the poet, folklorist, and translator Kailash Kabir, who has himself translated Detha's works into Hindi), observes in her introduction to *Chouboli and Other Stories,* Detha's writing involves both conservation and creation, notation and invention.

For decades, as part of his work for the organisation called the Rupayan Sansthan, Detha has been bringing together, as AK Ramanujan did, all the folktales he found told around him, and writing them up in the same language—Rajasthani—rather than the Hindi of which Rajasthani is often considered a poor cousin, thereby preserving and dignifying not just a corpus of oral literature but also the language in which it has been passed down over time. *Chouboli* asks us to understand it as a double act of translation: first, by Detha from oral Rajasthani into the written, and then by Merrill and Kabir from the written Rajasthani into English.

Many of these stories retain a trace of their origins in performance—the presence of an audience is implied in them in a way that written texts, aimed at the single private reader, are not. Merrill begins one story with a *chougou*, or a nonsensical rhyme intended to put listeners into a mood for storytelling. Some stories also make mention of the *hunkara*, or 'the grunts and hmms of approval that turn a telling into a two-way communication, a community event.'

'Just as eyes look more alluring outlined with kohl, and a brow looks prettier decorated with a tiki in sindur red, so is a story better told with hunkara,' declares the narrator of the cycle of stories called 'Chouboli,' in which a prince (actually a young woman in disguise) wins a haughty princess's hand with the power of his stories, which he tells in isolation, with only the princess as an audience, but with many objects around him, such as beds and necklaces, offering the *hunkaras* that send the story bounding forward. Many of the stories begin not with some significant fact about a character or event, but with some remark or claim about the nature of storytelling itself. 'Nothing happens to a story if all you do is listen,' begins the story 'A True Calling.' 'Nothing happens if all you do is read, or memorize word for word. What matters is if you make the heart of the story a part of your life. This story is one of those.'

At the same time, Detha likes filling out the oral stories of his culture—stories about princes and princesses, cunning thieves and shape-shifting tricksters, who in a modern scheme would qualify as 'flat' characters—with realistic touches and literary flourishes of his own, making them a reflection on manners, morals, and human nature that is recognisably the work of an individual mind. When the narrator of a story says that 'There's nothing in the world more sacred and more wonderful than freedom,' that is recognisably an emphasis of the writer.

The other great pleasure of these stories, for the English reader in particular, is the little swirls of local and proverbial detail folded into their situations. When a group of men each renounce a particular food, 'someone gave up touri root, another kaddu squash, and a third cucumber.' A jeweller fascinated by a female form fashions 'a set of thick mothiyou bracelets for each of her wrists and churau armlets to slide above her elbows.' A character is reprimanded for picking on somebody without reason with this proverb: 'When the potter isn't getting along with his wife, it's the donkey's ears he pulls.'

Merrill prudently does not bother to find (inevitably distorting) English equivalents for words like 'leela,' leaving us to confront directly the connotations of a line like 'The leelas of wealth are certainly most unusual.' Ramanujan thought that the folktale was infinitely adaptable, 'a travelling metaphor that finds a new meaning with each telling,' and in Detha's work the folktale sporadically seems to find in itself the energy to find not just a new meaning but a new self.

Certainly, in the best of these stories, 'Duvidha' or 'The Dilemma' (made by Amol Palekar into the film *Paheli* in 2005), a human predicament is so convincingly portrayed that we slow down our reading, wanting to savour the complexity of the situation. A pair of newlyweds are seen returning to the man's village. They stop to rest beneath a tree, where a ghost resides. The ghost is so taken by the girl's beauty that he falls in love with her. Strangely though, the husband, who should be experiencing something similar for his wife, is so caught up in the mercantile mindset of his community (Detha explicitly says he is a bania) that he can think only of trade and profit.

Shortly after, he sets out on a journey of five years because it is an auspicious time for business.

The ghost, still pining, sees the man heading away, engages him in conversation and learns of his story, and decides to take his form and replace him in the household he has left behind. But he is so much in love with the girl that he cannot bring himself to be duplicitous with her: he confesses everything. In turn, the woman, who has always been seen as an object and without desires of her own, cannot bring herself to reject this most extraordinary love from the beyond. The ghost and his beloved live as man and wife in the community for four years, when suddenly the real husband comes home. 'All the wealth in the world cannot bring back time past,' writes Detha, and his story appears to side with those people who value time and human relationships over material values.

In a story called 'The Dilemma,' the ghost finds that he is in such a difficult situation that he has to 'walk the fine edge between truth and untruth as skillfully as wise Yudhistir himself.' But between the folktale and the short story there is not a fine edge but often a yawning gap, and this is not so easily traversed. While these stories are often diverting, sometimes there is only so far a folktale can go on the printed page. Even so, this is definitely narrative work worth experiencing, especially when complemented by the insights of Merrill's own introductory essay on the work of translation and on the possibilities of an Indian English that contains words and concepts from other Indian languages. 'Armies march to the beat of drums,/ stories, to the rhythms of ohs and hmms,' goes one sing-song phrase or *chougou* in the book, and there are certainly many moments worthy of ohs and hmms in *Chouboli*.

# 17. Basanti's Dream: Reading Women in the Early Indian Novel

*Basanti,* by Annada Shankar Ray, Baishnab Charan Das, Harihar Mahapatra, Kalindi Charan Panigrahi, Muralidhar Mahanti, Prativa Devi, Sarala Devi, Sarat Chandra Mukherjee, & Suprava Devi, translated by Himansu S. Mohapatra and Paul St-Pierre (Oxford University Press, 2019)

When we browse the earliest Indian novels—novels published, say, between 1880 and 1910 in English, Bengali, Urdu, Odia, Malayalam—we cannot fail to remark their readers. I don't mean the readers *of* these novels: students, intellectuals, the educated upper and middle class—the natural constituency that early Indian novelists sought out. No, what is fascinating about these novels, when read at a distance of a century, is how often they contain scenes of *characters reading books*—very often western literature, and just as often novels. Sometimes the most important thing a protagonist does to assert themself in early Indian fiction is just read.

This was not just an ingenious kind of self-publicity—the desire of a new, imported literary form to validate itself by representing common people engaging with it. Rather, reading is often a controversial, provocative activity in early Indian novels, as sexual experimentation and drug-taking might have been in the novels of the post-Independence generation. To show a character—especially a woman—reading was to show her thinking, reasoning, reconsidering her position in society and her relationship to patriarchal tradition. It was to show her becoming an individual in ways newly sanctioned in the west but unfathomable or undesirable in the social world in which the early Indian novelists lived.

Reading, then, is rarely a benign detail in early Indian novels: it stands for a revolution within the spirit, and therefore, potentially, in society. As soon as a character is shown reading, we know that a fault line, a thread of self-consciousness and, potentially, of conflict and alienation, has been opened up between her and her world; they will never be joined up again in perfect comity, and even if they do, it is us, the readers, who will mourn the cost at which they have been brought back into line. Even the *tawaif* Umrao Jaan Ada in Mirza Hadi Ruswa's book by the same name loves to read, slowly substituting books for men as she ages, saying of her former admirers, 'When they began to drop out of my life one by one...I developed a taste for books.'

By showing their characters reading books, the early Indian novelists—almost always male, we must remember—wished to imply that these fictional (in every sense) women had the same aspirations to intellectual independence that they had themselves, as readers, witnessed in female characters of English novels of the day. A woman who read was a woman whom both the male hero—himself often somewhat alienated from tradition by an English education—could desire and the reader could love. She was a person who could validate the very existence of the novel itself.

This viewpoint, we see, is almost never shared by characters who represent figures of authority in the novels themselves. To them, to allow a girl an education, and especially an English education, is usually seen as fatally corrupting (although it was fine for men to study English) and radical. To allow them to read novels in English was to reach the heights of permissiveness. 'I lately found her reading an English book,' complains the old patriarch Panchu Menon of Indulekha, the spirited 16-year-old heroine of O. Chandu Menon's novel by the same name in 1890. 'She told me the story was only a made-up thing, but... just consider the consequences, my dear Panikar, if girls are allowed to read such trash.'

But even writers who did not share the general consensus among early Indian novelists that western education is good for young Indians—for instance, Bankimchandra Chatterji—can be found populating their books with images of women reading.

In *Debi Chaudhurani*, Bankim's most radical vision of a martial Bengali nationalism, the humble female protagonist Prafulla, cast out of her marital home by her in-laws, becomes a bandit in the forest under the tutelage of a Sanskrit-speaking brigand who teaches her to fight—and also to study the *Gita*. A program of reading, it seems, was essential for any woman who aspired to agency in the world. Only the choice of books differed.

This stark divergence at the turn of the century between the generations on the matter of female education and learning the language of the coloniser is both made a tragic crux and finessed for comic effect by the authors of *Basanti*, an Odia novel first published in 1931 and recently translated into English by Himansu S. Mohapatra and Paul St-Pierre. In *Basanti*, the disapproving matriarch Subhadra Devi—mother of the idealistic zamindar Debabrata, who seeks to marry the highly educated and capable, if orphaned and socially marginal, young heroine Basanti—is appalled by her son's choice of consort.

'Yes, it was good for daughters-in-law be well-read,' we read, following the lines of an argument still echoed in India nearly a century later. 'They ought to be able to sing the Bhagabata and read out *Kesaba Koili* and *Jema Dei Kanda* for their mothers-in-law. But then, heavens, what was all this! Learning English, learning Bengali, reading newspapers, singing—what on earth was all this!' Basanti's reading life is connected up to her lack of compliance with social norms for women. 'The thing she disliked most about Basanti was such a grown up girl, far from speaking softly in hushed tones from beneath a foot-long veil, wore nothing on her head and her words rang out loud and clear.'

But what is most exciting about this ironic recapitulation of the critique of 'reading girls' in *Basanti* is that it is not composed by an English-educated male writer with a progressive outlook (which would give such scenes a certain meaning), or even by a rebellious female writer with feminist leanings, of the kind who would arrive in Indian fiction within a generation. Rather, the novel is written collaboratively by a group of young writers who might be said to be the very kind of people of whom the first generation of male Indian novelists sought to produce an image in their writings.

Nine young Odia writers of the 1920s (six men, three women) come together in *Basanti* to write a story on the theme of gender and marriage for the youth of India. In keeping with the spirit of the novel form, always alive to the ambiguities latent within any idealistic project, the book is also a richly imagined scenario of the pitfalls that might lie in the path of this Indian new compact of love, compassion, and intellectual companionship in marriage.

At the beginning of the novel, we see young Basanti, a spirited, book-loving girl in the town of Cuttack, left orphaned when her beloved mother passes away. No matter: she has many well-wishers, and none more than the good-hearted college student Debabrata, who greatly empathises with her difficult position in the world. Debabrata loves reading, writing, and social work—and is apparently a feminist to boot. In an early scene, he is seen giving a speech to the student union of his college on 'The Duty of the Student Community with Regard to the Autonomy of Women.' He is laughed out of the room, partly because some of the other students allege that he thinks what he does because he is in love with Basanti.

Despite these challenges, Debabrata and Basanti come ever closer together, the only hurdle in their way being the sceptical figure of Subhadra Devi, to whose household Debabrata must return—and perhaps take Basanti—when he has finished his studies. Eventually, this is what happens, after Debabrata suddenly announces to Basanti that he has decided they are to get married—the first sign that he may not be as immune to the old complacencies of masculinity as he fancies.

The novel is a very sensitive rendering of what happens to an intellectually agile woman when subsumed by the hoary old pieties of family life because no other choice is available to her. Basanti's life in the village becomes a never-ending round of service to her mother-in-law, in the hope of earning her approbation. But this is merely to cede power to the institution and authority she has reluctantly embraced. Even Debabrata begins to feel guilty for suppressing his wife's individuality and intellectual spark, but nor can he root out his mother's set ways.

The writers of *Basanti* take turns to show how their heroine slowly loses her sense of self in her new surroundings. The two secure sources of solace in Basanti's life are her old friends and her books. In a key scene in the book, we see Basanti reading Rabindranath Tagore's *Gora*. She tells Nisa, her new friend in the village, 'As I was reading this book, the thought came to me that like the characters in this book we too could do something'—a sign of the early Indian novel's desire to light a lamp for a new path in Indian history by articulating new possibilities on the pages of a story, and also a glimpse of Odia writers fashioning their own pan-Indian novelistic canon.

Basanti thinks of starting a school for the village girls—an idea that sends her mother-in-law into a fury. Matters eventually come to a head, turning once again upon an act of reading or writing. Debabrata comes across an article written by Basanti in a literary magazine. There, she questions the pervasive patriarchal cast of the world and asks, 'Why is the idea that women are subordinate so lasting and all pervasive? Why has no one imagined a distinct and independent identity for women, separate from men?' Ideals clash with reality: he takes this as a personal criticism of him. When we hear him say, 'Now Basa, please tell me what kind of autonomous life you would lead that has nothing to do with me,' we know that, whatever the state of their marriage at a legal and social level, the marriage of minds that the two of them had once dreamt of is over.

*Basanti*, then, is a book about the recasting of the balance of power between man and woman in modern India. Most interestingly, it is written in a self-reflexive way that greatly deepens the relationship between reading, selfhood, freedom, and agency so prominent in the early Indian novel. While reading the novel, we are always aware, every time we start a new chapter and see that the narration has changed hands, that the men and women who wrote it come together in the book not just as writers but as readers. All nine of them were Basanti by turns and together.

In an echo of Prafulla's fate in Bankim's *Debi Chaudhurani*, Basanti, too, is cast out of the house by Debabrata. Eventually, the sundered couple are reunited—but in a somewhat melodramatic way that goes against the realistic spirit of the first half of the book, and that may have been a concession to readerly expectations.

Basanti's dream of a world in which women may have their own identity, however, is vividly impressed on our minds, as is her idea that men and women may reshape their relations by reading and reflection. Echoes of Basanti's dream can be found in Indian novels all the way through the 20th century, such as in Yashpal's *Jhootha Sach* (1955). There, the protagonist Jaidev, a journalist, mourns the loss of the great love of his life, Kanak, because of Partition, as the loss of a marriage in which both husband and wife would have been equals, if not in the eyes of the world, then certainly within their own home. 'Had she been there, they would have worked as one and achieved great new heights. Kanak's dream was to have a house of their own, both of them at their desks, writing and creating.' The new translation by Mohapatra and St-Pierre restores to the Indian novelistic canon a text that represents a kind of apotheosis—both in terms of the story and the conditions of its composition—of a grand theme of the early Indian novel: women who read so that they may imagine a new womanhood and thereby a new world into being.

# 18. Home and the World: Anuradha Roy

*An Atlas of Impossible Longing*, by Anuradha Roy (Picador, 2008)

The first, the most unassailable truth of life is change. And the essence of that change is often to be found in the memories that are always imperceptibly moving and shifting within us, the time that is ceaselessly passing, the body that is growing ripe and strong and then paling, the private and public faces that we sometimes will into being and that sometimes take even us by surprise. The Heraclitean epigram 'You cannot step into the same river twice' is justly famous not just because of its primary meaning—the river is always flowing, and what was present a moment ago is now gone—but also its secondary suggestion of eternal flux contained in that word 'you.' That *you* that steps into the river is also like the river.

Which art form walks with a lamp through this subterranean field? The novel, particularly the realist novel, a form we might think of as an education in human moods, feelings, and compulsions through the shape of a story that we live vicariously. The best realist novels rouse us to a state of heightened awareness and sensitivity and Anuradha Roy's first novel, *An Atlas of Impossible Longing*, the story of three generations of a Bengali family in the first half of the 20th century, seems just such a book. Roy's novel is as much about a house as it is about a family. Indeed, it shows us that houses, which hold themselves erect longer and witness more than people do and echo with human presence, cannot but be seen as beings in their own right.

Early in the 20th century, Amulya Babu, a Bengali entrepreneur, builds himself a huge house in the remote hamlet of Songarh, on the edge of a forest and beside the ruins of an old fort, with only a British couple for neighbours. His wife Kananbala detests the place because it is so far from Kolkata, relatives, and civilisation. While her husband finds the solitude and expanse of Songarh liberating, Kananbala is oppressed by it and slowly begins to lose her mind, shocking her family with sudden outbursts of spleen. Amulya and his wife are in search of a bride for their younger son Nirmal, and they find one from a town called Manoharpur, an only child raised in a vast, extravagantly built mansion by the edge of a churning river. The seasons come and go; one generation gives way to another. Suddenly widowed at a young age, Nirmal finds himself responsible not only for his daughter Bakul, but also for an orphan boy, Mukunda, whom Amulya had agreed to provide for.

Roy is especially good in establishing a character's relation to place: we always think of her characters in relation to a scene precious to them or resented by them. Here is Amulya Babu's bifurcated world of teeming town and hushed home:

> Amulya was the only Indian to have built his home in that area, in the wilderness near the miners' dwellings and fox-lairs, far away from the bustle of the main market, from the drums of Ram Navami, the speeches and tom-toms of patriots, the nasal calls of the maulvi, the discordant bursts of trumpet music at wedding processions, the sparklers and explosions of Diwali. He heard these noises all day at the factory. As his daily tonga clattered him towards his home each evening, he waited for that miraculous moment when the shouting town would slide behind, replaced by dark trees and an echoing stillness broken only by calls from the forest and birdsong at dusk.

Note that Roy does not say that the tonga 'clattered towards his home' but that it 'clattered *him* towards his home,' as if Amulya is himself a vessel of sounds and agitation on his journey towards peace. The noise-silence axis of this passage is thus evoked on every level.

And here is Kananbala's relation to the same place:

> The silence that to Amulya meant repletion locked Kananbala within a bell jar she felt she could not prise open for air. She had disliked it from the start: the large house with echoing, empty rooms, the wild, enormous garden where leaves rustled

> and unfamiliar berries plopped onto the grass. The want of visitors, the absence of theatre-shows and festivity. Instead, cow-bells tinkling, the occasional clopping of a horse's hooves, the ghostly throb of tribal drums far away. The croaking of a hundred frogs after rain, the inscrutable sounds from the forest at night. In Calcutta, in her rambling family home crowded with siblings and aunts and uncles, there was always the possibility of a chat, the comforting sounds of nearby laughter, gossip, clanging utensils, squabbling sisters-in-law, the tong-tong of rickshaw bells, the further-away din of the bazaar, the cries of vendors, the afternoon murmurs of a decrepit goldsmith who visited them with boxes of new trinkets and a tiny silver balance to weigh them on.

But this passage also suggests that perhaps Amulya Babu only enjoys his home and his grounds so much because he has a noisy day-world of business, conversation, and engagement that fulfils another side of him. Kananbala, on the other hand, subsists on the memories of the same sounds which Amulya Babu might find so annoying. All the genderedness of space in Indian society is evoked by this description of Kananbala's exceptional poverty of sounds and relationships, even within the prevailing constrictions of the female domain.

Indeed, the main theme of the novel might be the explosive relationship between people and the place they think of as home. Nirmal himself leaves home after the sudden death of his wife, entrusting Bakul and the orphan boy Mukunda to the care of his brother's family and a widow called Meera. As an employee of the Archaeological Survey of India, entrusted with digging up ruins across the country, Nirmal tries to leave the place of his youth and its scars behind him and make the world his home:

> It was a rare feeling, one that usually came to him, if it did, high on a mountain ridge, the immense folds and humps of hills and valleys falling away before him, edges muted in the evening air. At such times, he saw himself as if from the sky, an infinitesimal speck on a gigantic fold of earth,

> as inseparable a part of the mountains, pink sorrel and trees as were the flying squirrels that scampered up the deodars beside him.

When Nirmal returns home after several years to begin a dig on the site of the old fort, he finds that his daughter will not accept him as a father. And Bakul and Mukunda are inseparable in childhood, but as they reach the threshold of maturity, Nirmal is persuaded to send Mukunda to a boarding school to protect the innocence of his daughter. Mukunda never forgets this abandonment and resolves never to return to Songarh. After his studies he begins work as an assistant to a building contractor, and this is what occasions his bitter observation, 'I know all about houses and homes, I who never had one.'

Roy's slow-burning prose style proves germinal for a host of beautifully weighted observations. 'Beyond the house, in the memory of the day's light, the ruins of the fort were still discernible to those who knew it was there'—a sentence like that, with absences evoked as presences, encompasses a whole world of feeling and of mystery. When Mukunda, after a childhood supported by charity, rises to a position of some influence as a contractor and enforcer, he feels a new relationship with the world: 'After a lifetime of deferring to other people, now there were those who deferred to me. I saw in their faces my old faces.' And yet, Mukunda knows that there were things not only painful, but also admirable in his past life, and fears that with his rough work he is changing 'into someone my old self would have despised.'

One of the triumphs of Roy's construction is that, after two sections told in the third person by a voice standing above the characters, the novel suddenly switches, in the final section, to first-person narration through the voice of Mukunda. This is very apt, because of all the characters in the novel, his is the voice most worth hearing from the inside. Mukunda carries within himself a complicated tie of both attachment to and resentment of the old house at Songarh; he loves Nirmal and Bakul for protecting him and despises them for abandoning him; he has a wife and child of his own, yet longs for another woman. He harbours within him—as we all do to a greater or lesser extent—an atlas of impossible longing, and the contours of that terrain are mapped very memorably in this book.

## 19. Orhan Pamuk and the Shape of a Story

*A Strangeness In My Mind*, by Orhan Pamuk (Hamish Hamilton, 2016)

Mevlut Karataş is a kind of man every Indian reader will recognise: 'a songbird of the street.' Carrying a pole balanced across his shoulders, he peddles a mildly alcoholic yogurt-based drink called *boza* whose two syllables, sung by him in the farthest corners of Istanbul, make up a sonic universe at once plebeian and poetic. The slow-walking hero of Orhan Pamuk's novel belongs to the opposite end of the social spectrum from Kemal, the upper-class businessman whose travails in love and love-record-keeping were so vividly evoked in *The Museum of Innocence*. Mevlut's world is much grubbier and his life-focus, like those of so many new immigrants to the city, constricted by the daily battle for survival. But what Mevlut lacks in means, he makes up in manner. The grimness of his circumstances is redeemed by his innate capacity for happiness and his love of an urban universe whose moods he observes as closely as his own.

I always approach Pamuk with great expectations of pleasure and aesthetic fulfilment, for he has always revelled in spinning not just stories, but forms. Just as his protagonists are continuously provoked and unsettled by Istanbul, his readers too are always confronted with a challenge from the novel—not so much from the material of his stories, which are narrated with such lucidity and suffused with so much feeling as to draw us in at once, as their *shape*. The most abiding feature of his aesthetic is his awareness that while lives proceed in a linear way down the rail tracks of time, life stories need not do so and can, in fact, be made more intense and more satisfying—even more truthful—when subjected to loops, contrasts, and switches of perspective. One senses that, for Pamuk, the novelist's challenge is not just to tell a story, but to tell each story in a very unusual way and yet convince the reader that it cannot be told in any other way.

So, although *A Strangeness In My Mind* tracks Mevlut's life in Istanbul—and Istanbul's life in Mevlut—from the time he arrives in the city as a schoolboy all the way into his early 50s, the story begins *in medias res*, with a couple of episodes from his youth and middle age. Much later in the book, we see Mevlut growing into the man we have already met at the beginning, radiating the persuasive power both of a *human being* with a unique disposition and dilemmas, and a character in a *novel* that is using him to generate a life and time-scheme and house of meanings of its own. The idea of fiction as serious inquiry into the human condition and of fiction as a sophisticated game are always held by Pamuk in a lovely equipoise.

At the heart of the plot is a fascinating, endlessly ramifying incident that reveals a great deal about the nature of love, imagination, and time (perhaps the three most important words in Pamuk's fiction). At a wedding, Mevlut comes face to face with one of the sisters of the bride and falls in love right away. But when he asks one of his cousins who she is, he is given the name of her less attractive sister Rayiha, and proceeds to blur the name of one sister and the face of another for years. Unable to contemplate spending his life with anyone but 'Rayiha,' he pours his feelings for the distant girl back in his village into words, writing her love letters with copious help from his friends and letter-writing manuals.

Knowing that in a world of arranged marriages his status as a humble street-vendor counts for nothing, he eventually suggests to his beloved, again by letter, that they elope. Happily, she consents to the plan. In the dark of night, they make their getaway. It is hours before Mevlut has the long-anticipated pleasure of seeing the face that has served as an icon for his soul for so many years.

It is not the face of the woman of whom he has been dreaming for so long.

The shock is almost as soul-crushing for the reader as the hero. But does this mean that the love story has ended, or begun? Miraculously, exhibiting the capacity for empathy that makes him in turn such a sympathetic character, Mevlut cannot bring himself to disappoint the real (to him, the fake) Rayiha. He subdues the strangeness in his mind—the sense that his life's greatest project has gone totally off the rails—and sets himself to the not wholly unpleasant task of being a husband to this not unattractive woman who has dreamt about him for years only because of his own letters.

In time, he figures out how he was deceived: the cousin who misled him wanted Rayiha's more beautiful sister, Samiha, for himself. It is one of many occasions in the novel when Mevlut realises he has been made a pawn in someone else's great game—and then, that his own capacity for happiness remains undiminished. Before long, he has fallen in love for a second time, this time with the right woman; he feels like someone 'who has been admitted into paradise by accident.' Rayiha becomes the faithful and adept partner in all his life's humble projects: the building of a house, the preparation of food and *boza* to generate a livelihood, and the interpretation of Istanbul.

But what time bestows, it also takes away…

Among the advances made by Pamuk in this novel is his attention not just to the moral and material aspects of urban life, but also the municipal ones. He shows us how immigrants, in aspiring for a better life, drive the ferocious energies of a city; how networks of power and influence emerge in neighbourhoods; how land is grabbed and claims for space are negotiated; what kinds of arcane knowledge and cunning stratagems go into the work of administration. At one point, Mevlut realises that 'this city where he'd spent forty years of his life, where he'd passed through thousands and thousands of doors, getting to know the insides of people's homes, was no less an ephemeral thing than the life he'd lived here and the memories he'd made.'

Pamuk's great quality as a novelist has always been his ability to be an ambitious writer without being a difficult one. Partly, this comes from the very embodied quality of his stories: he is one of those writers who loves to 'do voices,' and therefore prefers to write his novels in the first person—sometimes from a single point of view, as in *Snow* and *The Museum of Innocence*, elsewhere in the more radical, revolving-door narration of *My Name Is Red*, where each chapter had a different narrator (in fact, the first speaker in the book is a corpse). But classical third-person narration has its own pleasures and freedoms, and all these possibilities are combined in *A Strangeness In My Mind* into a compelling new form. Although Mevlut's story is narrated in the third person, many of the other characters in the book interrupt the story, like ants swarming over a piece of bread, to retail vivid little monologues and reminiscences and maxims of their own, often addressing the reader directly.

Sometimes their tales have nothing to do with Mevlut, meaning that the story achieves a kind of equipoise between the preoccupations of the protagonist and those of the small society of family, friends, and customers of which he is a part. Most crucially, since Mevlut is the only character who is never seen speaking up about his concerns in this way, he retains a core of mystery and even majesty—as if the narrator, in taking on the task of interpreting him, were also admitting the impossibility of sketching all the shades of his soul.

## 20. Orhan Pamuk's Map of the Novel

*The Naive and the Sentimental Novelist,* by Orhan Pamuk (Penguin, 2011)

Every literary work of distinction has two parents: life on the one hand, and literature itself on the other. If, on the one side, a writer brings to his book all his experience of the world, of his knowledge of family, love, and friendship, his sense of time and fate and his view of human nature, then just as surely he brings to it a sense of his literary tradition based on his reading, the ambition of emulating or surpassing the books he loves best, and the particular stresses and patterns of his language.

For writers, life and literature exist in a symbiotic relationship, each nourishing and clarifying the other. Thus when Orhan Pamuk, the 2006 Nobel laureate for Literature, says in his book of essays *Other Colours* that 'I make the new world [of my novels] from the stuff of the known world,' that known world he is referring to is both the distinctive atmosphere of his upper-middle-class family and his teeming city, as well as the models handed down to him by his favourite writers. 'To read a dense, deep passage in a novel,' he writes, 'to enter into that world and believe it to be true—nothing makes me happier, more surely binds me to life.…I write because I believe in literature, in the art of the novel, more than I believe in anything else.' It is Pamuk's contention in his book *The Naive and the Sentimental Novelist* that the endlessly flexible form and questing spirit of the novel—seeking the revelations of both objectivity and perspectivism, delighting in ambiguities and secrets, and sifting the essential from the inessential in new and surprising ways—are the greatest of all mirrors to life.

Pamuk's title, one notices, emphasises the word 'novelist' and not 'novel,' suggesting that this is a book about the producers and processes of literature rather than the end product. Its six linked essays, offered up in a tone simultaneously conversational and schoolmasterly (they were originally a set of lectures that Pamuk gave at Harvard University in 2009), are preoccupied with what kinds of knowledge and expectation writers bring to the writing of novels and readers to the reading of them. Like all novelists, Pamuk loves dividing the world of novels into two, the better to illuminate the whole. Here, the principle of partition that he relies on derives from the 18th-century German writer Friedrich Schiller's essay 'On Naive and Sentimental Poets.'

The word 'sentimental,' at first glance and in English, appears allied with, rather than opposed to, 'naive,' so that title needs some explanation. Briefly, naive poets are for Schiller the naturals of literature, confident in their ability to understand the world, writing as if there was no gulf between the world and language, and seemingly innocent of literary technique, of the artifice that makes art seem real. The totally naive writer is both liberated and limited by his naivete: he cannot change anything about his work but must always just 'receive' it, as if from without.

The 'sentimental' writer, on the other hand, is the kind of artist who is deeply reflective and self-conscious, bringing doubt and scepticism to his reading of both world and work. He knows that art is always the result of certain decisions made in the realm of style and technique. 'Being a novelist,' declares Pamuk, 'is the art of being both naive and reflective at the same time.'

Readers can be divided into similar categories. Some may believe that novels are transcribed directly from their author's experience. Such readers aren't given to introspection about how their own act of reading brings the book to life. Others of a more theoretical temperament may be acutely aware of, and take pleasure in, the moves and patterns that the writer deploys to produce the experience of the text. Reading involves a different kind of creation from writing, and it is the reflective reader who approaches his task with ambition and awareness. And so for the both-naive-and-sentimental novelist, Pamuk seems to imply, the sentimental reader is more precious than the naive one, even if the latter group is usually bigger in size.

This is quite an interesting theoretical map, illuminating, for instance, the difference between literary and genre fiction, or the relationship between art and reality. Indeed, one of the great pleasures of Pamuk's novels is the way their narrators confidently braid theory and argument into story. One recalls the grizzled painter of miniatures in *My Name Is Red* explaining the divergent view of the human subject in Ottoman and Venetian art, or Kemal's meditations on Aristotle's theory of time, and on what love has done to his awareness of temporality.

If there is a criticism to be made of Pamuk's book, it is that it spends too long at the level of abstract argument and generalised assertion. It is not animated enough by the particularities and close reading that distinguishes the literary criticism of, for instance, Milan Kundera, another novelist who constructs provocative theories about the novel.

Pamuk the theoretician is, paradoxically, more compelling in his novels, where ideas might be thought of as a secondary layer under the primary one of story. In these essays, ideas are, so to speak, the main characters. The triads of nouns that are such a distinctive mark of Pamuk's sentences, for instance, seem a lot slacker here than in his fiction ('As our mind performs all these operations simultaneously, we congratulate ourselves on the knowledge, depth and understanding we have attained'), and a poetics of composition and reception is articulated for long stretches without actual novels being summoned to the scene.

We get some valuable points about how novelists actually verbalise a set of compelling images, how they are obsessed with visuals. For Pamuk, the roots of novelistic writing lie not so much in story per se as in a richly imagined point of view. ('The defining question of the art of the novel is not the personality or character of the protagonists, but rather how the universe within the tale appears to them.') He also observes that the novel is actually at its most political not when it works through explicitly political themes, but when it successfully realises the effort 'to understand someone.'

Readers may feel that they have already been schooled in these notions by Pamuk's novels, and that a certain conversational register that works in the lecture theatre becomes less satisfying when transferred to the page. Rather, it is when we come across the odd ringing assertion (*Anna Karenina* is 'the greatest novel of all time') or the mischievous put-down ('Zola is the sort of writer who thinks, "Oh, Anna is reading—so while she does that, let me describe the compartment a bit"') that the text really hums.

Although the book is perfectly competent and a pleasure to read, the demanding reader will feel that it is only in the last chapter, 'The Centre,' that Pamuk really hits his straps. This is where he advances his most interesting claim, namely that all real novels have a veiled locus. 'The centre of a novel is a profound opinion or insight about life, a deeply embedded point of mystery, whether real or imagined.' Further, it is important that this centre be hard to reach because 'if the centre is too obvious and the light too strong, the meaning of the novel is immediately revealed and the act of reading feels repetitive,' as with genre fiction.

The centre, crucially, is something that is not only searched for or perceived by the questing reader, but it is also the motor that determines the novelist's own perception of his text as he works through successive versions of it. And although it is the centre, it sometimes arrives last, and not first, in the process of composition, being, in Pamuk's striking image, 'manoeuvred into place' as the work's form and colours become clearer and brighter.

This is a matrix of ideas that only a novelist could plausibly express and defend. If such a thought appeared today in academic literary criticism from anyone other than, say, Harold Bloom, it would seem too fanciful, unprovable, woolly, conceived in a dream and not at the desk. But literary criticism is impoverished if it does not leave room for progress through metaphors such as this one, if it advances single-mindedly through rational argument. Many possibilities are activated when Pamuk asserts, for instance, that 'the difference between the *Arabian Nights* … and *In Search of Lost Time* is that the latter has a centre we are very aware of.'

It is as if Pamuk himself is roused by these ideas, for the writing in this last chapter has a higher pitch, and a continuous epigrammatic energy. ('Because Anna Karenina could not read the novel she held in her hands, we read *Anna Karenina* the novel.') One might say that *The Naive and the Sentimental Novelist* would have been a more balanced book if Pamuk had placed his idea of the novelistic centre itself at the centre of his book. But, appearing where it does, it ensures that Professor Pamuk exits the stage with a flourish.

## 21. Naguib Mahfouz and the Truths of the Novel

*Akhenaten, Dweller in Truth,* by Naguib Mahfouz, translated by Taghreid Abu-Hassabo (Anchor Books, 1998)

Akhenaten, an Egyptian pharaoh, also called the 'Sun King' or 'The Heretic,' ruled briefly in Egypt more than three thousand years ago. Akhenaten's peculiar appearance, as if part man and part woman, his inscrutable ways, and the wrenching changes he ushered into the life of his kingdom—shortly after coming to the throne, he overthrew Egypt's traditional polytheism and decreed the worship of a single god, the sun god Aten—brought him a notoriety that secured his place in history, where he still floats untethered to a single narrative or line of interpretation, a ghostly figure now perennially shrouded in ambiguity. Akhenaten's story nevertheless carries a certain resonance for all who hear it because it serves as a kind of archetype of a conflict running through the history of civilisation: the conflict between faith and freedom. The legend of Akhenaten is enhanced (because presented in a way that recreates the mystery that was Akhenaten, and also given a

thematic direction, a focus on one or two repeated words that is one of the ways in which novels are most truly novelistic), by the Egyptian Nobel laureate Naguib Mahfouz in his slender, glancing novel *Akhenaten, Dweller in Truth*.

Mahfouz's story is narrated from a vantage point relatively close in time to Akhenaten—through the eyes of a character who grew up in Akhenaten's Egypt, Meriamun, who becomes a second protagonist. We are not told Meriamun's exact age, but his thoughts and his language suggest he is in his early twenties, somewhat unformed, and hungry for experience. On a journey down the Nile with his father, himself a venerable man with 'a passion for knowledge and for recording the truth,' Meriamun espies on the river a gloomy and deserted city, which he learns is Akhetaten, the dead pharaoh's capital, where his wife and consort Nefertiti still lives in isolation. 'It all began with a glance, a glance that grew into desire, as the ship pushed its way through the calm, strong current at the end of the flood season.'

Meriamun's father calls Akhenaten 'the heretic,' but Meriamun is struck by the dead pharaoh's story and senses a narrowness in the verdict that history has passed upon him. He quotes to his father a saying by Qaqimna, a sage they both respect: 'Pass no judgment upon a matter until you have heard all testimonies.' Many of Akhenaten's friends, family members, and followers are still alive, and Meriamun's father is an influential man and can get them to open their doors to him. With his father's approval ('Your forefathers sought war, politics, or trade, but you, Meriamun, you seek the truth instead'), Meriamun sets out to meet all those who knew Akhenaten, and, as Qaqimna instructed, hear all testimonies.

Akhenaten is dead; each person that Meriamun meets tells him about the Akhenaten they knew. A basic framework of facts is established. Akhenaten's mother, Tiye, came from a commoner's family. Having married the pharaoh Amenhotep III, she then exerted great influence over the royal household. Akhenaten's name at birth was Amenhotep, like his father; it was only later, when he came to the throne, that he changed it to

Akhenaten. He was frail and feeble from birth, but when he and his healthier brother, Tuthmosis, contracted the same illness, it was Tuthmosis who succumbed to it and Akhenaten who survived. While he was growing up Akhenaten, although the heir-in-waiting, showed no interest in matters of government. Rather, his interest lay in spiritual matters: Ay, his tutor in his youth, recalls that it seemed to him that he was born 'with some otherworldly wisdom.' Before Akhenaten came to the throne, Queen Tiye had already declared her veneration of Aten, the Sun God, in preference to Amun, the master of all the deities in Egypt. As he grew mature, Akhenaten too began to believe in the pre-eminence of Aten. One morning, while watching the sun rise, he had a religious vision that affected him profoundly, and became convinced that the truth had been revealed to him—the truth that there was only one God, Aten. He resolved thereafter only to 'dwell in truth' and walk the path of love and non-violence, and though the pharaoh tried his best to draw him away from these beliefs, he remained stubborn.

One of Ay's two daughters, Nefertiti, was drawn to the prince and his beliefs, and they fell in love and were married. When the pharaoh passed away suddenly, his son came to the throne, upon which he changed his name to Akhenaten, and immediately set about purging Egypt of its plural religious traditions by decree, declaring that there was only one god, Aten. He toured his empire, preaching the new religion and proclaiming the message of love, and set up a new capital, Akhetaten, where he lived with Nefertiti and his closest followers and gave himself over to devotion. But there remained a disenchanted faction in the country, followers of the old beliefs and the old order. At the same time, the country's enemies pressed in at its borders, sensing an opportunity to invade it. But Akhenaten refused to send an army to the country's borders, saying he would confront the intruders himself with his message of peace. Finally, Akhenaten's chief of security, Haremhab, rebelled and declared his allegiance to a new pharaoh, Akhenaten's half-brother Tutankhamun. Akhenaten was deposed and put under house arrest, his capital was emptied of his followers, and the country successfully defended by the new regime. Egypt returned to its old traditions, and Akhenaten passed away soon after. The official reason for his death, a sudden illness, was contested by his wife, who continued to reside in the deserted capital, and his followers. The aberrant monotheistic religion dedicated to the sun god Aten died a swift death after the pharaoh's passing away and Akhenaten became established as a heretic in public memory.

These are the facts. Now what is the truth? As Meriamun covers the territory of Akhenaten's life over and over again with the people he meets, he encounters psychological explanations of his behaviour, speculations that he was a puppet in the hands of his mother or his wife, providential readings of history, accounts in which he seems remote and otherworldly contrasting with those in which he seems all too human, assertions that he was foolishly or tragically deluded milling with those that he was in possession of a higher truth and hence a martyr. Although the characters variously express anger, love, warmth, sadness, or bitterness, few, if any, speak complacently, as if confident of possessing the whole truth: they are aware that what they express is an account of a *relationship*, not a one-way stream of knowledge about the life of a man. The novel suggests that when we seek to establish something definite about human beings, we must resign ourselves to approaching only the threshold of truth, and not totally comprehending it: firstly, because we ourselves are implicated in the search and bring to it either beliefs or perspectives that are our own and that we cannot quite lay by, and secondly, because, even if we have had an opportunity to know the person closely or even intimately, and feel confident of a wide understanding and, therefore, a kind of objectivity, there is, nevertheless, still something about that person that we do not know about or is hidden from us—several people make some individual observation about Akhenaten that we could consider of importance but that others close to him seem not to know.

Nevertheless, the novel is not pessimistic about our desire to know the truth, our belief that we can ascend to the truth through effort. It does not regard Meriamun's 'desire to know the truth' as naive, but rather leads him to a more complex conception of it. In fact, something of what Meriamun will eventually understand is hinted at early in the novel, in his words to his father asking for letters of introduction to all those who knew Akhenaten: 'Then I could see the many facets of truth before it perishes like this city.' Truth here is not seen as something easily achieved or formulated; it has many facets, each of which must be discovered, after which it may not be further reducible. Also, it is significant that Meriamun speaks of the many facets of truth before 'it perishes' and not 'they perish': it is as if when even one facet of the truth is lost then the truth itself stands imperilled. Meriamun wants to take advantage of his historical proximity to the dead pharaoh to grasp the many faces of the truth before they begin to ebb away one by one, leaving behind a thinner, a more famished 'truth'—for instance, the current understanding of Akhenaten as a heretic.

But is not Meriamun only, in this novel, who is preoccupied with the idea of the truth. For that word was also the most important word in the whole world for Akhenaten, who believed he was 'a dweller in truth.' The novel achieves its charge through the interplay and contrast of these two conceptions of truth, which we might call the truth of reason and the truth of faith, a truth that prizes scepticism and one that resides in belief. We note the differing ways in which the two protagonists speak of the subject: Meriamun is a seeker of truth; Akhenaten, a dweller *in* truth. And through this contrast Mahfouz thrusts us onto rocky philosophical ground. Is it possible to make some judgment of the truth about Akhenaten without first making a judgment of Akhenaten's 'truth'—the vision that came to him and which he codified into a religious system and propagated as the only true way of knowing God? From what standpoint can one make such a judgment?

The novel form, itself a product of the waning of religious

belief in the world, has sometimes found this judgment easy; it is a form sceptical of absolutes, and for believers, religion is an absolute. But the great beauty of Mahfouz's novel is that it allows us to enter and inhabit not just the universe of Meriamun's worldly truth but also that of Akhenaten's otherworldly truth. For Akhenaten's opponents, his religion was a sham religion, the result of his hallucinations or else a piece of deliberate trickery; Toto, the chief epistoler in Akhenaten's chamber, thinks it 'the shrewdness of a man humiliated by his own weakness.' But these judgments are destabilised by the tutor Ay, who noticed the young Akhenaten's religious bent; by his wife Nefertiti, who confesses she was drawn to his beliefs 'as a butterfly is drawn to light,' and by the pharaoh's aged physician Bento, who was skeptical of his vision at first but then became a believer, and helped set up his capital at Akhetaten. Akhenaten's followers convincingly describe the ecstasy, the paradoxical wholeness of being that arrives from surrendering before the divine that, if at all we admit the authority of religion, we know as being one of the authentic experiences of faith. 'Every morning I compared what I heard in the temple of the One God to the liturgy of the old gods,' recounts Bento. 'I became certain beyond doubt that a stream of divine light was filling us with pure happiness. [...] Today, Akhenaten is known only as "the heretic." But despite all that was said about him, my heart still fills with love at the mention of his name. What a life he created for himself! Did he really devote his life to love?'

Difficult questions are not resolved in Mahfouz's novel, but addressed so compellingly from different angles as to give us a true sense of their difficulty. (It could be said that the novel's striking last paragraph is indeed a kind of resolution, but it is a private one, not to be generally applied.) Since no final judgment is passed on Akhenaten from the evidence Meriamun has compiled, one attitude towards Mahfouz's novel might be that Mahfouz has left it to *us* to make a judgment about Akhenaten. But this is to flatter ourselves. The novel is complete without the reader—complete in its recreation of the complexity and elusiveness of its subject, and also complete in the manner in which it is all-seeing, in the way in which it manages a omniscient, magisterial presence through nothing more than juxtapositions: of narrator and subject, and of different testimonies. Mahfouz's narrative method reminds us of 'the calm, strong current' with which the book began. He does not press a reductive idea of the truth upon us, and in doing so, reveals the truths that only novels can show us.

## 22. Irene Nemirovsky's Worldly Goods

*All Our Worldly Goods,* by Irene Nemirovsky, translated by Sandra Smith (Vintage, 2008)

Extended depictions of successful marriages are very rare in fiction. This is not just because good marriages themselves are rare, or because marital discord and misunderstanding is itself a favoured subject for fictional inquiry—an opportunity to observe the workings of the self as it rubs up against that other with which it is most intimate; a way to probe the gulf between the private thought and the public pose in adult life. In addition to all this, it must be said, it is difficult to bring out the richness of a fulfilling marriage in a way that is also dramatic. There is a reason why folk tales and romantic comedies end at the point of 'and they lived happily ever after'—because beyond this point lies more difficult, ambiguous terrain not just for the couple but also for the form.

This is why, when, four chapters into Irene Nemirovsky's novel *All Our Worldly Goods*, her protagonists, Pierre Hardelot and Agnès Florent, decide to consecrate the unspoken affection they have shared since childhood, and marry in defiance of Pierre's family, we ask: What now? We feel that Nemirovsky has either played her cards too soon, or she is setting these two young people up for a fall.

But remarkably, this is not the case. Nemirovsky's novel begins in a small town in France called Saint-Étienne at the beginning of the 20th century, and over the next three decades, everything around Pierre and Agnes will change—crises of livelihood, the death of parents, troubles with children, the horror of two World Wars in which Pierre and then his son are, respectively, mobilised—except for what is shared between them. The tenderness and awe that Pierre feels on his wedding night as he wakes up and contemplates the sleeping figure of his beloved runs like a winding thread across place and time all the way to the closing scene of the novel, in which, after many months of separation during World War II and of fearing the worst, Pierre and Agnes find each other still alive.

Nemirovsky's own life story is no less poignant. She was born in 1903, the daughter of Russian Jews who escaped just after the Russian Revolution and moved to France. In relative youth, she wrote a string of successful novels, but she was captured by German troops in World War II and met a terrible end at Auschwitz, Poland, in 1942. A notebook snatched up by her daughter as the family fled their house remained unopened for more than 50 years, when it revealed itself to be not a diary but a pair of finished novellas. This work, translated into English as *Suite Française* in 2006, proved an enormous success, and led to the republication and translation of Nemirovsky's earlier works, including *All Our Worldly Goods*. Contemporary fiction is all the richer for this belated injection of Nemirovsky's work into its bloodstream.

Nemirovsky's work is distinctive and unforgettable for many reasons. She is interested not only in individuals but also their milieu; *All Our Worldly Goods* also traces the fortunes of the Hardelot family and the business it owns, and repeatedly cuts away for a page or two at a time into memorable portraits of minor characters.

Further, Nemirovsky has the courage, both in this book and in *Suite Francaise*, to write about the present moment as if it were already historical. She began *All Our Worldly Goods* in

1940, when France was already occupied by German troops, and some of the action of the book takes place in the same year—indeed, we are given a fairly comprehensive portrait of what the war is like. The wonder of this would have been apparent to her first readers in French; reading it now, we forget that the war she is describing is the same war that took her life.

Lastly, like all the great realist novelists, Nemirovsky depicts life situations we are all familiar with and makes them come alive with some marvellous perception. For instance, Guy, Pierre's son, comes home on leave from the front, and is told by his wife, Rose, that she is pregnant. Guy cannot think of anything to say but 'I'm very happy' over and over again, but he does so 'without looking at her, feeling oddly shy,' and so much is contained in this paradoxical and yet truthful observation.

This moment parallels one from much earlier in the book, when Pierre comes home from the war (this is World War I) for the first time. Although he has arrived, we see Agnès standing still 'in the dark hallway, pressed against the door that was about to open'—she wants to hold on to this moment of delicious anticipation, because every moment after this will be turned towards her husband leaving again. Nemirovsky's writing is full of such delicate and daring surges, beautifully rendered by Sandra Smith's translation.

The title of Nemirovsky's book (*Les biens de ce monde* in French) is worth contemplating. At the most basic level, it gestures at the human need for material security and the use, within families and societies, of economic power as social force. Marriages are considered good or bad on grounds of class; Pierre's grandfather threatens to disinherit him when he decides to marry beneath his station; families are repeatedly shown gathering up their most precious possessions as they flee from war—all these are illustrations of the title.

But 'goods' can also be understood in a different way, as—to take a phrase in the novel itself—'all the good things of this world,' both tangible and ineffable. The trust and faith of relationships, the memories of sweetness and darkness we carry, the simple round of actions and exchanges that see us through the day—these, too, are our worldly goods, and Nemirovsky's novel successfully balances both these planes of existence to open out for us a vision of 'the good.'

## 23. Burning Life in the Novels of Irene Nemirovsky

*Jezebel,* by Irene Nemirovsky, translated by Sandra Smith (Vintage International, 2012)

Since the posthumous publication in 2004 of *Suite Francaise*—an unfinished novel of Tolstoyan scope and depth, about the experiences of French people on the run during the German occupation of France in 1940—the reputation of the French novelist Irene Nemirovsky (1903–1942), whose life was snuffed out in the gas chambers of Auschwitz, has reached heights that it never did during her own lifetime.

The depth of feeling, concision of expression, and agility of narrative technique of *Suite Francaise* were hard to forget. (The novel's wide-angle opening sentence is only four words: 'Hot, thought the Parisians.') They immediately stoked an intense curiosity in Nemirovsky's earlier novels, of which there seemed to be a great number. Nemirovsky was only 39 when she died, but she had published roughly a novel every year in a literary career that lasted only 16 years. How did she arrive at her extraordinary powers? What kinds of continuities exist between her early work and her later novels? Is it that the Nemirovskian narrator's apprehension of life and philosophical attitude towards it, which appears fully formed in the late books, comes into its own piece by piece, or in one great leap?

New translations of Nemirovsky's books, themselves arriving at the Nemirovskian rate of one a year from her translator Sandra Smith, are allowing readers in English to slowly put together all the answers to all these questions. Unlike Nemirovsky's first audience—the readers of her own lifetime—we go backwards into her work, reading books that are smaller in scale and emotional range than her final works, yet possessing their own distinct emphases and satisfactions (as also certain weaknesses). The latest of these works is *Jezebel*, written by Nemirovsky mid-career in 1936.

The very title of the novel offers a damning condemnation of its protagonist, the beautiful society lady Gladys Eysenach, whom we meet for the first time in a courtroom as she stands on trial for the murder of her much younger lover. This opening scene is unusual in Nemirovsky for the length of time—about 40 pages—for which the same frame is held. In most of her work, she cuts rapidly from scene to scene (and often forward in time too) as rapidly as in a film, but here we feel as if we are watching a play. The murder and its motivations are carefully reconstructed, and all the people in Gladys's life take their turn to speak. Although the accused often flinches, she does not deny the crime, one that exposes her as scheming and sexually predatory. There are the usual flashes of striking observation. When the judge asks Gladys to take off her hat, her chambermaid, sitting in the audience, moves instinctively to help her mistress, before she realises where she is.

Although the trial is for murder, it is also, we see, a prosecution by men of a woman, by bourgeois society of someone who has not conformed to its norms, and by the crowd of a scapegoat. It is about law, but beneath that it is also about morality and the complacence it engenders. Nemirovsky's work, even as it tracks the thoughts of individuals in the native mode of fiction, also often gives voice, more startlingly, to what people are thinking as a group, usually in a way that incriminates them. Here, when there suddenly appears on Gladys's face a sly expression that was 'the stock image of a murderer,' the crowd, we are told, 'felt even more confident that they had the right to judge her.' When the sentence is passed, the crowd leaves, satisfied. But the narrator wants to tell us some more.

The French filmmaker Jacques Becker once said, 'In my work I don't want to prove anything except that life is stronger than everything else.' He might have taken this thought from Nemirovsky. In *Suite Francaise*, when the teenager Hubert Péricand breaks down in impotent rage because he has not taken up arms against the Germans, the dancer Arlette Corail consoles him: 'What can we do?...first and foremost we have to live...to go on....' 'First and foremost we have to live' is a thought that echoes through the minds of many characters in Nemirovsky—Ada Sinner in *The Dogs and the Wolves*, David Golder in *David Golder*—who are conscious of all the beautiful things that life has to offer, of the ways in which these may be attained, of the enormous need in their own natures, and of the constant pressure of time upon existence. Life, for them, is stronger than everything else, and they will often transgress to keep the flame burning. There is only one one-word sentence in *Suite Francaise*, and that is 'Alive.'

Gladys Eysenach is someone who represents this lust for life at its negative extreme—someone who is motivated, but then gradually deformed, by the intensity of her need to cheat time of its taxes. A great beauty, she enjoys a glittering youth, marries well, has several love affairs after her husband passes away in middle age, and revels in her power over men, whose ardour is what gives her life its sweetness. 'Gladys was, and always would be, profoundly aware of her beauty. At every moment of every day she felt it was her inner peace.' But she cannot stand anything that shows up her real age. Naturally, this leads to an attempt to deny that her teenaged daughter Marie-Therese is growing into a woman herself. (Nemirovsky may have drawn this detail from the conduct of her own mother Fanny, who dressed her daughter in children's clothing until Irene was well into her teens.)

When Marie-Therese wants to marry early, Gladys implores her to wait a few years, just so that she may enjoy her own youth a little longer. When, later, her daughter dies in childbirth, Gladys has the baby sent away because it reminds her that she is now a grandmother. We see Gladys thinking, as a twenty-year-old: 'Leave me alone! I want my pleasure!' Forty years later, she is still thinking the same thing. She cannot bring herself to go through the stages of adult life gracefully, and thus turns herself not only into a monster of egotism, but also eventually into a figure of pathos.

In the novel's most wrenching and grotesque scene, we see Gladys camped one night outside the home of her Italian lover, Aldo Monti. Monti has repeatedly beseeched Gladys to marry him, but she always refuses, fearing that his regard for her will disappear when he finds out her real age. Monti is not at home, and at dawn he appears with Jeannine, the wife of one of his friends, a woman less than half Gladys's age. Gladys is enraged, and is just about to confront the couple, when something stops her. It is the realisation that youth will win anyway. 'Jeannine could cry,' she reasons. 'Jeannine wasn't even thirty. Her tears would make Monti feel tenderness towards her. But she, Gladys, couldn't forget that tears made her make-up run down her cheeks.'

*Jezebel* is a slighter work than some of Nemirovsky's other novels. At times the narration has a somewhat perfunctory air and Nemirovsky might herself have conceded that the story becomes claustrophobic because it hews too closely to the protagonist's perspective. (This problem is solved in later books by a stronger narratorial voice and beautiful short diversions into the lives of minor characters.)

But the effort invested in the novel's structure and its plotting yields rich rewards. Nemirovsky loves the lash of an uncoiling plot, and the challenges of distracting the reader from perceiving the shape of things before the moment of revelation. Also on display is the trademark panache in the exposition of a demanding story that absorbs over 40 years in the life of the protagonist. Indeed, it is a kind of beautiful paradox about *Jezebel* that narrative time should be managed so expertly in a story about a woman whose tragic flaw is that she does not know how to control time.

## 24. Jose Saramago and the Small Voice of History

*The Elephant's Journey*, by Jose Saramago, translated by Margaret Jull Costa (Harvill Secker, 2010)

In Jose Saramago's novella *The Tale of the Unknown Island*, the protagonist—an unnamed everyman figure—asks a king for the gift of a boat so that he may go out 'in search of the unknown island.' The king is sceptical. Isn't it well established that no more unknown islands exist? But the man stands his ground. In a remark rich with metaphorical meaning (one might even take it as the reason why writers write novels), he insists that there is always another unknown island to be discovered.

Finally, the man has his way. Saramago also gives him a love interest: the humble cleaning lady of the royal palace, who decides that after a lifetime of swabbing the royal floors she would rather be part of a voyage. No other crew member can be found, but this does not seem to be a problem. The story takes its leave of us with an image of the two lovers painting the name of the boat on the prow. The narrator has long been setting up his triumphant finish: 'Around midday, with the tide, The Unknown Island finally set out to sea, in search of itself.'

Of the many great exponents of the novel in the 20th century, Saramago was one of the few who really made the form his own. In his books, the story never arrives to us neatly organised, crafted, and finished, cleansed of narrative detritus. Rather, like the boat in *The Tale of the Unknown Island*, the story is always in search of itself, trying to arrive at an understanding of itself, remarking on its own difficulties as it goes on.

At first this disorients us. We resist the writer's rough and ready ways. But then, when we begin to see the possibilities of the mode, they begin to delight us. The narrator is always the most powerful presence in Saramago's novels, now speeding the action along, now slowing it down, making a luminous observation one moment ('We are, more and more, our own

defects and not our qualities'), then succumbing to a page or two of pure pedantry. The narrator's love of irony, empathy for the marginalised, and undercutting of the grand narratives of history establish a direct line between him and the author, a lifelong and outspoken communist. Saramago's protagonists are almost always ordinary people who distinguish themselves by some gesture of protest or defiance at the iniquities and awesome arm-twisting power of time, history, or convention. Kings in his stories are usually the characters with bit parts.

Most distinctive in Saramago's work, though, is the style. His narrators revel in the role of master of ceremonies, insisting on it through the very form of their prose, which swallows up the talk of the characters into long, rolling, idiosyncratic sentences. (When Saramago uses direct speech, he does so without quotation marks or indentations.) The typical Saramago sentence can seem almost Jamesian in its love of ripples and qualifications, but it employs no other punctuation than the full-stop and the comma, and creates the illusion of something spoken rather than written. In Saramago, it is as if the folktale met modernism.

This narrative method naturally risks falling into self-indulgence and corrosive doubt—the arid self-reflexivity of the French nouveau roman of Robbe-Grillet and Sarraute. But Saramago vaults this chasm by virtue of the scale and the thrilling conceits of his stories, which roam widely over Portuguese and European history and are never happier than when juggling metaphysical speculations. In *The History of the Siege of Lisbon*, a proof-reader of a historical work changes the entire shape of the Portuguese history by inserting the word 'not' at a crucial moment in the text. *Blindness* imagines an unnamed city struck by a mass epidemic of sightlessness, thereby illustrating just how fragile and hard-won is the civic peace that a portion of humankind now takes for granted. In *Death at Intervals*, death (a character, named, like most of Saramago's characters, with her initial in lowercase) suddenly abandons her work of taking human beings away from this world. First there is jubilation among human beings at the prospect of immortality, and then consternation as the larger implications of eternal life start to emerge.

Saramago's new novel, published posthumously and translated by his excellent long-time translator Margaret Jull Costa, is called *The Elephant's Journey*. For two years Solomon the elephant, a gift to King Dom Joao III from one of his colonies in India, has been languishing in Lisbon along with his devoted keeper Subhro. Solomon's arrival, we hear, initially caused a great stir in Lisbon life before he fell, like all fashionable new diversions, from favour with the elite.

It is the middle of the 16th century and Protestantism has recently shaken the foundations of Western Christendom. Dom Joao III wants to send a present to the Duke of Hapsburg, Maximilian, who has embraced the new faith. But the gift cannot have any savour of Catholicism, and so Dom Joao fixes—taking the irresolute suggestion of his flighty wife—on Solomon. The elephant must now travel on foot, by land and by sea, down rivers and over the Alps, to Vienna.

And so we embark on a picaresque tale in the manner of Cervantes, to whose school Saramago certainly belongs—albeit one told in slow motion, as if keeping time with the stately pace of its protagonist, who often holds up the travelling party because he wants to take a nap.

Solomon causes a great stir in towns and villages along the route, becoming, like in the old fable about the elephant and the three blind men, many things to many people. Some villagers, overhearing bits of a conversation about the elephant-headed god Ganesha, come to believe that Solomon is God. One priest nearly loses his life in trying to exorcise the devil from Solomon's soul. Another tries to enlist the elephant in performing a cunningly man-made miracle, just so that the authority of the Catholic Church may be reaffirmed. (Many of Saramago's best jokes are those aimed at the vanity of church and state.)

But the book's pleasures are mainly rooted in the narrator's playful spirit and his rejection—repeatedly played for laughs—of most of the rules of conventional novelistic exposition. We hear a voice that is gnomic, dryly witty, rich in proverbs and zany maxims. ('The same thing happens with good ideas, and, on occasions, with bad ones, as happens with Democritus' atoms or with cherries in a basket, they come along linked one to the other.') It is a voice given to gusts of whimsy and anachronistic observation, fastidiously laying out all the possibilities of a situation with qualifiers ('in the unlikely but not impossible event of,' 'always assuming that'), and then breaking up this rhythm with sudden pistol shots: 'He went plof and vanished. Onomatopoeia can be so very handy.' When I came across the simple declarative sentence 'The snow began to fall' at the end of one chapter, I was astonished and made a mark in the margin.

'It must be said that history is always selective,' says the narrator at one point, 'and discriminatory too, selecting from life only what society deems to be historical and scorning the rest, which is precisely where we might find the true explanation of facts, of things, of wretched reality itself. In truth, I say to you, it is better to be a novelist, a fiction writer, a liar.' This is as close as Saramago comes to articulating a philosophy for his fiction. In *The Elephant's Journey*, it is the stoical mahout Subhro whose experience—like that of other figures outside the grand narratives of the past, like Raimundo Silva in *The History of the Siege of Lisbon*, or Baltasar and Blimunda in the novel of that name—allows us to access what the historian Ranajit Guha calls 'the small voice of history.' Such works should never go plof and vanish.

## 25. Dancing Lessons with Bohumil Hrabal

*Dancing Lessons For The Advanced In Age*, by Bohumil Hrabal (New York Review of Books, 2011)

One of the minor arts of the novel is the art of the title, of a word or a phrase that successfully broadcasts the sense and spirit of the whole work. Novelistic prose has all the time in the world to unfurl its nature, but titles, if anything, belong to the universe of poetry, to its mode of tightly wound suggestion. We carry within our minds, at best, a few sentences of any prose writer's work, no matter how distinguished it is. But good titles ring on forever.

Sometimes, of course, a title can prove to be, disappointingly, the most intriguing bit of a work, a cover charge that yields no reward in the establishment to which it gives access. But on other occasions, titles are not only thresholds to narrative worlds of the greatest density and distinction; they are the whole work in microcosm. Such, at any rate, are the titles of the great 20th-century Czech novelist Bohumil Hrabal (1914–1997). Even in translation, where they surely lose some of their colloquial charge, the phrases *Too Loud a Solitude*, *Closely Observed Trains*, *Pirouettes on a Postage Stamp*, *I Served the King of England*, and *Dancing Lessons for the Advanced In Age* are flares that light up the teeming, gusting worlds, red with carnival and bursting with suppressed laughter, from which they emerge.

At one point in *I Served the King of England*, one of Hrabal's most perfectly realised works, the protagonist, a small waiter named Ditie, is seen moving from a big hotel in Prague to a small but plush establishment in the countryside called the Hotel Tichota. He arrives with his suitcase in the middle of the day, but mysteriously the hotel and its grounds are absolutely deserted, the only sound being that of the wind, 'which smelled so sweet you could almost eat it with a spoon.' Perplexed, Ditie turns and is about to leave, when suddenly he is stopped in his tracks by a piercing whistle: 'It blew three times as if it were saying, Tut tut tut, then gave a long blast that made me turn around, and a short blast that made me feel a line or a rope was reeling me in, pulling me back to the glass doors.' Even sounds in Hrabal's world are as perfectly measured and varied as the sentences that then describe or translate them. The entire universe rains meanings upon the fevered brains of his heroes.

Hrabal's protagonists are also agents and enablers of the central force in his work, which he termed *pabeni*—loosely, shooting the breeze. He is a kind of poet of the beer garden, gathering up folk wisdom, old maid's tales, testosterone-fuelled exaggeration, and street chatter into perfectly formed monologues delivered by characters he called *pabitels*. A *pabitel*, he explains in a note to his early work *The Palaverers*, 'is a person against whom there is always welling up an ocean of intrusive thoughts. His monologue flows constantly....As a rule, a pabitel has read almost nothing, but on the other hand has seen and heard a great deal....He is captivated by his own inner monologue, with which he wanders the world, like a peacock with its beautiful plumage.'

Thus, although Hrabal's fantastically vivid narrations throb with incident and anecdote, they are paradoxically often plotless, taking delight in their very aimlessness and susceptibility to suggestion. The series of 'little men' in his work—Ditie, the paper compactor Hanta in *Too Loud a Solitude*, the train dispatcher Miloš Hrma in *Closely Observed Trains*—achieve a gentle subversion through their very earnestness and naivete, blowing the pompousness and absurdity of the world's structures and doctrines into bubbles of the strange and the surreal. Although Hrabal worked under the aegis of a communist regime in an age of 'socialist realism' in literature, about the only doctrine sounded in his work is the exuberant conclusion of the unnamed narrator of *Dancing Lessons for the Advanced In Age*: 'Mother of God, isn't life breathtakingly beautiful!' Taken in the context of its time and literary environment, this is not so much a declaration of a complacent aestheticism as a reproach to a world that hums with, to adapt one of Hrabal's titles, too loud a certitude.

The most important word in Hrabal's work might, however, be not so much a particular concept like *pabeni* or the repeated emphasis on the delights of sense life, but the humble conjunction 'and.' Since his narratives thrive on an effect of copious simultaneity, of a dozen balls of incident being juggled in the air at the same time, the word 'and' is the well-oiled hinge through which this sense is circulated. Like Jose Saramago, Hrabal loves run-on sentences and enormously long paragraphs, though in Hrabal these things are not meant to mime a primitive 'folk voice' as in Saramago, but to produce an onrushing river of richly embroidered and seemingly unstoppable incident.

This principle of composition reaches its logical conclusion in Hrabal's early and daringly experimental work from 1964, *Dancing Lessons for the Advanced in Age*. The entire novel is told in a single sentence. Once we begin, we are allowed no pause for breath. In his life, Hrabal worked variously as a warehouseman, a railway dispatcher, an insurance agent, and even as a waste-paper collector, in which incarnation his fellow novelist Josef Skvorecky first met him, finding him, in a detail that might have come straight out of Hrabal's own work, 'saving the proofs of a Thackeray novel from the rubbish.' The unnamed narrator of *Dancing Lessons* is similarly diverse in his vocations, telling us about his tumultuous exploits as a cobbler, a brewer, and a soldier, even as he retails to us his application to the real world of the lessons he has learnt from his favourite books (one on the interpretation of dreams, another a book of wisdom on marriage).

Stories and characters come sailing out of nowhere, such as the tale told to the narrator by some truckers about a dentist they see while they are racing one another down a hill: 'He'd left his umbrella in his office, and just as he was sticking his key into the door one of the [lorries] burst a spring and barrelled smack into the office and it lurched away from the key, the whole office, and he was left standing there with his key in the air.' In Hrabal it is not the key that misses the door, but rather the door that escapes the key. Elsewhere, we find human hands blown off by grenade explosions slapping people as they fly, and a flock of turkeys blown to bits by a careering express train coming down, part by part, at stations all the way down the line.

As typical in Hrabal, we see from numerous amorous exploits 'how a real man trembles like a frog about to leap whenever he sees a beautiful woman,' and are led through parades of comic complaint: 'Why will no one see that progress may be good for making people people, but for bread and butter and beer it's the plague, they've got to slow down their damn technology.' Never has the workaday world of bread and butter and beer been rendered so lyrically as in the work of this essential writer, every phrase of whose narrations both assert and prove his contention that 'the world is a beautiful place, don't you think? not because it is but because I see it that way.'

## 26. Daniyal Mueenuddin's Duniya

*In Other Rooms, Other Wonders,* by Daniyal Mueenuddin (Penguin, 2010)

'In this game of love, women have immense power...much more power than we do,' writes the Scottish painter Jack Vettriano, whose works often depict couples netted by one another, oblivious to the world. 'They can really tie us up in knots. We're animals by comparison.' It is a long stretch from Vettriano's coolly erotic portraits of beautifully dressed men and women, bright in their own power, to the lawless longing, veiled wooing, insecure dependency, and difficult mingling of unequal partners in Daniyal Mueenuddin's short-story collection *In Other Rooms, Other Wonders*. But the root feeling is the same. Many of the best moments in Mueenuddin's book involve men who are 'wholly masculine'—that is, secure in their place and well-stocked with capital in a man's world, confident that they know what life is—being humbled by a power that disarms their own strength, being surprised by eros or by an emotion that they fear is love. Two of the eight stories in Mueenuddin's book take their titles from the names of their female protagonists, and at least two more could have.

Mueenuddin's linked stories—this has now become a convention in short fiction, but in this one instance the material demands it, for the characters are part of an ancient and elaborate hierarchy—wind their way leisurely through the great Lahore house and even bigger country estate of KK Harouni. A pillar of Pakistan's old feudal order, Harouni rules over a world 'as measured and as concentric as that of the Sun King at Versailles.' But Harouni is now aged and enfeebled. Unable to watch over his holdings with the same care of old, he is squeezed of his riches by his extended family of servants, retainers, managers, and workers (many of whom figure as characters in their own right, and are therefore granted a higher status in Mueenuddin's construct than that of their master, who only cares for them insofar as they contribute to his comfort and standing).

But Mueenuddin's stories are fascinating not only for what is present in them—the beautifully relaxed, wheeling exposition that recalls the work of Jhumpa Lahiri, the love of the natural world expressed in ripples of memorable language, the dramatisation of the jagged route that human beings take towards understanding themselves and others—but also for what is absent, which is a criticism of the feudal order through which these stories wander. His gaze is curious but uncritical; he sees the world as his characters, who mostly accept the rules of the game, see it; it is as if the world can only be this way. His interest, in fact, is in those individuals who are secretly ambitious in a world where everybody is expected to know their place; his gaze halts upon those who want to rise, and those who can raise.

In the story 'Provide, Provide' Harouni's elderly and opportunistic estate manager Jaglani, who has long been appropriating his master's property, takes as his mistress a married woman, Zainab. Zainab gives him whatever he asks for by way of service and bodily pleasure but stoically, as if performing a duty. When she says she must return to her husband, Jaglani impulsively decides to marry her, although he has a family and children. Shrewdly unpacking his reasoning, Mueenuddin tells us that Jaglani feels he is so powerful that 'now he deserved to make this mistake, for once not to make a calculated choice.' Jaglani's new marriage brings him pleasure and pain in equal measure; he finds that 'although he had made a career of fearing no one,' he fears his wife, and 'yet his love kept increasing.' It is only later, when the deed has been done and its consequences have taken hold both in his home and in his mind, that Jaglani begins to regret his actions. Now he cannot even go back to the estate, which he loves, without being reminded of his folly. Here is a paragraph from Mueenuddin:

> Yet Dunyapur has been spoiled for him by the presence of Zainab. He minded very much that he had given his sons a stepmother of that class, a servant woman. He minded that he had insulted his first wife in that way, by marrying again, by marrying a servant, and then by keeping the marriage a secret. His senior wife had never reproached him, but after Jaglani told her she quickly became old. She prayed a great deal, spent much of her time in bed, stopped caring for herself. Her body became rounded like a hoop, not fat but fleshed uniformly all over, a body thrown away, throwing itself away, the old woman sitting all day in bed, dreaming, muttering perhaps when left alone. He reproached himself for taking his eldest son's daughter and giving her to Zainab, transplanting the little girl onto such different stock. Secretly, and most bitterly, he blamed himself for having been so weak as to love a woman who had never loved him. He made an idol of her, lavished himself upon her sexual body, gave himself to a woman who never gave back, except in the most practical terms. She blotted the cleanliness of his

> life trajectory, which he had always before believed in. She represented the culmination of his ascendance, the reward of his virtue and striving, and showed him how little it had all been, his life and his ambitions. All of it he had thrown away, his manliness and strength, for a pair of legs that grasped his waist and a pair of eyes that pierced him and that yet had at bottom the deadness of foil.

Among the many satisfactions of this passage is the way in which the pleasure of the thought—a kind of Macbethian regret at an audacious dream gone sour—is paralleled and improved, the two linking hands, as prose writing of a high order almost always does, by the acuity of Mueenuddin's syntax. It is worth thinking about the impact of phrases which effect small, rueful inversions like 'how little it had all been, his life and his ambitions' and then, immediately after, the similar, 'All of it he had thrown away, his manliness and strength.'

And also the sentence: 'Her body became rounded like a hoop, not fat but fleshed uniformly all over, a body thrown away, throwing itself away, the old woman sitting all day in bed, dreaming, muttering perhaps when left alone.' This observation is an example of a very characteristic and striking register of Mueenuddin's prose, which is a sentence that seems about to close, to expire, until it suddenly takes a new breath and then runs on strongly again, as if it has seen something new late in the day (here the anticipated close might be 'a body thrown away,' and the revival 'throwing itself away,' which both changes the tense and, through repetition, better indicates the effect of continuous stress this is having on Jaglani's mind). Here is another example of this kind of sentence, from the story 'Lily': 'It wearied her that this memory came now as she turned and stood, appraising Murad's clothes, loafers with unfortunate tassels, pressed jeans, white shirt tucked in—resembling somehow an army officer out of uniform, the effect touching to her, sincere, a gentleman calling on a lady.'

'Provide, Provide' works itself through to an exceptional conclusion that features neither of the principal characters, thereby greatly enhancing its beauty and strangeness (a strangeness seen again in 'Nawabdin Electrician,' a story about a man shot by a thief, and who lies on the road thinking he is going to die, remembering, of all things, 'the smell of frying fish'). In his attention to the minds of Zainab and Jaglani, or that of Husna, the impoverished distant relation who, in the title story, infiltrates the household and then the affections of Harouni himself, Mueenuddin serves up a series of masterful character studies embedded into the massive edifice of Harouni's world.

In keeping with the need for economic security or love of luxury revealed by so many of his protagonists, Mueenuddin's writing has a heavy, beguiling materiality. 'The hard blue sky stood enormously tall over Paris,' he writes at one point, throwing us right into the scene with that unusual adjective 'tall,' which is a tautology—what else could the sky be other than high, or tall?—and is yet expressive, here, of a sense of freedom and possibility being experienced by the narrator. Describing Nawabdin's prowess with tampering with electrical meters, Mueenuddin offers this bouquet of explanations: 'Some thought he used magnets, others said heavy oil or porcelain chips or a substance he found in beehives.' When Husna begins to live with KK Harouni, she hoards a secret stash of goods in 'two locked steel trunks, which she filled with everything from raw silk to electric sandwich makers.' A couple make love in a small hotel in the French countryside: 'The loose bedsprings made long rusty sounds, like a knife leisurely sharpened on a whetstone.'

In Mueenuddin's hands the material realm often seems to take off, almost become ethereal: 'Nawab would fly down this road on his new machine, with bags and cloths hanging from every knob and brace, so that the bike, when he hit a bump, seemed to be flapping numerous small vestigial wings; and with his grinning face, as he rolled up to whichever tubewell needed servicing, with his ears almost blown off, he shone with the speed of his arrival.' Some works of fiction, by their excellence of craftsmanship, singularity of worldview, and richness and precision of language, announce themselves instantly as classics, and I'd say this book is one such.

## 27. Junichiro Tanizaki's Memorable Maids

*The Maids,* by Junichiro Tanizaki, translated by Michael P. Cronin (New Directions, 2017)

Novels, like life, tend not to take much notice of maids. In most novels, domestics serve only to open and close doors, make meals, or assist with the toilette of those who have attained true selfhood. At best, they might pass a message between lovers or stumble upon some conspiracy. They are cogs in the plot, efficiently playing an enabling role in the story as they do in life.

What a pleasure, then, to come across a story in which maids occupy centre stage from beginning to end and are as clever and capricious as any bourgeois heroine. To many followers of Japanese fiction, myself included, Junichiro Tanizaki (1886–1965) is the greatest Japanese novelist of the 20th century and *The Makioka Sisters* (1949), his book about the familial and marital dilemmas of four sisters of an upper-class family (in which maids stand by in the shadows), the greatest Japanese novel.

While at work on his masterpiece, Tanizaki was also engrossed in translating into a modern idiom a foundational work of Japanese literature—a book written by a woman on the far side of the millennium. *The Tale of Genji*, a richly detailed story about the life of the sybaritic prince Genji and his lovers in the imperial court of the Heian dynasty, was written by a lady-in-waiting, Murasaki Shikibu, at the turn of the 11th century. Some scholars call it the world's first novel.

The book's storyline—Genji's roving eye means he does not limit his attentions to women of blue blood alone—requires

many detailed portraits of accomplished women in service, women much like Murasaki. And while it would be a stretch to call them maids, their example seems to have given Tanizaki—the rare male novelist more comfortable writing about women than men—the idea of re-presenting the bourgeois world of *The Makioka Sisters* from the point of view of the kitchen rather than the salon.

Published in 1963, and set in what was then the recent past, *The Maids* is Tanizaki's final novel. It is also—as Michael P. Cronin's translation, the first into English, shows—one of his best. Loosely organised but written with Tanizaki's usual narrative brio and sly intimacy, *The Maids* is a homage to the work of the humble in making a house a home.

In this case, the household is that of the elderly novelist Chikura Raikichi and his wife Sanko. This prosperous couple own and rent a number of homes in the Osaka-Kobe region and deploy a retinue of maids across them like pawns on a chessboard, judging them by their housekeeping, cooking, account-keeping, and general tractability, but also by their liveliness, conversational skills, and aesthetic sensibility.

Without exception, the maids all come from the same region, Kansai, in the extreme west of Japan. They speak a dialect much removed from 'the smooth, clipped Tokyo way of speaking,' and even have in common a certain regional style of peeling vegetables. Here we see Tanizaki's skill not just as a novelist but also as an ethnographer, taking great pleasure in the specifics of time and place.

The maids' congested quarters in the main house, a room off the kitchen 'only four and a half mats in size,' becomes a domestic subculture not just of class but of thought, feeling and memory. To understand these women as individuals, the narrator seems to be saying, we need to make the journey—the reverse of the one they themselves have made—to the place where they come from.

'Raikichi,' we are told, 'liked to have a lot of maids around—he said it made the house bright and lively.' But Tanizaki's lifelong focus on feminine allure and male erotic obsession, from early novels such as *Naomi* to the late work *Diary of a Mad Old Man*, is here reprised in a subdued, autumnal key.

Raikichi is clearly the aging sensualist, drinking in the freshness and innocence of youth to keep up his interest in the world. But when sexual scandal finally erupts in maidland, there is no male hand in it. Sayo and Setsu, two maids who have left Raikichi's for another household, are discovered by their new mistress in the throes of passion. It is society that is shocked by this, not the narrator, who in a perfectly weighted detail gives us the two girls in their room, 'seated in careful composure' and with their bags packed, waiting to receive notice.

Other maids, such as the beauteous Gin, make eyes at the tradesmen who visit the house and make use of the family telephone to advance their amours. And some girls just fall in love with themselves. When the maid Koma is taken to a department store with a closed-circuit television setup, she is thrilled to see herself on TV, 'and she [rides] the escalator again and again, watching herself.' That Koma is not alone in her abundant self-regard becomes apparent when, in an allusion that works on many levels, we meet the maid Yuri, a great reader who owns 'a complete set of Tanizaki's adaptation of *The Tale of Genji*.'

Tanizaki's focus on the pleasure and drama of everyday life is so all-encompassing that when the eruptions of history intrude in the form of the second Sino-Japanese war and World War II, they ring, as desired, like pistol-shots at a party. As men are drafted into wartime service, many maids are sundered from potential husbands; others rush back home to help their aging parents.

But time has many gears. Even without these cataclysms, we come to see—Tanizaki is an insistently elegiac writer—that the world is always in flux. By the end of the story, we are in the 1960s. Domestics now stay in service no longer than a year or two, and the very word 'maids' has become archaic, replaced by 'helpers.' Tanizaki's great success is to make us see how it is not only the masters who mourn the passing of such a world, but also the older generation of maids.

## 28. Sandor Marai and the Soul

*Portraits of a Marriage,* by Sandor Marai, translated by George Szirtes (Knopf Doubleday, 2011)

'It was not my muscles she was weighing up, but my soul,' decides Peter, one of the characters in Sandor Marai's novel *Portraits of a Marriage*, as he proposes marriage to his maid Judit while she stokes the fireplace, then tries to interpret the long silence that is her response. It is an inflammatory silence, more provoking than speech, that causes him, for the first time in his life, to lose all control of himself.

'The soul': novelists might be divided into two camps based on what they think of this word, whether their narrators or their characters use it with irony or in faith. The camp of Marai—if we wanted to cite a contemporary, it would be Orhan Pamuk—believes passionately in this word as the something that adult conversation, and therefore novelistic narration, must never shirk from. In the work of most novelists, a thought such as Peter's would actually seem like an instance of the writer laughing at the character, through a violent, almost bathetic juxtaposition of the corporeal with the ineffable. But here we know that it is not just the character taking life seriously, but also the writer.

*Portraits of a Marriage*, translated by the Hungarian poet and critic George Szirtes, is the fifth novel, after *Embers, Casanova in Bolzano, The Rebels*, and *Esther's Inheritance*, by Marai to appear posthumously in English in the last decade. Reading a few pages of any of these shows that they are the books of a writer who was an adept of a great variety of situations and structures in politics, society, culture, and, finally, 'human relationships' (another favourite phrase in Marai). Marai was born in 1900, in the twilight of the Austro-Hungarian Empire, saw out the two World Wars in Hungary, then fled to Italy after persecution at home by the Communists in the 1940s. From his books we can see why he was resented; characters in his novels are repeatedly sceptical of the prospect of human beings making themselves new through revolutionary principles, or of violent justice ever settling into the promised peace. Marai might be considered a kind of conservative.

Marai finally ended up in America, where personal and artistic freedom seemed to him to have reached the other extreme, ending up in a mass of trivialities the very obverse of the moral seriousness attached to the word 'art' in hierarchical or totalitarian regimes. (This difference, seen from the American side, is what so attracts Philip Roth to his lesser-known contemporaries in East Europe in his book of interviews *Shop Talk*.) But perhaps Marai would have been disappointed anywhere, because even when set against novelists more or less of his time and from his own part of the world who shared something of his spirit—Kafka, Musil, Hermann Broch, Joseph Roth, Witold Gombrowicz—he seems unusually serious, rigorous, and fervent, forever linking particulars to universals and realities to ideals.

The signal quality of Marai's work is that it is not just the writer or the narrator who is invested in formulating a theory of human nature from the particulars of the story being told. His *characters* are equally committed to such a project: each one of these eloquent people is a psychologist, a poet, a prophet, and a philosopher, and knows it.

People in Marai are passionate generalisers, distillers of experience, forever funneling the 'I' of their life stories into the 'we' of what they are convinced are immutable human laws. They are never happier than when they have opened out their soul's sails in a long monologue (against these effusions, Marai's actual dialogue always seems clipped and sparse). In a fine comic moment in *Portraits of a Marriage*, Judit, who has been telling her lover her life story over the course of a whole night, discovers at dawn that he has fallen asleep. The reason why this is a particularly good and sly joke is that at the end of this riveting novelistic night, the reader is certainly wide awake.

Marai's novels have no need of continuous incidents, because a single dramatic event—a quarrel between two old friends in *Embers*, a betrayal by a lover in *Esther's Inheritance*—is enough to keep his protagonists preoccupied for years, decades, the whole of their lives. The same event is seen first from the point of view of the actor and the acted upon, the betrayer and the betrayed, the man and the woman (male and female nature are always very distinct things in Marai), each time memorably cast into a new mould that brings to bear upon the incident all the important facts and themes of the speaker's life. Marai's protagonists are, through marriage or adultery or rivalry, thrown into bruising dyads or triads, and then return to solitude to process their experience. Some of literature's greatest romantics are to be found in Marai, and their romantic character, it seems fair to warn the reader, is contagious.

*Portraits of a Marriage*, one of the most original pieces of novelistic architecture in Marai, is actually a portrait of the discontents of two marriages: those of Peter, the scion of a business family, first to the middle-class woman Ilonka and later to the servant Judit. Each of the three reflects on what happened between them, producing, it seems at times, a combined portrait not of three but of nine people. The urgency with which they speak, their love of 'tiny but vital details,' and their 'passion for truth' (in *Embers* there is a fine line about the quest for 'that other truth that lies buried beneath the roles, the costumes, the scenarios of life') become, in their own way, a kind of narrative energy. Only the most confident of novelists could trust in his work in this way. Here is Peter speaking of Judit, sex, union, nature, childhood, all in the same reverie:

> Jungle and half-light, strange cries in the distance—you can't tell whether it is a man screaming by a well, his throat ripped open by some predator, or nature itself screaming, nature, which is human, animal, inhuman at once—bed entails all that. This woman knew all that was there to be known. She had the secret knowledge: she knew the body. She knew self-control and the loss of self-control. Love for her was

> not a series of occasional meetings but a constant return to a familiar childhood base: a blend of homecoming and festival; the dark-brown light over a field at dusk, the taste of certain familiar foods, the excitement and anticipation, and under it all, the confidence that once evening came, there would be nothing to fear in the flight of the bat, just the road home at dusk. She was like a child tired of playing, making her way home because the light in the window was calling her to a hot dinner and a clean bed. That was love as far as Judit was concerned.

Marai delights in stacking the odds against his characters, throwing them into a spot from which it will take them all night to extricate themselves. Why does Judit, when she knows that she has Peter completely under her spell, suddenly disappear without a trace for two years, forsaking all that she could win from him? Why does she then return and take it? Why does Peter suddenly play a trick at dinnertime one day on Ilonka with a friend, pretending that it is the friend who is Ilonka's husband and not him? Why is Ilonka suddenly filled with profound respect for Judit on discovering her crime, admiring how 'she wanted it all, life entire, destiny with all its dangers?'

Marai's characters often respond to situations in the most irrational, the most surprising fashion, and then pop up afterwards to justify their behaviour in an enormously persuasive way. They are dangerous and seductive in the way the novel was once believed by moralists to be dangerous and seductive, having the mysterious power to convince or corrupt. Page after page goes by, filled out by the writer with streaks of exquisite perception ('Being human beings is not a responsibility we can avoid, but we can, and do, tell an awful lot of lies in trying to fulfil it') and lines of throwaway brilliance ('He could listen the way others shout'; 'The only people capable of being at peace are people who live in the moment'; 'Six is the best age for dogs and for wine') and majestic paradoxes. These are speakers who gather the reader up in the nets of their worldview so powerfully that one believes, with them, that this is the way life really is—until they are contradicted by those of whom they speak and from whom they seem to have learnt what they know.

Of a writer whom she meets on travels, Judit observes that he seemed motivated almost wholly by lust—but not ordinary sexual lust. Rather 'it was the world that brought on his lust, the fabric of it; word and flesh, voices and stones, everything that exists [that] is tangible and, at the same time, impossible to grasp in its meaning and essence.' This seems an accurate self-portrait of Marai himself, a writer just as capable of devoting a long passage to the importance of pimiento-filled olives as the notion of joy to the meaning of culture. *Portraits of a Marriage* confirms Marai's retrospective status as one of the 20th century's great writers of fiction.

## 29. Alaa Al Aswany's Egyptian America

*Chicago,* by Alaa Al Aswany, translated by Farouk Abdel Wahab (Harper, 2008)

'Praise the Lord who created beauty in a hundred ways!' declares a character in Alaa Al Aswany's *Chicago*, and a similar attitude might be discerned in the writer's attitude towards the many protagonists of his sprawling narration, whose particularities and quirks are so elaborately taxonomized as to seem like extracts from state dossiers. Equally fascinated by both sexes, alert to the tinkle of class and race in human commerce, aware of the consolations and the deceptions of religion, and interested above all in the question of the human body and its agitations, the narrator of an Aswany story seems to flutter above the world of his creation, hearing, noting, murmuring.

Aswany's novel achieves something surprising, which is to turn a great city in the American midwest into a little Egypt. It begins, most unconventionally, with a short history of Chicago city, and then suddenly dives into the lives of a set of Egyptian doctoral students and emigrants resident in the city, some freshly arrived, others naturalised Americans. In Aswany's previous novel, *The Yacoubian Building*, an apartment block served as a microcosm of Egyptian society; here, that crucible is Chicago, home to a set who have eagerly left home for better prospects, and yet carry that home in their hearts.

Are Quranic injunctions even more compelling in this strange and godless world, or are they in some way refuted by this carnival of liberty and licentiousness? Can freedom of speech and political allegiance make for a platform from which to question the suppression of these rights in the motherland? Should one's goal be the pursuit of excellence in science and learning, or is it that, as one character claims, 'all success outside one's homeland is deficient'? Can whites and nonwhites meet on an equal footing, or must they perform an encounter replete with hypocrisies? These are the questions Aswany's protagonists—a devout woman from a peasant background who continues to wear the veil, an arrogant student fixated on outperforming his colleagues, a political radical who thinks of himself as a poet, a professor who has rejected everything Egyptian and goes to baseball games on weekends 'wearing his cap backward,' a Christian Copt hounded out of Egypt—ask themselves and each other.

Indeed, there are at least three levels of conversation in Aswany's work. The simplest one is that between the characters, who feel a deep need to talk and are roused by the prospect of conversation in their mother tongue about themselves or the motherland. They debate politics and religion, banter till they find they have fallen in love, quarrel and fall silent, long for or dread the sound of another's voice. But, on a second level, they also constantly talk to *themselves*, and Aswany reports these justifications, interpretations, changes of heart, and arcs of argument almost as speech. Here is the male chauvinist Tariq Haseeb vexed by the behaviour of his girlfriend:

> He rang her number again and she didn't answer. When he tried one more time, she hung up. So, it was obvious. She

> was playing the role of the angry paramour. She wanted him to come running after her, humiliating himself. 'Impossible!' he muttered. [...] Who did she think she was? He said to himself: This peasant girl wants to humiliate me? What a farce. So, she doesn't know who Tariq Haseeb is. My dignity is more important than my life. From now on I am going to delete her from my life as if she never existed. Before I met her what did I lack? I was working, eating, sleeping, enjoying life, and living like a king. On the contrary, ever since I've met her I've been anxious and tense.

Those 'so's are like the hinges of Haseeb's thought, showing us the moment at which a situation begins to bristle with private meanings that seem irrefutable to the person in whose being they take root.

And lastly, there is always in Aswany's work a kind of implied conversation between the narrator and the *reader*, a way in which we feel as if we are being taken into confidence. A character is described at length and then the narrator stops to ask, as if describing the world of the jellyfish to a room of students, 'Have we learned everything about Safwat Shakir? There are still two aspects to his life we have not touched upon...' After detailing the grinding work schedule that Tariq Haseeb observes, the narrator asks: 'Does that mean Tariq Haseeb does not have any fun? Not true. He also has his little pleasures...' We feel in *Chicago* as if a host is asking if we are enjoying ourselves at an evening at his house.

Aswany's storytelling is also marked by its sensuality. From the self-denying student who allows himself an hour of recreation to watch wrestling and pornography to the lapsed poet whose voice and wholeness of self is restored by sex, everywhere we see the animal self lurking beneath the trained, dressed, and tutored body-in-the-world, aching to unsheathe itself. If Aswany's women sometimes seem implausibly beautiful and voluptuous, they at least have more selfhood and agency than Salman Rushdie's sex goddesses. His warm-blooded, sometimes voyeuristic narration is clearly a man's work, but it has a Chaucerian love of human tints and foibles that redeems its faults.

Some of the twists and reversals in *Chicago*, as also its circling focus, make us in agreement with the character who feels 'as if he were watching an Egyptian soap opera.' Aswany's rolling cast of characters and panoramic vision tell us that he wants to investigate the human condition on the grandest scale and, as in soap operas, he wants to make the spectator feel like part of the family. His book resides firmly within the mainstream of popular fiction, but it is also an unusual and striking post-9/11 American novel.

## 30. Herta Müller's States of Fear

*The Appointment,* by Herta Müller, translated by Michael Hulse and Philip Boehm (Macmillan, 2010)

To read the work of the Romanian novelist Herta Müller is to feel instantly that the lights of one's everyday world have been switched off, and that one is in a place of danger, of an amorphous dread. Müller's protagonists, powerless but mildly peeved individuals living under the yoke of a tyrannical regime, are the agents of this immersion into paranoia. Perennially watched, or suspecting they are being watched—for even the most innocent bystanders 'might be doing a little spying on the side'—they are themselves ever-watchful, living, even at their most secure, in 'a tousled state of fear.'

The most common kinds of social interaction in Müller's world are interrogation, observation, or conspiracy—power and the attempt to subvert power. Material life is abject, private life narrowed down to a set of desultory gestures, and small spurts of emotion or sensory stimulation take on a heightened significance in these novels, which enact, through the very texture of their bleak and enigmatic sentences, the debilitation

of human personality in a world in which every person feels incarcerated and choiceless. 'What am I taking away from this country by going to another?' the narrator asks her interrogator in Müller's novel *The Appointment*. The answer, of course, both tragic and exhilarating, is 'oneself,' for without subjects, there can be no dictatorship.

The *Appointment* opens with a scene of coercion. 'I was summoned,' begins the narrator, a young factory worker whose name we never get to know. Desperate to leave the country, she has been caught sewing notes into the linings of men's suits bound for Italy, entreating the buyer to marry her. This real 'crime' has become, in turn, the foundation for fictitious ones. The narrator's supervisor, an older man called Nelu who is upset with her for spurning his advances, has concocted some new notes on the same lines as her own, signed off with a spiteful touch—'Best wishes from the dictatorship'—and passed these over to the authorities. State power and sexual resentment spin a web around the protagonist, and she and her boyfriend are now entrapped. Her summoning engulfs her totally, and is thus aptly her introduction. As we see her taking a tram on her way to her menacing appointment, she tells us that 'today I'm carrying a small towel, a toothbrush, and some toothpaste in my handbag.'

Like *The Land of Green Plums*, perhaps Müller's best-known novel in English translation, *The Appointment* proffers a series of plangent, elliptical vignettes of life under the regime of Nicolae Ceausescu, Romania's dictator between the years 1974 and 1989. In these novels Ceausescu is never mentioned by name; rather, his reign is treated almost as a fact of life, like the coming and going of the seasons or the onset of old age and decrepitude.

Unlike many novels in the 20th century's vast library of the literature of totalitarianism, Müller's books do not offer us a redemptive map of the struggle to keep hope and humanity alive under conditions of the worst physical or psychological oppression (of the sort we associate with the Russians Aleksandr Solzhenitsyn and Vasily Grossman), or else concoct a kind of grotesque comedy from the convulsions of their embattled lives (of the kind found in the work the Chinese novelists Mo Yan and Ma Jian). Their words and situations replicate, rather than contest with a vivid rhetoric of their own, the banality and the stupor of a life lived to the tune of empty slogans (in *Green Plums*, workers' choruses play all day long from loudspeakers attached to the walls of student dormitories) and reflexive persecution.

A network of causes and effects is not drawn out; the stoical protagonists just accept that the air is bad, and try to keep going a life that, in the words of one character, is 'just the farty splutter of a lantern, not even worth the bother of putting your shoes on.' These are books that, in effect, make the same demands of their readers as the life that they depict makes of their protagonists, with gradually accumulating tensions suddenly being muffled by anti-climax. Like JMG Le Clezio, the novelist who won the Nobel Prize the year before her in 2008, Müller is one of those independent-minded writers who don't so much reach out to the reader as ask to be reached.

*The Appointment* is stretched out upon a frame of double time: the present moment, in which we see the protagonist taking the tram to her interrogation early one morning, watching the people around her and making guesses about their lives with a practised eye, and, balanced against this, the swoops and circles of memory as she lives what may be her last hours of freedom. She remembers her father, a bus driver whose affair with a vegetable seller is part of a recurring pattern in the book in which older men prey on young women; her friend Lilli, who was shot dead on the border while trying to flee with her lover, a retired army officer; her ex-husband, who nearly threw her off a bridge when he found out she wanted to leave him; and her lover Paul, whom she first met at the flea market while trying to sell her wedding ring.

In one of the novel's best moments, the narrator tries to imagine what might have gone through the mind of the young border guard whose bullet took the life of her best friend.

'When he fired, he was just a man on duty, a miserable sentry under a vast heaven where the wind whistled loneliness day and night,' she thinks. 'Lilli's living flesh gave him shivers, and her death was heaven-sent, an unexpected gift of ten days' leave... Perhaps a woman like me was waiting, someone who, although she couldn't measure up to the dead woman, could nonetheless laugh and caress her man in the grip of love until he felt like a human being.' By extinguishing the life of a human being, then, the guard, under the incentive scheme of a perverted order, has his own prospects for humanity returned to him.

Müller documents the slow descent of her protagonist into paranoia ('I've been listening to the alarm clock since three in the morning ticking ten sharp, ten sharp, ten sharp'), and the small obsessive gestures and dependencies of someone in trouble ('Once the nut's been cracked, it loses its power if it opens overnight.') Sometimes this kind of work risks shrinking into mannerism. Her narrator spends almost unreasonable amounts of time thinking about things like the precise colour of apples or leaves or the surfaces of windows. This is a world in which the life of objects almost equals that of human beings—a theme amplified in Müller's Nobel lecture, appended here to the text of the novel, in which a handkerchief laid out upon a staircase becomes Müller's office after she is thrown out of her workplace.

Indeed, at one point the protagonist finds, wrapped in a piece of paper inside her handbag, 'a finger with a bluish-black nail,' and cannot figure out whether this object, in its own grisly afterlife, connects to life or to death—'whether the whole person was dead, or just his finger.' It is this strange mingling of the quotidian and the macabre that one remembers when one puts down the work of this difficult but distinctive writer.

# 31. Orhan Kemal's Autobiographical Realism

*My Father's House* and *The Idle Years,* by Orhan Kemal, translated by Cengiz Luhal (Peter Owen Books, 2008)

Novels are a source of comfort and psychological sustenance to their readers, but they can be so to their writers too. This is especially true for writers working in an autobiographical mode. The novel, here, is like a beam turned in upon oneself, lighting up old shadows and nooks—or it might be thought of as a mirror in which one's old faces successively appear. The forward march of the narrative is, in this case, also a backward journey into time, and the slow time and fruitful agitation of writing throw up memories long submerged.

These are the speculations occasioned by *The Idle Years,* a novel first published in two parts in 1949 and 1950 by the great Turkish writer Orhan Kemal (often referred to as 'the Turkish Dickens') and now newly and strikingly translated by Cengiz Luhal. Although it is sometimes a mistake to link a writer's books too simply to his autobiography, it would seem that a discussion of *The Idle Years* would at least begin with such a reading.

The unnamed narrator of the book is the son of a charismatic political agitator who is sent into exile with his family after falling foul of the Turkish regime in the 1920s. Brought up in a large house with all the comforts of life, the protagonist is suddenly pitchforked into a life in which the family is always on the move, money is scarce, and the father's temper thunderous. He is forced to work at menial jobs and begins to keep the company of a set whom he has previously seen only from afar, and with no consideration of their miseries: workers, vagabonds, and prostitutes. He is constantly hungry, and when granted a good meal through luck, comradeship, or charity, not only eats ravenously but also remembers every dish and every helping for days. He is often consumed by despair and by shame, but most of all loathes the heavy hand and bellowing voice of his father.

This story broadly follows the contours of Kemal's own youth, and it might be seen as part of that library in literature in which writers mull over the weight placed on their lives, in both good and bad ways, by their fathers: the early novels and later autobiographical meditations of VS Naipaul, for instance, or Franz Kafka's anguished *Letter To My Father*, or even the essays of Kemal's famous countryman Orhan Pamuk (whose Nobel Prize acceptance speech is called 'My Father's Suitcase,' and who has written a short, admiring foreword for this book).

Indeed, the first part of *The Idle Years* is called *My Father's House*, and its closing movement is one in which the protagonist resolves to leave that house and returns from Beirut to his homeland to strike out on his own. In one of the novel's best passages, the narrator returns to his hometown, Adana, hot with stories of his itinerant life to tell his childhood friends, only to find that nothing is as it used to be. The place the heart thinks of as home is a pillar to one's self but fragile on its own terms.

Kemal's novel beautifully evokes the world-changing ardour and angst of youth, the consolations of friendship, the aches and burns of love, and the redemption of constant misery and hardship by small acts of kindness or brief interludes of escape. He is considered a great writer of dialogue, and in Luhal's translation the reader can see why. Many of his characters are real talkers, but they talk in a stop-start and naturalistic fashion, leaping from one subject to another, or revealing some particularity of their character through a repeated emphasis. They don't always know what they are saying, though characters in other kinds of novels seem to.

*The Idle Years* ends with a scene in which the protagonist, still impoverished, marries his beloved wearing a borrowed suit, shoes, and tie. The newlyweds are excited by the beautiful gifts that they have been given, and begin to construct a castle of dreams upon them, only to find out that the groom's grandmother borrowed them all from family and friends to give the wedding a glitter, and that the goods must now all be returned. This episode is symbolic of the whole story, in which hope and yearning are always trying to break free of the chains of reality, and disappointment is quickly forgotten. The last line of Kemal's novel—'So we carried on with our lives, appreciating all that we had'—seems both an observation of a fact and a piece of friendly advice to the reader.

## 32. Cricket in New York with Joseph O'Neill

*Netherland,* by Joseph O'Neill (Pantheon, 2008)

Cricket and life are two very different things but often to lovers of the game they seem the same, or at least to inhabit a continuous plane of existence. The contest of bat and ball seems a smaller version of the great game of life; the variability of pitches, weather and match situation a symptom of the workings of chance in all human affairs; the effort to impose oneself on the rectangle of brown within the circle of green emblematic in some mysterious way of the human condition in general. 'For what was an innings if not a singular opportunity to face down, by dint of effort and skill and mastery, the variable world?' asks Hans van den Broek, the stoical and embattled protagonist of Joseph O'Neill's novel *Netherland*, and we know right away what Hans means. Indeed, Hans is totally adrift in the larger 'variable world,' and for a brief period cricket is his only means of hanging on at the crease on the pitch of life.

O'Neill's novel has its home in the scattered cricket fields of New York, one of cricket's earliest centres. (As one character in the book points out, the first international cricket match was played between the USA and Canada in Manhattan in the mid-19th century.) Although Hans is a Dutchman married to an Englishwoman, Rachel, his work in banking has brought him to New York, where very soon he begins to inhabit 'the nativity New York encourages even its most fleeting visitor to imagine for himself.'

But soon Hans' world begins to collapse around him. Rachel feels their marriage is unsatisfactory and wishes to move back to London with their young son, Jake. Hans is unable to dissuade Rachel and, taking the blame for a shared crisis, is left with a great burden of rejection and failure. A family man, he is now cut loose from all his moorings. His arc is a classic trope in the American novel, that of the limping and dejected loser struggling with his intransigent nature in an environment of exuberance, optimism, and self-reinvention. Hans shares many similarities, for instance, with Tommy Wilhelm, the protagonist of Saul Bellow's great short novel *Seize The Day*. Both live in hotels, both are estranged from their wives and torn from their children, and both are, 'to anyone who could be bothered to pay attention, noticeably lost.' (This is from O'Neill.)

Hans used to play some cricket as a boy in Holland and, one day, taking up an invitation after a chance meeting with a Pakistani cab-driver, he goes to a weekend club game at Staten Island and finds himself the only white man in a motley crowd of Indians, Pakistanis, Sri Lankans, Bangladeshis, and West Indians. This should be disconcerting, but the sense of being pulled out into a new set far removed from his usual world is a relief to him, and he finds playing cricket again immensely calming. O'Neill evokes this mood in his majestic description of 'the sights and sounds and rhythms of a full day's cricket, in which unhurried time is portioned out by the ticking of ball against bat.' Cricket, in this description, is a kind of restorative clock set to a more languorous speed than others, encouraging everybody to slow down and appreciate the big picture and the finer details of life.

It is at the cricket, too, that Hans meets an older Trinidadian man called Chuck Ramkissoon, a great dreamer and schemer who talks 'incessantly, indefatigably, virtuosically,' is a master of the grand pronouncement ('Women are responsible for the survival of the world; men are responsible for its glories'), and has a plan for building a cricket stadium in Brooklyn. The stadium, in Chuck's optimistic view, will make New York a centre of world cricket and restore the game to its lapsed prominence in American life. Hans finds succour in this unlikely brotherhood of men brought together by a shared love of the great game, and in the companionship and infectious enthusiasm of Chuck and his starred-and-striped motto of 'Think fantastic.'

*Netherland* is an impressive achievement on every level, from the stream of beautifully weighted and sonorous sentences that ripple across the pages to the larger architecture of narrative time and of plot. Here is Hans explaining (and thereby making an apparently simple matter dense) why he cannot slog the ball like the rest of his teammates, because cricket represents a force of continuity within his own fragmented self:

> Some people have no difficulty in identifying with their younger incarnations. Rachel, for example, will refer to episodes from her childhood and college days as if they'd happened to her that very morning. I, however, seem given to self-estrangement. I find it hard to muster oneness with those former selves whose accidents and endeavours have shaped who I am now. The schoolboy at the Gymnasium Haganum; the Leiden student; the clueless trainee executive at Shell; the analyst in London; even the thirty-year-old who flew to New York with his excited young wife; my natural sense is that all are faded, by the by, discontinued. But I still think, and I fear will always think, of myself as the young man who got a hundred runs in Amstelveen with a flurry of cuts, who took that diving catch at second slip in Rotterdam, who lucked into a hat trick at the Haagse Cricket Club. These and other moments of cricket are scorched in my mind like sexual memories, forever available to me and capable, during those long nights alone in the hotel when I sought refuge from the sorriest feelings, of keeping me awake as I relived them in bed and powerlessly mourned the mysterious promise they held. To reinvent myself in order to bat the American way, that baseball-like business of slugging and hoisting, involved

> more than the trivial abandonment of a hard-won style of hitting a ball. It meant snipping a fine white thread running, through years and years, to my mothered self.

'These and other moments of cricket are scorched in my mind like sexual memories'—this is very fine and apt. And let us look at this paragraph again, and all its pauses and qualifications, the way in which the sentences seem to keep interrupting themselves: 'I, however, seem given to'—'But I still think, and I fear will always think…'—'These and other moments of cricket are scorched in my mind like sexual memories, forever available to me and capable, during those long nights alone…'—'It meant snipping a fine white thread running, through years and years…'

This is the characteristic cadence O'Neill has forged for his colourless and yet extraordinarily interesting protagonist's narration, and much of the pleasure of *Netherland* is in catching the delayed gratification of these stretched-out sentences: 'Those circumstances were, I should say, unbearable,' or, (moving from two pauses to four very even ones, which in this case also dramatise the peace of the moment) 'Not knowing what to say, I got up and stood next to him, and for a while we surveyed, twenty-two floors down, the roving black brooms of four-dollar umbrellas,' or to a mix of short and long pauses: 'Perhaps the relevant truth—and it's one whose existence was apparent to my wife, and I'm sure to much of the world, long before it became apparent to me—is that we all find ourselves in temporal currents and that unless you're paying attention you'll discover, often too late, that an undertow of weeks or years has pulled you deep into trouble.' The writing in *Netherland* has its own temporal current, a kind of slow, rapt murmur, and it does not take very long before we are pulled deep into the text by these rhythms.

# 33. Never Give All the Heart Outright: Edna O'Brien

*Saints and Sinners*, by Edna O'Brien (Faber and Faber, 2011)

'Is there a place for me in some part of your life?' a married man asks a woman in 'Manhattan Medley,' one of the stories in the Irish writer Edna O'Brien's *Saints and Sinners*. By asking for a place not in someone's life, but in a part of her life, the man suggests that he wants things to happen slowly, less dramatically than affairs usually do. By speaking of a sliver and not of the whole, he perhaps indicates too that, realistically, all that he can offer is a part of his own life.

'We did not have a garden, we had ploughed fields and meadows,' says a girl about her family in another story, 'My Two Mothers.' 'Somehow I thought that a garden would be a prelude to happiness.' Although she longs for the pleasures of a garden to call her own, the girl still seems to divine that her childish desires can be but a threshold to some ideal state, not happiness but a prelude to it. These are people who seem preternaturally aware, even when in the grip of heightened feeling, of how obdurate life is, of how something may be changed or attained only by small steps, not grand sallies. Even the children are, by observing the world of adults, already adults, and the stories they narrate in O'Brien's work are adult stories.

*Saints and Sinners* is the late work of a writer—late in terms of O'Brien's own age, a vivid 80, but not in terms of any diminution of her sensibility—to whom we owe some of the most beautiful, limpid, and resonant English prose of the 20th century, especially that of the great *The Country Girls* trilogy and the stories later collected in *A Fanatic Heart*. Across these stories can be found all of O'Brien's signature characters and narratorial emphases. There are the questing, emotionally dissatisfied female protagonists of small Irish towns and villages, longing for escape from boredom or stiflement; the women who think about their love affairs and the girls who watch the love affairs or marriages of their mothers. There are, too, the hardened men who want to escape from feeling or have succeeded in deadening it through drink or desolation.

There is the landscape of fields, mountains and marshes, described in language that brings out all their strangeness (from 'Inner Cowboy': 'The bogs were more peaceful, stretching to the horizon, brown and black, with cushions of moss and spagunam and the cut turf in little stooks, igloos, with the wind whistling to them, drying them out.') And there is the society both roused and distorted by what O'Brien has elsewhere called 'the hounding nature of Irish Catholicism.' 'I was full of fears, thought everything was a sin,' remembers the old man Rafferty about his youth in the book's opening story 'Shovel Kings.' 'If the Holy Communion touched my teeth I thought that was a mortal sin.'

There is O'Brien's very precise attention to the colours and textures and emotional valency of objects, as when we are shown, in 'Old Wounds,' a woman turned out of her house by her son, who wanders down the road 'carrying her few belongings and her one heirloom, a brass lamp with a china shade, woebegone, like a woman in a ballad.' And there is the affection for people who dream and at the same time attend conscientiously to life's duties and try to do little things well, such as the mother who, despite being poor, applies icing on a Christmas cake with 'the rapture of an artist.'

All these things are presented through a style that knows how to be ornate without being mannered and how to be plain without being plebeian. O'Brien achieves an effect of naturalness and spontaneity through a palette of options as simple as the omission of a comma where one is expected, and as complex as a clause in a sentence that seems unrelated to anything before it, as if seeking to surprise the very sentence of which it is a part.

Consider, for instance, Miss Gilhooley, the protagonist of the story 'Send My Roots Rain,' which borrows its burnished title from a poem by Gerald Manley Hopkins that

Miss Gilhooley loves. Miss Gilhooley finds herself abruptly abandoned by a man with whom she has had a passionate affair, but remains possessed by him. Maddened by her pent-up yearning, she goes to see a psychic to see if there is a future for them. Encouragingly, the psychic foresees them 'setting up a house together….She drew a picture of their future life together, one or the other, whoever got back first of an evening, kneeling to light a fire and praying that the chimney would not smoke, though at first it would, but in time that would clear, once the flue had its generous lining of soot.'

'Though at first it would, but in time that would clear'—the psychic seems to take her story much further out than she needs to, into a level of detail that should interest nobody, not even Miss Gilhooley. But it is only by her doing so that her story becomes real to Miss Gilhooley even as, on another plane, we comprehend how the writer's narrative ingenuity has made the story real to us. The psychic's crafty story also illuminates the craft of story. Miss Gilhooley is gulled by the psychic, but so are we, who are nowhere as susceptible.

In O'Brien's stories men and women are always blazingly, defiantly, men and women before they are human beings. These are stories that everywhere ask us to think about what it is that constitutes their difference, a difference which undergirds both their mutual attraction and their ultimate incompatibility. Men and women feel differently, think differently, want differently, as a consequence of their biological and emotional differences, and this fact is not something to be evaded or simplified, but rather to be both experienced and rued. This sentiment may be accused of being essentialism, but in O'Brien's stories it has always seemed, from the situations laid out before us, more like realism.

'Never give all the heart outright—who said that?' asks Mildred, the rambling, slightly disordered narrator of the marvellous story 'Madame Cassandra.' 'I have read that men have cycles just like us women…we have cycles because of the presence of the uterus—hence we are subject from time to time to hysteria—whereas men's cycles do not answer to the womb or the moon but to their own dastardly whims…they simply go on and off the creatures they call women.'

The story is about Mildred's visit all the way from a village up to Dublin to meet Madame Cassandra, some kind of psychic or healer, about an affair her husband is having. Madame Cassandra, however, refuses to see Mildred, but even in inaction she precipitates the story's denouement. On the train back from Dublin, Mildred runs, of all people, into her own husband, and finds that he 'looked at me almost with wonder, as if he was seeing me in some way altered, his wife of twenty-two years leading a secret life, having a day up in Dublin, a rendezvous perhaps.' Mildred knows now, as they return home, that there is 'a little agitation at the core of both our hearts,' and it does not matter if her husband's rendezvous is real and her own is fiction, as long as her knowledge of the whole exceeds his. This is just one of many unusual closes and catharses in the work of this sensuous, rueful, and sublime writer.

## 34. Knowing How to Do It: Kazuo Ishiguro

*Nocturnes,* by Kazuo Ishiguro (Faber & Faber, 2009)

In one story in Kazuo Ishiguro's new book *Nocturnes*, the narrator, a small-time musician who plays in cafés, looks around at his supporting cast and explains, 'Playing together every day like this, you came to think of the band as a kind of family.' Of course, it is not only among musicians that music generates feelings of intimacy, tenderness, fraternity—a kind of higher awareness of both the present moment and an overarching continuity. To an extent that the rational side of our minds can never fully explain, our moods sometimes vault dramatically when we hear a melody, the tremor in a singer's

voice makes a hundred memories or regrets come flooding back, and the shape of a tune can make the most banal phrases appear as if they are exploding with significance.

In his new book, Ishiguro, who in his youth nurtured dreams of being a singer-songwriter, conjures up a set of stories about the power of music to bind, console, and heal. The word 'nocturne' means 'a musical composition of a dreamy character.' It struck me that the protagonists of the stories here are not just players of nocturnes; their lives are themselves nocturnes. Some of them are young musicians of modest talent who know that they will never be stars; others are middle-aged drifters whose lives are gently washed by regret. Ishiguro explores the implications of this for their self-perceptions, their friendships, and their marriages in a way that is simultaneously tender and comic.

Like a just-plucked guitar string, these stories are never stable or stationary. There is a twist or turn, usually minor but slowly expanding in significance, on nearly every page, as the narrators (all the stories are told in the first person) work out, sometimes not very well, what is happening to their lives. In the story called 'Nocturne,' we see a middle-aged saxophonist, Steve, whose career has come to a standstill not because he is not good enough, but perhaps because he is not good-looking. Steve's wife eventually falls for the charms of a richer and better-looking man, but both of them feel so guilty that her paramour offers, as a kind of compensation, to pay for some plastic surgery for Steve. Steve's agent thinks this is quite a good deal, given that Steve is going to lose his wife anyway. After some resistance, Steve finally succumbs and gives himself a new face in the mirror.

Recovering after his operation, Steve finds himself in the room next to the celebrity Lindy Gardner, who is one of those children of the media age who are famous despite having done nothing of significance. Seeing that he and Lindy are now in the same boat, Steve realises 'the scale of my moral descent.' But the despised Lindy turns out to be surprisingly good company, and eventually turns into a kind of confessor figure for him. Ishiguro's deceptively light and easy touch draws the reader in right away, and much of his dialogue is of an exceptionally high order.

Another story, 'Malvern Hills,' offers the pleasures of a familiar Ishiguro device: that of the unreliable narrator. This kind of story features a complex first-person narration where, although we have no other information than that which is being provided by the person telling the story, we can nevertheless tell that he or she is not interpreting life accurately. When carried out skilfully, this makes fiction more stimulating and rouses the reader to activity, because it is as if we are reading a story and constructing an alternative version of it at the same time. Simultaneously, we come to understand, philosophically, how our sense of the world depends so much on subjective perception.

The narrator of 'Malvern Hills' is a young, self-involved, hard-up songwriter who goes to spend the summer in a hotel in the countryside run by his sister and her husband. Although he is the one who is being helped out, he quickly comes to resent the few duties thrust upon him, and feels that the artist in him is being suffocated. 'It seemed clear I'd been invited here on false pretences,' he thinks, and we laugh at this and commiserate with him at the same time.

At a number of points in *Nocturnes*, the characters express a preference for popular music—evergreen ballads, Broadway hits, the work of 'those old pros [who] knew how to do it'—over more challenging and difficult forms. The idea behind these gestures is that we often overlook the extent to which music we think of as 'easy' is itself the result of great craft and discipline. After six novels, Ishiguro is now an old pro, and as these smoothly tossed-off and beguiling stories demonstrate, he too knows just how to do it.

## 35. Boyd Tonkin's Novelistic World Tour

*The 100 Best Novels in Translation,* by Boyd Tonkin
(Galileo Publishing, 2018)

Over the last century and a half, the novel has become the preeminent prose storytelling form around the world: a torch that passes from country to country, language to language, lighting new fires of story everywhere and finding, or fashioning, new audiences. It follows, then, nobody counts as a serious reader of novels who does not self-consciously seek out novels in translation.

Many of our great novel-reading experiences are actually the result of the work of two artists, not one. How would we know Chekhov in English without Constance Garnett, or Proust without CK Scott-Moncrieff, or Garcia Marquez without Gregory Rabassa? How would the Arab novel have travelled to Anglophone shores without the pioneering work of Denys Johnson-Davies? As the British literary critic Boyd Tonkin argues in his exciting new book *The 100 Best Novels in Translation*, translators are the great travel agents and bridge-builders of the novel form, allowing books written in one language to be read—with pleasure approximating or, by some reports, even exceeding that supplied by the original—by readers in many others.

And since no one language or country has a monopoly on novelistic excellence, every reader knows a majority of their favourite novelists in the words fashioned by their translators. In fact, without translators to give them new material to feed on, even novelists would be stuck with models solely from their own linguistic tradition. Behind every successful novelist lies a platoon of translators.

And although the Anglophone world is extremely rich in translators, a sad consequence of the dominance of English in world affairs has been the marginalisation of works in translation.

But here comes Tonkin to remedy that. For many years the literary editor of the British newspaper *The Independent*, Tonkin has always been a committed proponent, in a literary culture all too often unconsciously insular, of the pleasure and power of the cosmopolitan tradition of the novel and the translators that make it come alive. Uniquely, the Independent Foreign Fiction Prize, an annual prize he helped found, awarded its prize money equally to author and translator.

Now he presses his decades of reading world literature into a literary panorama of great geographical sweep and intellectual charge, making a list of his favourite novels in translation across 400 years, from Cervantes to Balzac, Mario Vargas Llosa to Orhan Pamuk (one of the rules of the game is that no author is allowed more than one book). Here is a book that makes a hundred other books come alive.

In fact, more than a hundred, as Tonkin often points to more than one translation of a novel, pointing to the relative merits of each in a way that might disconcert those readers who want him to recommend 'the best translation.' Certainly, many versions exist of the first book on the list, Cervantes' *Don Quixote* (1605), 'the acknowledged pattern-book or seed-bank which germinates every branch of Western fiction.' But if Tonkin is to be taken at his word, Edith Grossman's 2003 translation is the most readable of them all, and the most faithful to Cervantes's style.

For all those of us who loved novels in our youth but have sacrificed their pleasures to the demands of family, work, and tweeting, here is a book to make you fall in love all over again. In almost every essay, Tonkin says something illuminating and memorable. In Marcel Proust's great novel sequence *In Search of Lost Time*, 'Not quite all human life is here. All human feeling is.' In his essay on Naguib Mahfouz's *Cairo Trilogy*, he gets to the heart of what has made the novel such a good traveller when he says that the books 'enact a dialogue between Egyptian ways of being and European ways of knowing.' Each essay has many wonderful quotations from the books themselves, allowing the reader direct access to the novelist's style and sensibility. How I wish I'd had this book when I was a literature student 20 years ago. It would have saved me so much work.

Tonkin is at his most revelatory in his selections from 17th and 18th century novels, and then again in the final decades of the 20th century. I only found him somewhat limited—and more than a touch Eurocentric—in the middle. The core of his list is made up of novels from between 1920 and 1960. Here there are too many predictable choices—and too many men. I'm not convinced that Sartre, Camus, and Mann are as essential as Tonkin thinks. And there are a host of great Italian writers (Buzzati, Pavese, Bassini, Svevo) whom one might also consider not indispensable, especially when one sees there are so few novels from the Indian subcontinent (two), Africa, or the Arab world.

Tonkin is too hung up, one might say, on European ways of knowing European ways of being. A cosmopolitan literary critic brought up in Delhi, Rio, or Cairo would probably add many other novelists to such a list (Gopinath Mohanty, Jorge Amado, Nawal el-Saadawi, Malika Mokkedem) while still covering the great European tradition. But this is a small cavil at a large and generous project. As Tonkin shows, we are living in a great age of translation, with many of the great classics of old also being presented in exciting new versions. ('Translations, notoriously, age faster than their originals.') We need people like Tonkin to bring the big picture into focus—and it is our responsibility to refocus it to make big pictures of our own.

# 36. Narratorial Forgiveness in Vasily Grossman and Fakir Mohan Senapati

*Everything Flows*, by Vasily Grossman (Harvill Secker, 2010)
*Six Acres and a Third*, by Fakir Mohan Senapati (Penguin, 2006)

On the moral spectrum of actions available to any human being, forgiveness is one of the most difficult and demanding and, when it does manifest itself, one of the most surprising. Forgiveness requires of the person who forgives a self-gathering and self-giving, an immense moral exertion and clarity in response to some grave injustice. Although it is seen as a way of ending a cycle of injustice or retribution, forgiveness is in fact literally 'un-just' in its own way, for almost by definition it is not expected of the person who grants it, and were it not given, we would actually seek to sanction or prosecute the agent to whom forgiveness is being granted. Forgiveness is, if not morally troubling, then certainly morally demanding, both of the person who gives it and of those who witness it. In its surprising leap of faith and redemptive possibility, it is cleansing and cathartic, but at the same time it makes us all uneasy about our own resentments and our own clogged search for justice.

Forgiveness is all the more taxing because it asks something of the forgiver beyond mere assertion. When we say that we seek revenge for some injury done to us, nobody doubts that we do, in fact, seek it. But when we say that we forgive someone, we are required to present by word, deed, or gesture—such as by our tears—some unmistakable token of that decision, and nor can we later retract our forgiveness. (This is what makes us often so reluctant to forgive.) It is as if forgiveness itself does not forgive half-measures. Like love, forgiveness requires that we make ourselves vulnerable—vulnerable in front of those who may have already violated our dignity or vitiated our trust. And forgiveness, for all its force and moral grandeur, need not always be positive, for just like the wrongs that precede it, forgiveness may also be sometimes extracted by coercion, or be given as a consequence of sheer exhaustion in the face of an unrelentingly cruel and pitiless adversary. Last, in some especially complex cases, forgiveness can itself be a kind of revenge.

For all these reasons, forgiveness gives us human beings at their most human: paradoxically at their most vulnerable and their most powerful in the same instant. Although it is completely human not to want to forgive, we are never more aware of our power as human beings and moral agents than when we do so. And for all these reasons, forgiveness as an emotion, a practice, a journey, a personal and political question, is something that interests all human beings and in turn all the humanistic disciplines. But I want to focus in this essay on some particularly interesting instances of forgiveness in literature.

Literary narration, by its very nature, shifts continuously between the descriptive and the analytical in ways that draw us in as readers into the moral frame of a situation in a particularly compelling and immediate way. Further, literature is often very interested in systems of moral accounting that go beyond merely legalistic notions of justice, in a way that is analogous to the operation of forgiveness itself, which aspires to something greater than merely to even out the moral score.

Now, the simplest way of studying revenge and forgiveness in literature would be to analyse situations where characters visit great injustices upon others. But studying such stories would not be substantially very different from studying instances of injustice and forgiveness in real life. Perhaps a more interesting question to ask at this juncture is: is there a kind of forgiveness in literature that is specific to narrative art?

What I find fascinating is that revenge and forgiveness in literature need not always be horizontal, between one person and another within the field of the story, especially in novels. For novels have another kind of (often invisible) human presence inside them: the narrator, who serves as a mediating presence between the characters and readers and passes moral judgements on one of—sometimes both—these groups. Now to formulate my question. In a novel, is it possible for narrators to forgive guilty or sinning characters, perhaps even when other characters don't do so? How can we tell that they are doing so, and what does it mean within the field of meanings of the book? Given that the characters are 'real' in a way the narrator is not (and in a different way the narrator, as a proxy for the writer, is real in a sense in which the characters are not), what are the ethical and philosophical implications of such acts of forgiveness?

Here are two examples of acts of narratorial forgiveness in novels. The first is from the great Russian novelist Vasily Grossman's *Everything Flows*.

Like Rip Van Winkle, Ivan Grigoryevich, the protagonist of *Everything Flows*, leaves society a young man and returns elderly, bowed, and perplexed. His exile has not been one of sleep, but of 30 years in Stalin's Gulag for a trivial offence. His life has been shredded by the state: his mother is dead, his lover long ago married someone else. In a striking passage, he goes to Moscow to see his cousin, the prospering scientist Nikolay, and his wife Maria Pavlovna. They are the only kin he has; yet by welcoming him, they risk being drawn into the terrible world of the sentenced and the stigmatised that they have taken such pains to stay clear of. Yet they cannot refuse outright to meet him. Nikolay offers Ivan a confused welcome, while Maria Pavlovna worries that 'if Ivan did use their bath, they'd never be able to get the bath properly clean again, neither with acid, nor with lye.' (That last qualifying phrase about acid and lye might have been left out by a lesser writer, but it brilliantly brings alive Maria Pavlovna's pinched hospitality.) And now we come to a very interesting moment in the book. While Ivan knows nothing about the reservations of his hosts, we see Maria Pavlovna being condemned for her behaviour by her husband Nikolay. We read:

> Nikolay Andrevich was angry with his wife. All the same petty thoughts, each one of them, had passed through his own mind before she had said so much as a word. This had happened many times before. What he saw in his wife were

> his own weaknesses, though he did not understand this; he was unable to grasp that it was his own failings, rather than his wife's, that made him so very indignant. But then, because of his love for himself, he was also quick to calm down; forgiving his wife, he forgave himself.

In this very complex passage, two kinds of judgment and in fact two kinds of power relations are at work: one, that of Nikolay with respect to his wife, and two, that of the observing narrator with respect to Nikolay. In fact, the narrator is the agent through which Nikolay's judgment of his wife is turned back upon himself, for we are told that Nikolay himself 'did not understand this.' Maria, Nikolay, and the narrator occupy concentric moral fields, each one fitting into the other a bit like Russian dolls. We see that Nikolay forgives his wife, but what might be a morally generous gesture is immediately problematised and made ironical, because we see that the person Nikolay is forgiving is not his wife but really himself. We see how forgiveness can actually be something as petty as that which it deigns to forgive; it is a kind of consoling self-deception. At the same time, the narrator's touch is gentle enough that we are left in some doubt about whether, in laying bare Nikolay's self-deception, the narrator is *only* condemning him, or rather condemning him and himself forgiving him at the same time with the exculpatory phrase 'though he did not understand this.' Perhaps, recognising the limitations of human nature, even the narrator condemns and forgives in the same breath.

And an even more interesting example of narratorial forgiveness appears in Fakir Mohan Senapati's *Six Acres and a Third*. In this work, we swiftly realise that the protagonist Ramachandra Mangaraj, a moneylender introduced to us as 'a kind and pious man,' is actually a scoundrel and villain, as deficient morally as he is wealthy in material things. Yet Mangaraj serves as a mock-hero, because the novel takes the form of an extremely sly satire. As Mangaraj's venal deeds pile up and we see how he is feared and detested by the people of his village, the narrator continues to praise him, thereby pressuring the reader into a state of moral fervour: the contrast between what is observed by the reader and what is asserted by the narrator is so great that we are compelled to read against the grain. The narrator schools us in the hermeneutics of suspicion: what he says, we are never to believe.

But just as we, following the cues abundantly supplied by the narrator, have turned completely against Mangaraj, something strange happens. His wife, Saantani, who till this point has been only a marginal presence in the book, suddenly passes away. We know that Mangaraj never treated his wife well. But now:

> Sitting near Saantani's body, Mangaraj gazed listlessly at her face. Tears rolled down his cheeks. No one had ever seen Mangaraj shed tears; this was the first time people saw him cry. They believed that he was incapable of love, affection, shame, and decency; they believed that for him money was everything, that day and night, he thought about nothing else. Had Mangaraj ever understood the heavenly sweetness and beauty of conjugal love? Had anyone ever heard him utter a word of affection to Saantani? Why, then, should he grieve for her today? Nonetheless, we trust that he was now feeling the pangs of separation. Having observed Mangaraj, we conclude that he was overcome with sorrow, as well as repentance. Did he repent because he sensed a connection between his misdeeds, his neglect of Saantani, and her death?

The narrator now proceeds to expand the frame of the judgement:

> In physical appearance, no two human beings are completely alike. So too does their nature also differ. At times, under the pressure of a strange combination of events, the faculties of the mind come to life. Who could have foreseen that Jagai and Madhai, who were drunkards and lechers, would become great devotees of Lord Krishna? Saul, who was an enemy of the Christians and cruelly persecuted them, was later transformed into Saint Paul. On the contrary, all the merit earned by the great rishi Viswamitra, through harsh

> austerities endured over thousands of years, was destroyed by a single amorous glance from Menaka. Consider carefully these sudden changes in human character, their root cause, and their meaning. The Brahmos teach, 'Condemn the sin, not the sinner.' How can we tell whether the emotion that inspires remorse in men was not now awakened in Mangaraj's heart?

Here, three-fourths of the way into the book, is the first sign of a break or fracture in the narrator's hitherto quite sure-handed method. Thus far, although Mangaraj lorded it cruelly over every other character in the story, he was always securely enclosed within the satirical frame that the narrator had with such delight set up around him, and could never escape it just as his victims could never escape him. Finally, even we as readers had come around to believing that there was no redeeming quality about Mangaraj. And if in fact the narrator had taken a sceptical view even to this situation, we would have quite willingly accepted it and interpreted Mangaraj's grief as mere showboating. But instead, the narrator suddenly and surprisingly humanises Mangaraj by insisting that he feels not just grief, but repentance; in a way, Mangaraj is seen silently asking forgiveness of the woman who has just departed for good.

To put it another way, the narrator not only complicates our view of Mangaraj, he also admits to his own fallibility as an interpreter of human beings, and greatly deepens the moral complexity of the story. Narratorial forgiveness becomes the foundation in these novels for a much more capacious, self-reflexive view of human nature. We might even say, taking a cue from Grossman, that the narrator, in belatedly forgiving Mangaraj, like Nikolay Andrevich in Grossman's book, suddenly both perceives and forgives himself.

## 37. The Indian Novel as an Agent of History

People experience their lives as embedded not just in time, but in history. And we deploy a variety of modes and instruments to make a personal map and mood of history: individual experience and cultural memory, political ideology and historiography, myths and legends, the news on TV and the chat at the barbershop. Among these ways of constructing or examining the past, a somewhat late-arriving one in India—only about 150 years old—is the novel.

But what is so noteworthy about the novel as a lens on history? It might be argued that even as a form of story, let alone history, the novel does not enjoy great currency in India, for it is neither an indigenous form nor a mass one. Cinema has far greater mass appeal, and the stories and narrative conventions of epics like the Ramayana inform everyday life and moral reasoning much more than any novel does (notwithstanding the apparent desire of nearly every educated Indian to write a novel, ideally bestselling).

Yet if the novel deserves to be studied as a site of Indian history, it is because Indian history itself is one of the great subjects of the novel in India. A preoccupation with Indian history—its pleasures and possibilities, its continuities and its fractures, its burdens and its freedoms, its shape and its mysteries—is a thread running through the work of some of the greatest Indian novelists of the past century and more, across more than two dozen Indian languages and literary traditions. In the great diversity of narrative forms and interpretative cruxes generated by the Indian novel, there lies, waiting to be unpacked by the active reader, a wealth of wisdom about Indian history—and therefore about how to live in the present time as an Indian and a South Asian, as a modern person of the 21st century and as a citizen of the first century of Indian of democracy. (Some of these possibilities are apprehended or activated by characters in novels themselves, allowing us to experience vicariously, or in advance of actual historical fact, difficult dilemmas and choices in our own lives.)

Consider Fakir Mohan Senapati's enormously sly, satirical and lightfooted novel *Six Acres and a Third* (1902). The plot of Senapati's novel revolves around a village landowner's plot to take over the small landholding of some humble weavers. But this is also the Indian village in the high noon of colonialism, and the first readers of Senapati's story would have delighted in the many potshots taken by the narrator against new and perplexing British institutions or perverse intellectual fashions, administered and advanced by a new class of English-educated Indians. 'Ask a new babu his grandfather's father's name, and he will hem and haw,' the narrator chirps, 'but the names of the ancestors of England's Charles the Third will readily roll off his tongue.'

The story appears to be generating, then, an argument about history and about political resistance. India must rid itself of its colonial masters, it seems to say, because they have delegitimised many of the traditional knowledge systems and truths of Indian society, and in the process made the modern Indian self-imitative and inauthentic. (The argument persists in today's debates about 'westernisation.')

But this raises a new question, one that is not lost on Senapati. Was traditional Indian village society itself ever very wise, just, or balanced? As the story progresses, we see that anti-colonial sentiments have not blinded the narrator to the need to subject his own side to the scrutiny of satire. When we hear that 'The priest was very highly regarded in the village, particularly by the women,' and that 'The goddess frequently appeared to him in his dreams and talked to him about everything,' the complacency and mystifications of Brahmanical Hinduism are also laid bare, as is the credulity about those who would place their faith in such a system.

Senapati's irony is particularly effective *because* of its double-sidedness, and leads to a point useful as much in our time as his own. That is: criticism of a clearly marked-out 'other' (to Indians in the early 20th century, the British; to Hindu nationalists today, Muslims and Christians) often legitimises a sweeping and complacent faith in one's own worldview; that the search for truth or meaning in history must remain a charade if not accompanied by the capacity for self-criticism. The novel's argument, buried in its details and never overtly stated, is liberating not because it is comforting or inspiring, but precisely because it is disenchanted. Fiction shows us how human beings are themselves fiction-making creatures, and must therefore take special care to scrutinise what they believe to be foundational truths.

A different kind of novelistic irony—cosmic rather than comic—radiates from *This Is Not That Dawn*, the English translation of *Jhootha Sach,* the Hindi novelist Yashpal's thousand-page novel from the 1950s about Partition. The story tracks the lives and loves of Tara and Jaidev, a pair of siblings, across the worlds of Lahore and New Delhi in the years both before and after Partition. In so doing, Yashpal's novel generates dozens of alternative views of that cataclysm from viewpoints male and female, Hindu and Muslim, Indian and Pakistani (at the very moment that these new highly charged and adversarial identities are coming into being), prospective and retrospective.

Each character's position or dilemma carries its own distinctive charge of hope, memory, conviction, doubt, naïveté, prejudice, fatalism, cynicism: a vast narrative collage of human beings swimming valiantly with and against the tides of history. If the narrator himself has something to say about the logic or validity of the breaking up of India, it remains parcelled out among the characters and must be intuited by the reader.

In fact, although the book faces up squarely to the tremendous violence and horror of Partition, the feeling we take away from Yashpal's novel is not that of an entirely tragic story. Of course, Partition destroyed a particular shared and longstanding, if uncodified, sense of what it meant to be Indian. But as we perceive from the quest of the protagonist, Jaidev Puri, to start his own newspaper rooted firmly in a rejection of religious partisanship of either a Hindu or Muslim stripe, what it means to be Indian would, in a new democratic and secular republic, have entailed building upon a new foundation in any case. At certain junctures in history, the novel shows us, tragedy and moral progress may be inseparably mingled.

But of course, as we can now see more than seven decades later, the new Indian republic has faced many challenges in remaining secular (and indeed democratic). Perhaps, in retrospect, we might say that it asked too much of the first citizens of independent India, who might have preferred political independence while remaining wedded to their old ways of social organisation. A splendid insight into the tensions between the hierarchical imperatives of Hinduism and the egalitarian impulses of the new Indian democracy might be found in the novels of the great Kannada novelist UR Ananthamurthy, and nowhere more convincingly so than in his early novel *Samskara* (1965), published when Ananthamurthy was just 33.

*Samskara* is, as the title indicates, about rites for the dead. Its plot turns on the dilemma posed by Naranappa, a man even more troublesome dead than alive. Naranappa is a member of a small agrahara, or settlement, of brahmins in rural Karnataka. The brahmins are, for the most part, almost stereotypically true to type: they live off alms and donations, perform rituals for the rest of the community, interpret the sacred books, and uphold through both poetry and penance the values of an ancient (and apparently eternal) hierarchical social order.

But Naranappa has gone rogue, profaning the tradition, provoking his neighbours with orgies of drinking and meat-eating, living in sin with a woman of a lower caste. There is no taboo he has not traduced. If he has not been excommunicated, it is only because the agrahara's leader, the wise and compassionate scholar Praneshacharya, has long waged a war to reform his demoniacal nature. When Naranappa suddenly passes away, a question of profound significance comes up, one on which the entire world order seems to turn. Must the dead man be cremated with all the respect due to a high-born Brahmin? Or will the brahmins who survive him themselves be polluted by performing the last rites of someone who devoted himself to 'kicking away at brahmanism'? It is Praneshacharya who must decide. Confused, the man widely known as 'the Crest-Jewel of Vedic Learning' turns to his palm-leaf manuscripts for guidance. What precedents exist for a conundrum such as this?

Upon the horns of this beautifully counterbalanced conflict—dead against the living, hedonism against self-restraint, profaner against pardoner, sexuality against textuality—Ananthamurthy sets down an allegory of Indian history with a particular resonance for the 20th century, and indeed the one after. For although the novel appears to be set in the unchanging Village Time of old India, in actual calendar time we are somewhere in the 1950s, in the levelled world of the new Indian democracy that has made its touchstone not the books of revelation, but a constitution thrashed out by human beings.

Slowly, our view of the dead man's misdemeanours changes colour. Perhaps Naranappa, underneath the obvious provocation of his saturnalia, represents the spirit of the new freedom, blowing away the fossilised thinking sanctified by the centuries. In openly falling in love and living with a low-caste woman, Naranappa shows a greater humanity than that required merely by 'keeping the faith.' Unlike his compatriots, flapping cantankerously in manacles of jealousy and moralism, he thinks on his feet and with his body.

Even the spotless Praneshacharya finds himself morally discombobulated by the age: his righteousness is founded upon a deep social conservatism, and he thinks through the foundational categories of purity and pollution which find no place in the new social compact. The brahmins, we see, are prisoners of history, huddled in a cocoon of hypocritical piety; never daring to live beyond the 'duties a brahmin is born to.' Teaching all other castes to keep their own boundaries, they preside over a sterile society, when the age demands a new moral creativity. When they face a dilemma, they delve into their palm-leaf manuscripts, not into themselves. Praneshacharya begins to perceive this, but is powerless to act upon his intuition. Until his body does. On a trip deep into the forest to seek out an answer at the feet of a god, he encounters Naranappa's voluptuous companion and ends up sleeping with her.

Now Praneshacharya, too, is a sinner, forced to confront his own repressed carnality. 'I suddenly turned in the dark of the forest,' he ruminates. Smarting with shame but rapt with a strange exhilaration, he takes to the road, both running away from himself and in search of himself. Ananthamurthy's finespun prose, rendered in exquisite cadences by his late translator AK Ramanujan, tracks with great rigor the inner monologue of Praneshacharya as he arrives at a new vision of the self. And as we follow Praneshacharya there, we see that we have reached a point not just metaphysical but metafictional. In place of the Sacred Books, perhaps it is the novel that contains the wisdom and the doubt that India needs for a new age in its history (which would make Ananthamurthy a kind of novelistic Naranappa). It's a startling story, one as provocative for its time and place as those of Cervantes, Sterne, and Diderot must have been in theirs.

As these examples show, the work of novels is not confined to mere representation of historical realities (although this is where they may start). Rather, a novel may be a creative intervention in history in its own right—an actual *agent* of history, passing on to the reader who passes through its narrative field both its diagnostic powers and visionary charge. Indeed, from Bibhutibhushan Bandyopadhyay to UR Ananthamurthy, Bankimchandra Chatterjee to Kiran Nagarkar, Qurratulain Hyder to Salma, Phanishwarnath Renu to Amitav Ghosh, novelists have generated some of the most layered and sophisticated visions of Indian history produced in the last two centuries. Yet as a group, they fall into no school or political camp—some of them possess a conservative rather than progressive sensibility. What unites them is their interpretative power and their ability to illuminate the particular historical crux they focus on.

It would appear that there is something inherent in the novel form—the persuasive power and freedom of a story when compared to a discursive argument; the prospect of linking the world of the self with that of the community and society; the freedom to rove in spaces of the past that we cannot access by means other than that of the imagination; the potential to think dialectically in exchanges between characters or switches in perspective between the narrator and the characters—that makes the space of the novel a particularly fertile ground for historical thinking.

And when they are themselves reinserted into the canvas of Indian history, it seems to me that the projects of the Indian novel and that of Indian democracy (both fairly new forms in Indian history) appear uncannily similar—and perhaps similarly unfinished. As Indian democracy has over the last seven decades sought to fashion a new social contract in a deeply hierarchical civilisation, so the great Indian novel has attempted not just to address but also to form a new kind of reader/citizen, alive to both the iniquities and the redemptive potential of Indian history.

# PART TWO

# 38. Jawaharlal Nehru as a Writer of English Prose

*The Oxford India Nehru*, edited by Uma Iyengar
(Oxford University Press, 2007)

'I am not a man of letters,' wrote Jawaharlal Nehru in one of his fond missives from jail to his daughter Indira. But of course he was. All through his lifetime, Nehru lost no opportunity to write. His words took the form of drafts and resolutions for the Congress party, essays on the great issues of the day for newspapers and journals, and letters to friends, family, and colleagues in the Independence movement. When he became Prime Minister, Nehru wrote a long letter addressed jointly to his chief ministers every fortnight, containing his deliberations on 'the internal and international situation.' It is clear that for Nehru, words put down on paper were a way of making sense of the chaos and profusion of the world.

But Nehru was also a man of letters in a more abiding sense, as readers of any of his major works (his autobiography, *Glimpses of World History*, and *The Discovery of India*) know, and as *The Oxford India Nehru*, a selection of his most representative speeches and writings, once again proves. That is to say, we can read Nehru not just for his ideas and for insights into his personality and politics, but also for the way in which expressed himself, for the rhythm and grace of his English. 'At its best,' wrote the editor Frank Moraes, one of Nehru's best biographers, 'Nehru's style shows a vigour and clarity as pleasing and compelling to the ear as to the mind.' Indeed, Nehru was among a handful of Indian writers, among which Gandhi and Tagore are also prominent, who found a way to domesticate what, for most other Indians born in the 19th century, was an alien and tripping-up tongue, a language that could of course be learnt, as did many young people desirous of making good under the Raj, but could never be used with the same vigour or pliability.

'English made the empire,' observes the historian Sunil Khilnani, 'but [Gandhi and Nehru] showed how it could be used to unmake it—how the language could be a tool of insubordination and, ultimately, freedom.' The two men, neither of them professional writers, shaped the place and form of English in India in three decisive ways. Gandhi was born in 1869; Nehru died in 1964: their lives encompassed a linguistic century that stretched from the English of legal petitions and imperial proclamations, of diwans, pleaders, and officers of the early Raj, to the official bureaucratese of the Five-Year Plans and the ministries of the independent Indian state. The sheer bulk of their spoken and written words (combined, the published work of Gandhi and Nehru exceeds 150 volumes), as well as its historical span, ensured for the English language a countrywide currency. Second, though often ambivalent about the function of English in India, they kept a political commitment to English as a language of public communication. English may have been 'the language of the enemy,' yet both wished to accommodate it alongside other Indian languages, recognising it as a vital link not just to the wider world but also between Indians themselves. Finally, the forms in which they wrote—autobiographies, public and private letters, journalistic essays and articles, and works of history—helped to define how these genres came to be understood and used in India, by their contemporaries and those who came after.

Although he sometimes chose a romantic and elevated tone that could grow monotonous, there is never in Nehru's work that tendency towards vagueness and bombast, the use of clichés and archaisms, that to this day disfigures so much Indian prose in English. Indeed, Nehru deserves to be seen, independently of the political man, as one of the best Indian prose writers of the 20th century.

Uma Iyengar's selection of extracts for *The Oxford India Nehru* organises Nehru›s work by theme rather than by chronology, grouping together Nehru's thoughts on Indian history and culture, on Gandhi, on India before and after Independence, on the changing world situation, and so on. The great preoccupations and leanings of Nehru's work quickly emerge: his rationalism, his natural egalitarianism and his commitment to democratic institutions and practice, his impatience with, if not outright contempt for, religion, his espousal, after the fashion of his times, of socialism, his sometimes qualified admiration for and complicated relationship with Gandhi, his keen interest in world politics, his sense of India as one indivisible composite culture and his desire to overlay upon it 'the garb of modernity.'

Many of these thoughts are still relevant—in fact, sometimes Nehru seems to be speaking more to our times than his own. Attacking the demands made by various communal organisations in 1934, he writes that communalism is 'another name for social and political reaction,' and that 'it has often sailed under false colours and taken in many an unwary person.' Writing in 1953, he remarks that although nationalism can be a rousing and unifying force, one of the problems with it is 'the narrowness of mind that it develops within a country, when a majority thinks itself as the entire nation and in its attempt to absorb the minority actually separates them even more.' Objecting to the very name of the Backward Classes Commission, he writes, 'It is as if we are first branding them and then, from our superior position, we shall try and uplift them.'

In more than four decades of writing to persuade, engage, describe, attack, defend, reminisce, synthesise, and understand, Nehru wrote upon every possible subject, from cow slaughter to public health to the national flag and anthem to divorce. ('Divorce,' he opines with characteristic clarity, 'must not be looked upon as something which makes the custom of marriage fragile.') Iyengar even includes a letter to his chief ministers on the subject of brooms, observing that the commonly found short-handled ones make for tiring and backbreaking work and encourage 'a certain subservience in mind,' and insisting that municipal sweepers be supplied with long-handled brooms.

Here, from *The Discovery of India*, is a classic example of Nehru's elevated style: a sentence expansive and multi-claused, yet syntactically balanced and clear in sense, and proceeding steadily from specifics to generalities, generalities that exemplify his professed humanism and universalism:

> The story of the Ganges, from her source to the sea, from old times to new, is the story of India's civilization and culture, of the rise and fall of empires, of great and proud cities, of the adventure of man and the quest of the mind which has so occupied India's thinkers, of the richness and fulfilment of life as well as its denial and renunciation, of ups and downs, of growth and decay, of life and death.

The only phrase among these sonorous cadences that jars slightly is 'ups and downs,' which is a favourite Nehru phrase.

Nehru becomes a more interesting writer, we discover, when irked or riled; the expression of annoyance or dissent adds muscle to his writing. Here, for example, is a paragraph from one of a series of letters he exchanged with the Englishman Lord Lothian in 1936 over the future direction of India. In it he attacks Lothian's argument that Indian people should stick to constitutional methods of protest:

> You refer also to the 'constitutional road' in India. What exactly is this constitutional road? I can understand constitutional activities where there is a democratic constitution, but where there is no such thing, constitutional methods have no meaning. The word constitutional then simply means legal, and legal simply means in accordance with the wishes of an autocratic executive which can make laws and issue decrees and ordinances regardless of public opinion. What is the constitutional method in Germany or Italy today? What was this method in the India of the nineteenth century or of the early twentieth century or even now?...The mere fact that it is impossible for the great

> majority of the people of India to make their will effective shows that they have no constitutional way open to them. They can either submit to something they dislike intensely or adopt other than so-called constitutional methods. Such methods may be wise or unwise, under the particular circumstances, but the question of their being constitutional or not does not arise.

Nehru's brilliant rhetorical tactic is to ally 'constitutional' to 'democratic,' and to insist that one is nothing without the other. Cutting and hacking away sentence by sentence, he leaves his adversary with no ground to stand on. And in an essay in the *Tribune* early in 1934, he launches a broadside against organisations motivated by communal considerations:

> What are communal organizations? They are not religious, although they confine themselves to religious groups and exploit the name of religion. They are not cultural and have done nothing for culture, although they talk bravely of a past culture. They are not ethical or moral groups, for their teachings are singularly devoid of ethics and morality. They are certainly not economic groupings, for there is no economic link binding their members and they have no shadow of an economic programme. Some of them claim not to be political even. What then are they? As a matter of fact they function politically and their demands are political, but calling themselves non-political, they avoid the real issues and only succeed in obstructing the path of others.

Even today one would be hard-pressed to find a more cogent critique of the Rashtriya Swayamsevak Sangh.

Nehru had a naturally metaphorical cast of mind. He is often found on these pages comparing history to a great river. Indeed, he thought a lot about history, and felt keenly the pressure of history. In a speech to the Contituent Assembly in 1947, he imagines himself 'standing on the sword's edge of the present between the mighty past and the mightier future'—a particularly good metaphor, because it suggests how fraught with uncertainty the present is, possessing the power to cut sharply even as attempts are made to work with it. Elsewhere, he likens the taking of risks to the exhilaration of climbing mountains, while those who hold back, desiring safety and security, are seen as living in the valley, 'with their unhealthy mists and fogs.' This metaphor shows, among other things, Nehru's love of mountains, for most people would hardly go along with his negative characterisation of valleys.

Although he read widely and well, Nehru was curiously not much given to quoting from the works of other writers—perhaps because he spent so much time on the move or else in prison, with limited access to books in either case. Despite frequent references to the defects and excesses of capitalism and the merits of socialism, for instance, he can only be found quoting Marx once on these pages. Also, Nehru's relationship to his reading was intensely practical, a means of learning something about the world past or present. He liked to read travellers' accounts—Hsuen Tsang, Marco Polo, Ibn Battutah—and surveys of history and society—Marx, Oswald Spendler, Reinold Neibuhr. But we know that he disliked reading novels, saying they left him 'mentally slack.' Gandhi appears to have been a more adventurous and open-minded reader, fond not only of the *Gita* and the works of Tolstoy, Ruskin, and Plato, but also of Walter Scott, Jules Verne, and Goethe.

Perhaps it is to these tendencies we may attribute one fault of Nehru's writing, which is a fondness for generalities and groupings and a disregard for bracing and often necessary specificities. Consider that, although he travelled widely for decades on end, and was a captivating speaker who drew huge crowds, his references to the Indian peasantry almost always take the form of the generalized description—'the sunken eyes and hopeless looks of the people,' 'the starving peasant' for whom 'hunger gnaws at his stomach.' There is no account in his letters or essays of an actual conversation with a peasant whose name is provided and who is seen as more than a downtrodden man or a hungry stomach, although it would have doubtless strengthened the force to his work to incorporate into it such figures and voices.

Yet the most stirring sentences of 20th-century Indian writing in English are Nehru's: the opening lines of his speech to the constituent assembly at the hour of India's independence. It was a situation made for a man of his talents and predilections. 'Long years ago we made a tryst with destiny, and now the time comes when we shall redeem our pledge, not wholly or in full measure, but very substantially. At the stroke of the midnight hour, when the world sleeps, India will awake to life and freedom,' he begins, before moving onto a majestic seven-part sentence. 'A moment comes, which comes but rarely in history, when we step out from the old to the new, when an age ends, and when the soul of a nation, long suppressed, finds utterance.'

Nehru never wrote a better or more deeply felt line. It was what he had been waiting to say all his life.

## 39. My Work Would Be Mainly to Make You All Work: Gandhi's Autobiography

*The Story of My Experiments with Truth,* by Mohandas Karamchand Gandhi (Navjivan Trust, 1968)

Halfway through Part II of his autobiography *The Story of My Experiments with Truth,* we see the young Mohandas Karamchand Gandhi, still only 24, preparing to leave South Africa in 1893 after the successful resolution of the court case that originally took him there.

Gandhi has, by this time, won not just the respect but also the love of the Indian community in South Africa. His unusually stringent and holistic approach towards authority, law, and morals, his keen interest in matters well outside his brief such as racial discrimination, religious division, diet and sanitation, and his enthusiasm for petitioning and pamphleteering, organising meetings, and travelling has made him many friends and admirers. In Natal, his friends, and the merchant community in particular, try to persuade him to stay back and set up a legal practice there. They are willing not only to send private legal work his way, but also organise funds for the 'public work' of reform and improvement that so preoccupies him. Gandhi mulls over their offer, and then refuses the second part of it. He explains: 'My work would be mainly to make you all work. And how could I charge you for that?'

*My Experiments with Truth* was first published in English translation in 1927, and it still commands the power, just like its author did in his own person, to make us work should we come within range of it, to make us newly reflective, newly ambitious. It is, as Gandhi himself writes, not 'a real autobiography,' but a spartan, goal-directed one, closely focused only on those incidents and encounters in his life 'which bear upon the practice of truth.' It reflects its author's impatience with inessentials, and his constant search for first principles; it is rich in lessons and maxims, in speculations about root causes and deep connections, and in an infectious moral restlessness and urgency. It can sometimes be vexing and crankish, as in the author's obsession with matters of diet and sexual self-control, or his imputation of a divine will at work in the most mundane matters. But as Gandhi himself writes, 'The useful and the useless must, like good and evil generally, go on together, and man must make his choice.'

The *Autobiography* was written or dictated in haste, during the fallow years of the 1920s, when the energy of the independence struggle had subsided somewhat but the demands on Gandhi's time remained immense. It was published piece by piece from 1925 onwards in Gandhi's Gujarati weekly *Navajivan* (which explains the book's often arbitrary division into dozens of three and four-paged chapters). Gandhi's faithful associate, Mahadev Desai, translated it almost concurrently into English, supervised by Gandhi himself, but the paradox remains that the autobiography of one of India's greatest writers of English comes to us in an English translation by another hand. The copies found in most Indian homes are the homely, cheap editions published by Gandhi's own press, The Navajivan Trust, but they are in keeping with the spirit of the author, who honoured substance and economy over show and style.

Notwithstanding the fact that most of it is set in England and South Africa, the *Autobiography* is the most quintessentially Indian of books. Indeed, it might usefully be prescribed as the foundational book for anyone approaching Indian life or literature for the first time. This is in part because of the range of fundamental Indian experiences, across both public and private spheres, with which it engages critically—that of travelling in third-class railway compartments across the length and breadth of India, of agonising over the filth and squalor of public and community spaces, of walking through temples and observing religious festivals, of reflecting on the inequity of power relations in Indian life all the way from marriage (beginning with the author's own marriage) to caste and class.

But it also demands to be read because of Gandhi's own creative attitude—the insight offered by his specific strategies and responses—as a negotiator between the forces of tradition and modernity, as a seeker of a common ground where inter-religious dialogue can take place, and as an enthusiast when it comes to the multiplicity of Indian languages and systems. At different points in the book we see Gandhi trying to learn Tamil, the better to deal with indentured labourers from south India in South Africa; speaking in Hindustani at a Viceregal meeting, where the accepted practice was to speak in English; and trying to win over a predominantly Muslim audience in faltering Urdu. Gandhi always goes one step further than one would expect in dealing with the other; when we read him he always seems to be saying to us, 'You can do it too.'

Among the aspects of Gandhi's nature that emerge most clearly from the autobiography are his considerable talents as propagandist, pressman, and editor. Gandhi's *Collected Works* run into a hundred volumes, yet relatively few writings were conceived as independent books—they all made their first appearances as pieces in newspapers and periodicals, often those run by Gandhi himself. Although Gandhi began to read newspapers only in his teens, very early in his career he seems to have become conscious of the enormous power of the printed word to disseminate information, to stoke reflection, to offer considered criticism, and to forge durable relationships on a mass scale without the necessity of reader actually meeting author.

But—and this is characteristic of him—he also saw in the written word a means of holding himself to the highest standards of fairness and justice (which are only other words for what he would have understood as 'truth'). Writing about the journal *Indian Opinion*, which he ran for over a decade in South Africa, he recalls:

> Week after week I poured out my soul in its columns, and expounded the principles and practice of Satyagraha as I understood it. During ten years, that is, until 1914, excepting the intervals of my enforced rest in prison, there was hardly an issue of Indian Opinion without an article from me. I cannot recall a word in those articles set down without thought or deliberation, or a word of conscious exaggeration, or anything merely to please. Indeed the journal became for me a training in self-restraint…The critic found very little to which he could object. In fact the tone of Indian Opinion compelled the critic to put a curb on his own pen.

Here, as at many other points in the book, we see Gandhi advance a sophisticated understanding of the dialectical relationship between one's own actions and those of others, such as when he says, 'My experience has shown that we win justice quickest by rendering justice to the other party.' And sounded here, too, is the idea of responsible speech and action through self-scrutiny which is one of the root ideas of Gandhian ethics and is explained elsewhere in the book: 'Man is man because he is capable of, and only in so far as he exercises, self-restraint.' Gandhi often asks the impossible of us, but his appeal is in the radical possibilities he opens out before us; he expands our moral arena. We come away from Gandhi with an enhanced view of our relationship to others and to the world.

The word 'God' appears dozens of times in the *Autobiography*, and God clearly has pride of place in Gandhi's worldview. But what kind of God is he? Sometimes Gandhi speaks of God in a way that would strike the secular reader as strangely angular, but which is in fact characteristic of the pious, by ceding the very human agency that has so assiduously been forged in hostile circumstances. ('Thus God laid the foundations of my life in South Africa and sowed the seed of the fight for national self-respect.') Sometimes the word appears in notes of gratitude towards a mysterious higher authority who seems to be watching over him ('Only vaguely I understood that God had saved me on that occasion'—the occasion being a visit to a prostitute that ends in Gandhi fleeing the scene); sometimes as the end of a human ideal or endeavour ('I worship God as Truth only'; 'I had made the religion of service my own as I felt that God could be realised only through service'); and sometimes as a retreat of language and intelligence before the mystery and ineffability of the divine ('I have no word for characterising my belief in God'). Most notably, this is not a God who belongs to a particular faith; he is a God available to any person who seeks him. How did Gandhi, a practising Hindu, arrive at such a God?

The *Autobiography* offers a very comprehensive record of the development of Gandhi's views on religion. Gandhi was brought up in a staunchly Hindu household. But because the first years of his adulthood were spent as a student in England (he almost did not go abroad because his family feared that he would lose caste by crossing the seas) and then as a lawyer in South Africa, in these years he kept the company of Christians far more than he did that of Hindus. Indeed, he had a sustained encounter with Christianity—attending church service with friends, reading the Gospels, debating the nature of Christ and of salvation, trying to resist attempts to convert him—and with Theosophy before he came to Hinduism in any sustained or coherent way. About his first stint in South Africa, he writes that 'it was Christian influence that had kept me alive in the religious sense.' He first read the *Bhagavad Gita*, for many the core text of Hinduism, at the behest of two Theosophist friends in England, in an English translation by Edwin Arnold.

This awakening of the religious spirit led Gandhi to explore, through his 20s, the intellectual heritage of Hinduism through correspondence with Indian mentor-figures, and to also read widely on other religions. The reading, he reports, 'fostered in me the habit of putting into practice whatever appealed to me in my studies'; as in other fields, Gandhi is a great improviser in religion. But although Gandhi was soon to be persuaded by what he calls the 'beauties' of his own faith, Hinduism, and came to regard the Gita as 'the book par excellence for the knowledge of Truth,' there remained in his thought a Christianised view of sin and salvation. At the same time, the roundabout, unorthodox, and graduated route by which he arrived at his Hinduism made his creed both a liberal and critical one in itself, and genuinely open (and not just 'tolerant') towards others. 'In matters of religion beliefs differ,' he writes, 'and each one's is supreme for himself. If all had the same belief about all matters of religion, there would be only one religion in the world.' This would seem to be the starting point of peaceful coexistence in a multifaith society, yet individuals of all persuasions still have difficulty subscribing to this simple and dignified idea, which are both an endorsement of belief and a check on religious coercion.

Characteristically, Gandhi can be found in the *Autobiography* interpreting the word 'religion' not just as belief in God, adherence to scripture, rituals, and doctrine, but 'in its broadest sense, meaning thereby self-realisation or knowledge of self.' Looking at his own book similarly in the broadest possible perspective, we can situate it within a venerable tradition of the most ambitious human seeking and questioning. *My Experiments with Truth*, with its insistent questioning and refashioning of both self and world, and its pursuit of 'the higher law of our being, the voice of conscience,' might be seen not just as the central book in modern Indian literature, but amongst the most Socratic books in world literature.

## 40. Dr Nagaraj's Trysts with History and Fiction

*The Flaming Feet and Other Essays: The Dalit Movement in India,* by DR Nagaraj (Permanent Black, 2010)

Two voices suddenly pipe up midway through *The Flaming Feet*, the Kannada writer DR Nagaraj's book of essays on the history of the Dalit movement in India. They are those of BR Ambedkar and Mahatma Gandhi. For once we see them not spoken about, but speaking in their own voices, as if restored to life. Nagaraj, a great lover of fiction and a skilled interpreter of its capacity to tell the truth about the world even more powerfully than discursive argument or autobiographical testimony—unusually for an Indian observer of society and politics, his work is full of references to Indian novels—is found here taking the fiction writer's license to compose 'two imaginary soliloquies.'

It is 1997, the 50th anniversary of India's independence—an independence about which both men were, from the very beginning, and for different reasons, sceptical. Ambedkar and Gandhi occupy adjoining rooms in heaven, and look down somewhat disconsolately on an India that has moved on. Ambedkar speaks of his immense antipathy to religious superstition and myth-making, and acknowledges that 'my intimate enemy, that Gujarati Bania Mr. Gandhi, also does not like these things,' even if Gandhi is always seen as a man of religion. Gandhi, meanwhile, is found contemplating 'how *Hind Swaraj* would be if my nextdoor neighbour, the learned Babasaheb, had written it,' and thinks that Ambedkar, a trained economist and the quintessential rationalist, would have found an enormous array of statistics to improve the argument.

Perhaps no one in the pantheon of Indian intellectuals had earned the right to appropriate Gandhi and Ambedkar in this fashion more than Nagaraj. Although clearly written from a perspective sympathetic to the Dalit viewpoint, Nagaraj's essays repeatedly dramatised, with the deepest empathy and attention to detail, the epic clash between the two over the kind of society and polity that would finally grant Dalits a life of dignity and self-respect.

For Gandhi, this would happen only if high-caste Hindus examined their consciences, took account of the historic wrongs committed against Dalits, and experienced 'a conversion of the heart' that made them redress these injustices. Gandhi's method seemed idealistic, and time has shown it to be overly optimistic. But it was in its own way practical, trying somehow to identify 'simultaneously both with caste Hindu society and the untouchable' so as not to lose one or the other. Nagaraj grants that this was an enormous step forward for upper-caste Hinduism, but remains sharply critical of it. He holds that the Gandhian project had no real role for untouchables themselves, once again making them spectators to history in a drama in which high-castes were the chief protagonists, experiencing the guilt of a tragic hero and acting upon it. The Gandhian appellation for Dalits—'Harijan,' or the child of God—was not a generous but a patronising one.

In contrast to Gandhi's language of conscience (what Nagaraj acutely calls the mode of self-purification), Ambedkar spoke the language of rights and of political agitation (or the mode of self-respect). While Gandhi wished to bind Hindu society into a refashioned whole, Ambedkar's vision was of a complete break with Hindu society and all its encrusted modes of viewing the beleaguered and alienated masses on its margins. Ambedkar wanted the Dalit to stop being a subject in history and start becoming an agent, thereby 'eliminating dependence on mercy and benevolence.' The modern systems of democracy, rights, political suffrage, and the nation-state allowed Dalits pathways to all this, while the traditional village panchayat never had.

This bifurcation in views set up one of the pivotal clashes of modern Indian history: the disagreement in 1933 between Gandhi and Ambedkar over the issue of separate electorates for untouchables, which Ambedkar desired deeply. By launching a fast unto death in Yeravada Jail over this issue, Gandhi forced Ambedkar's hand, and had his own way. But even if Gandhi won the immediate battle, the larger war over the next eight decades for the Dalit view of self and the world has been won by Ambedkar, whose vision of aggressive self-mobilisation and minoritisation has found a variety of expressions in Indian politics and public life, especially since the 70s.

But, Nagaraj acknowledges, even if Dalits have won themselves new rights and greater security, especially from upper-caste violence of the more overt kind, the result is not so much a rapprochement as a kind of detente. The structure of caste society remains basically unchanged from the top. The peace achieved is a fragile one—it needs a dose of Gandhi to convert it into something more meaningful. In this way, as the scholar Ashis Nandy remarks in a short foreword, Nagaraj attempts heroically to reconcile Ambedkar and Gandhi. This posthumously published book is a memorable examination of the Dalit encounter with history and modernity, suffering and healing.

One of the pleasures of reading Nagaraj is his constant awareness of local contexts and frames to ideas which, over time, we have come to see in a somewhat general or pan-Indian way (this applies even to the word 'Dalit'). Here he is, for example, on the specific roots of Ambedkarism in Maharashtra and in ideas Ambedkar adapted from his western education, and on other 'proto-Dalit' movements which over time have become invisible in history:

> Untouchable activism, finally, came into being only with the arrival upon the scene of Ambedkar, a Maharashtra Mahar untouchable. However, the proto-Dalit phase is under-studied in modern Indian history; in this phase, and afterwards too, many other models of lower-caste revolt were active and disappeared only after the decisive victory of Ambedkarism over other competing discourses to define and shape the identity of Dalit politics. For instance, in order to get an accurate and comprehensive picture of the

> emergence and consolidation of Shudra identity in general and Dalit identity in particular, we must study the insider culturalist-rebel model of Narayana Guru, the religious reformer of Kerala; the model of Manguram of Punjab; and the South Indian model of gradualism. Only then will we arrive at a deeper understanding of the specific strengths of the Ambedkarite paradigms.

Another virtue of Nagaraj's work is his reluctance to restrict himself solely to an empirical style of argument. He is an adventurous rather than a safe writer. Sometimes he advances by applying a vivid metaphorical imagination to the reading of history, and very often he uses examples from Kannada novels, plays, and poems to illustrate particular cruxes and dilemmas in Dalit thought and the representation of Dalits. (In an essay on representations of Gandhi, Nandy writes of how he follows in the tracks of Nagaraj, 'who loved to claim, following William Blake, that stylised exaggeration could be a path to wisdom.') *The Flaming Feet* is full of allusions to the work of Shivaram Karanth (whose 1931 novel *Chomana Dudi* Nagaraj calls 'perhaps the earliest Kannada novel to explore the theme of untouchablity'), Kuvempu, UR Ananthamurthy, Devanuru Mahadeva, and the radical Dalit poet Siddalingaiah. These allow us to glimpse a literary universe with very different themes and tropes than those thrown up by Indian fiction in English. Although Nagaraj very rarely offers close readings of literary texts at the level of word or phrase, he is frequently stimulating and provocative when looking at them at the level of ideas and thought systems. Here he is, for instance, on Devanuru Mahadeva's Kannada novel *Kusumabale*, which he compares to Ananthamurthy's much more well-known English novel *Samskara*:

> While studying the narrative technique of the novel, an inevitable question came to my mind. Does the cosmology of lower castes mean the death of the realist novel?...I have always been nagged by the doubt that realism can provide full justice to the collective psyche and worldview of the lower

> castes. Even at its best, realism can only, in our context, reflect and accommodate the rationalist and empirical worldviews of the modern middle class. It can only deal with untouchability as a theme. The life of untouchables and other lower castes—in a total sense—has always remained outside the patterns of realism. If images are the distillation of worldviews, then naturally realism can only create images out of human situations. Images do not appear there as the synthesis of myth and history. Realism can only transform history into fiction. In fact, the realist novel is even seen as a fictional strategy to appropriate a form of history wherein, for example, a cot cannot be made to talk in an autobiographical vein. In *Kusumabale*, as in folk tales, by contrast, an ill-used cot tells the story of the decadence of the family to which it belongs.
>
> Such restrictions [placed on writers by the realist novel] do not merely reflect the aesthetic rules of a narrative game. They are basically the restrictions of philosophy and ideology. Even if the realms of experiences and worldviews barred by realism seek entry into the fictional world, they are permitted only after making sure that they do not wreck the narrative. It is without argument that their philosophical explanation has no legitimacy in this context: irrational structures are allowed, but only in order to be monitored by the inbuilt rationality of the realist novel.

This is literary criticism of the highest order, playing for the highest stakes possible: the question of whether an apparently ambitious, capacious, and celebrated narrative mode, now the default method of fictional narration, is not in the end subject to limitations of perspective and imagination that undermine its putative project. Wouldn't a novel where a cot can also speak (one thinks of the objects, like coins, that speak so eloquently in Pamuk's novel *My Name is Red*) be able to show us a truth, or give us a way of looking at the world, that shakes off the pinched legacy of realism? After reading Nagaraj, I put his book on the topmost shelf of the single bookcase in the room where I live and work, and while many other writers arrive and depart from that station, there he always stays.

# 41. Mukul Kesavan's Nationalist Exceptionalism

*The Ugliness of the Indian Male and Other Propositions,* by Mukul Kesavan (Permanent Black, 2008)

Mukul Kesavan's voluble essays take up a set of subjects which typically lend themselves to cliches and pieties—Indian secularism, nationalism, history, cinema—and refurbish them with a series of arguments and linkages that really set the brain ticking. The particular pleasure of Kesavan's work in the essay form is that the drama of Indian history is enhanced, in his telling, by the drama of thought. The writing constantly asks questions to itself, wheels and roves in search of adroit juxtapositions or historical parallels, hammers away at key points. A historian by training, and one of our sharpest columnists, Kesavan is also distinguished by the breadth of his expertise: he is equally at home on each of the subjects that make up what might be called the holy trinity of Indian public discourse: politics, cricket, and cinema (or more properly, Bollywood).

The material of *Ugliness* is arranged much like the way a team traditionally built an innings in one-day cricket. Early on, the tempo is more relaxed, the style of the play more various. Kesavan declares his disdain for Indian documentaries, asserts that the Indian male is not only born ugly, but hones that trait through regular practice (on which more later), and dissects the various kinds of patriotism found in Hindi cinema. He can be seen attending a political rally in Uttar Pradesh, looking at statues in Madras, enjoying a junket in Australia, bathing in Istanbul. It is only in the last section of the book, 'Politics,' that his tone rises to a kind of slog-overs crescendo, with a constellation of high-octane arguments about the distinctive colour and character of Indian secularism and nationalism. This is where the book is most interesting and, one might surmise, enduring.

Kesavan's argument runs something like this. Indian secularism is not only highly unusual (all the neighbouring states in South Asia privilege one religious community or another), it is also confused, to its disadvantage, with the Western version of that practice. The origins of Indian secularism lie not in the battle to separate the church from the state, as in the west, but in our anti-colonial national movement, and in particular, the strategies forged by the Indian National Congress. Unlike the other provincial political bodies that sprung up in India late in the nineteenth century, the Congress, from the very beginning, was self-consciously and pluralistically 'national,' of a mind to represent all the classes, religions, and communities of India on the common plank of anti-colonialism. 'The uniqueness of Congress' nationalism,' writes Kesavan, 'is its near-complete freedom from mystical and mystifying notions such as blood, soil, or national essence which are the stock-in-trade of narrower patriotisms':

> The Congress, as its name suggests, saw itself as a cross between a party and a parliament (or at least an assembly of representative Indians). Typically, till 1939, members of the Hindu Mahasabha and the Muslim League could be members, even presidents of the Congress. For the Congress, being secular meant making different types of Indians equally welcome; secularism in this context was a way of being comprehensively nationalist. [...] The emotional charge of Congress nationalism came from anti-imperialism—not the myth of a suppressed identity waiting to be born.

Even if, in the beginning, the Congress' pluralist definition of nationalism was strategic, designed to bring the largest number on board in a Noah's Ark kind of way, over the 60 years of the independence struggle, it became something like a reflex. Thus it was that, despite the horrors of Partition, India did not go down the road of being a Hindu nation. Our secular constitution, in Kesavan's telling, enshrined this liberal and hospitable nationalism in law. Although the Congress itself has been unable to live up to its legacy, the historical triumph of the

Congress, writes Kesavan, 'is that every party must now lay claim to the virtue of being secular. The meaning of secularism can be contested (truly secular/pseudo-secular), but it is a value, like democracy, that no mainstream party can publicly repudiate.' Every nationalist thinks his country is unique and incomparable; but Kesavan, movingly, thinks even Indian nationalism is greater than any other: he is a nationalist exceptionalist.

Because we don't fully appreciate the ingenuity of the Congress' construction of nationalism, argues Kesavan, we tend to confuse it with the more pedestrian, majoritarian ideas of nationalism that have forged nations around the world. Paradoxically, it is this race-and-religion conception of nationalism, which we bypassed, that is now advocated by a powerful force in Indian politics: the BJP and its allies. Although many secular Indians are horrified when their friends and family members support what they see as the bigotry of the BJP, the fact is that BJP supporters rarely think of themselves as communal, only as nationalist. And indeed, if we look at the history of the nationalist movements of Europe, it is possible to credit this argument. Hence,

> Since the dominant sense of nationalism the world over is derived from the European experience, when a Hindu chauvinist arguing for the primacy of Hindi asks rhetorically, 'Doesn't France have a common language?', the French example begins to seem a sound nationalist precedent for supporting Hindi. When he asks, 'Don't the English acknowledge that their culture and morality are derived from Christian values?', this becomes a persuasive reason to support the demand that all Indians acknowledge that they are constituted by Hindutva. The proper secularist response to this is that the nationalism of Gandhi that won us our freedom as a nation state and shaped the pluralism of our constitution has very little in common with this hectoring, homogenizing patriotism. These derivative arguments don't apply. They're irrelevant because they aren't rooted in our experience of the freedom struggle; they don't emerge from our nationalist practice.

'For secular Indians, the dreadful track record of intolerant nationalisms and their failure in containing secession or managing dissent is a gift,' Kesavan argues. 'Instead of reflexively denying the BJP's claim to nationalism, secularists should ratify this claim enthusiastically. They should then distinguish it from the nationalism of Gandhi and the freedom struggle, and encourage an undecided public to study the self-destruction that BJP-like chauvinisms wreaked on countries misguided enough to harbour them'—in neighbouring Sri Lanka, for example, where an aggressive Sinhala majority and an embattled Tamil minority have been locked in a murderous conflict for decades. The day Indians accept that those in the majority deserve to have their beliefs and sensibilities deferred to by the rest—the prevailing climate in the rest of South Asia—our marvellous pluralist experiment will have foundered. 'Invisibly, we shall have become another country'—that is the ringing close of Kesavan's book.

The density of Kesavan's engagement with these questions, and the sophistication of his responses in general, is perhaps intentionally absent in his irreverent title-essay. 'Some years ago I was struck by the contrast between the beauty of Hindi film heroines and the ugliness of Hindi film heroes,' he writes. The explanation for this is simple: Indian women are radically better-looking than Indian men. Indian women are, to Kesavan's eye, 'delicate and vivid,' Indian men 'coarse, dull, and squab-like.' Their ugliness is accentuated by their deficiencies of hygiene (nose-picking, crotch-scratching), hair (moustache-wearing, nose and ear-hair growing) and other assorted personal and sartorial habits.

In fact, if the ugliness of the Indian male resided only in the list drawn up by Kesavan, Indian women or columnists might not be too fussed, since some of these deficiencies are surface-only and can be reversed with a little grooming. The real ugliness of the Indian male resides not in his face, but in his mind: in his willing or unknowing endorsement of patriarchy and chauvinism. But Kesavan's jocular survey of surfaces and appearances, his refusal, for a change, to probe any deeper, makes for a sly variation in a first-rate collection of essays. The Indian male may be ugly, but in certain instances his writing is remarkably fine.

## 42. Shashi Tharoor, Banally in Love with India

*The Elephant, the Tiger and the Cellphone,* by Shashi Tharoor (Penguin, 2007)

A newspaper column is, as demonstrated by its best practitioners, a minor but nevertheless demanding art form, the essence of which is to give memorable expression to the topical by linking it to deeper realities. Those who carry it off most successfully on the Indian scene—Ramachandra Guha, Vir Sanghvi, Priya Ramani, Girish Shahane, Santosh Desai, Mukul Kesavan—delight and provoke us not only with their command over their subject but also their flair for shrewd generalisation and the economy and lucidity of their expression.

Sadly none of these qualities are visible in Shashi Tharoor's *The Elephant, the Tiger and the Cellphone*, a ragbag of columns and op-eds in which ancient platitudes, second-hand insights, and limp witticisms are aimed at the reader with marvellous conviction. Tharoor has never been a very good columnist anyway, so his unwise (but in some ways perfectly characteristic) decision to gather up his jottings only serves to expose more clearly his shortcomings in the realm of both thought and expression.

Let us begin with the thought. India, pronounces Tharoor, is an ancient civilisation of great diversity and richness, 'a conglomeration of languages, cultures, ethnicities,' 'a land of contrasts.' Our pluralist ethos is our greatest strength, yet because we have so many differences we often lapse into anarchy and division. Our economy is booming and our middle-class expanding; the cell phone is the symbol of this economic revolution. But a large chunk of our population still languishes in poverty, and if we don't attend to this problem then, in Tharoor's laboured metaphor, the elephant which is turning into a tiger may turn back into an elephant.

Tharoor asks us to mark also that elected leaders are often corrupt and unprincipled, and a blot on the name of democracy. Corruption is so endemic that the size of the black economy is probably as large as that of the white economy. Cricket emerged in a foreign land, but its spiritual home now is India. Cinema: movies are the great Indian national pastime, and Bollywood dominates popular discourse in India. Health: Indians are somehow acutely conscious of personal hygiene but unmindful of public sanitation. The mango: the mango is the king of fruits, but it sells at prices that make it the fruit of kings.

Tharoor's interpretation of particulars is as dismaying as his stultifying generalities. Nowhere is he more wearisome than when composing elaborations on his favourite theme: the Nehruvian idea of India's unity in diversity. Take his reflections on the rise of the cricketer Irfan Pathan. That Pathan, a Gujarati Muslim and the son of a muezzin, could play for India and attain the popularity he did in the wake of Gujarat 2002 is for Tharoor 'a testament to the indestructible pluralism of our country.' This logic is dubious in itself, but a further advertisement of pluralism, Tharoor avers, is the Indian team itself, a champion side 'including two Muslims and a Sikh, and captained by a Hindu with a wife named Donna.' Tharoor here fatuously confers an honorary Christianity upon Sourav Ganguly's wife Dona to fill up a blank in his pluralist headcount.

Elsewhere, Tharoor recounts an incident, which he knows only through the testimony of 'two American scholars,' of a Muslim girl whose father refused to let her play one of Krishna's dancing gopis in a play, but had no objection to her playing a stationary Krishna holding a flute. Anybody can see that this story is marked by doubt and confusion (and distaste for low activities like dancing) as much as assent, but for Tharoor it is 'a lovely story that illustrates the cultural synthesis of Hinduism and Islam in northern India.' Tharoor sees himself as a proud carrier of the Nehruvian torch, but is oblivious to how complacent and patronising a Nehruvian he is.

Nor is Tharoor much more edifying when talking about another of his pet subjects, 'the new India.' Watching the excitable cricketer S. Sreesanth slog a bullying South African fast bowler over his head for six and follow it up with a frenzied war dance, Tharoor is convinced that this incident epitomises 'all that is different about the new India'—bold, fearless, confident. As the flagbearers of the bold new India and the secular and pluralist India respectively, Sreesanth and Irfan Pathan may, to go by Tharoor's reading, be the most meaningful pair of new-ball bowlers in the history of cricket.

Of course, we have still not approached one of Tharoor's main subjects, one that looms almost as large in the book as the India he loves so. This topic begins with the same letter as India and stops right there: it is the 'I.' Tharoor is a highly energetic and committed self-promoter. In fact, some of the most ingenious writing in his book takes the form of his acrobatics of self-aggrandisement.

Consider these two examples. Coming across a photograph of a sadhu chatting on a mobile phone at the Kumbh mela, Tharoor remarks that this contrast 'says so much about the land of paradoxes that is today's India—a country that, as I wrote many years ago, manages to live in several centuries at the same time.' In another passage about India as a land of contrasts and extremes, Tharoor closes a paragraph with the lines: 'Any truism about India can be immediately contradicted by another truism about India. I once jokingly observed that "anything you can say about India, the opposite is also true."'

What is going on here? In these lines we find not one but two Shashi Tharoors—Shashi Tharoor present and Shashi Tharoor past—supporting each other in confirmation of the most trite observations. Tharoor is not only saying something that all of us keep saying, but also insisting that he said the very thing earlier, as if by a continuous process of self-quotation he can lever the thought into the domain of his personal copyright. *The Elephant, the Tiger and the Cellphone* abounds with such predictable moves out towards India on the one hand and preening gestures in towards the self on the other.

Not all of Tharoor's book is so tedious. In one chapter he argues persuasively that Hindutva, an ideology without any genuine relationship to Hinduism even if it shares the same root word, is in effect a separatist movement, one that appeals to a majority rather than a minority. Another section offers some useful profiles of little-known or neglected figures. But most of Tharoor's writing is just noise. Although we know from Tharoor that 'anything you can say about India, the opposite is also true,' there is little chance about the same polarity of opinion about a work so banally, so fatally, in love with India as *The Elephant, the Tiger and the Cellphone*.

## 43. Talking History with Romila Thapar

*Talking History*, by Romila Thapar, with Ramin Jahanbegloo and Neeladri Bhattacharya (Oxford University Press, 2017)

Human beings live not just in time, but in history. History is an account of the events of the past, but it amounts to much more than that, for it is also a theory of cause and effect, a source of identity and consolation, a narrative that includes some and excludes others. History not only influences the present, it is also influenced by it: we go to history in search of answers to questions that are of importance to us now. History may have taken place, but it is never finished. It remains a dynamic entity, capable (like memory) of generating new meanings.

These and many more insights into the nature of history pop up in *Talking History*, a freewheeling, book-length conversation about the practice and the politics of history with Romila Thapar. Thapar is the doyenne of Indian historians, someone who has lived and worked in two centuries and taken readers into the India of many more, from the world of the Indus Valley civilisation to that of the *Ramayana*, that of Ashoka to the medieval Kashmiri historian Kalhana.

Even at 90, she is still very much a vivid and forceful presence on the Indian intellectual scene, not least because of the ascent in recent years of the Hindutva school of history and its votaries, whose keenness to dismiss her as 'anti-Hindu' and a 'Marxist' is grudging acknowledgement of Thapar's stature. Her discussants here are the Iranian philosopher Ramin Jahanbegloo (now virtually an honorary Indian after having produced several such book-length dialogues on themes in Indian life with other intellectuals) and the historian Neeladri Bhattacharya.

Here is a book to initiate any lay reader into the subtleties and difficulties of the historian's craft. Although it is not Thapar's aim to say that history is best understood only by historians, she does want us to appreciate that history is hard: not an open plain, but a dense forest. Finding one's way around the terrain of history is not easy. Much depends on the intellectual resources, scepticism, imagination, and even self-restraint we bring to the quest.

And just as everything—monarchy or slavery, a word or a world view, tea or coffee—has a history, so, Thapar reminds us, does the writing of history itself. The study of history-writing is called historiography, and from it we see that there can be many ways of thinking about the past, some compatible with one another and some not. The *Ramayana* may have much to tell us about ancient India, but in its literal form it is not admissible as history, even if some people think of it as such.

Over 300 pages, Thapar takes us on a journey through Indian historiography over the last 50 years as it has attempted to interpret themes and events that take place over a span of

at least five millennia. These are questions of great import over which much ink—and sometimes blood—continue to be spilt. Is it true that Indians lack a sense of historical consciousness, as claimed by writers on India across a whole millennium, from Alberuni to James Mill? ('Contesting this,' says Thapar, 'has been my lifetime project.') Was the defining historical event of ancient India an invasion, or waves of migration, from the north-west, of the Indo-European peoples that we now call the Aryans? Or, as some writers today would have us believe, were the Aryans indigenous to India and migrants *out of* India to the West? What kinds of linguistic, archaeological, and literary evidence are admissible in the court of these debates, and must the historian ask different types of questions of each kind of source?

Some of the best pages in the book are those in which Thapar shows how history, even when not motivated by any overt ideological agenda, gradually becomes aware of its own biases and develops new eyes and ears for the past. For instance, since so much of what we know about the past comes from textual evidence, elite groups that had control over the writing of those texts come to dominate our view of the past. The default version of Hinduism we project on to the distant Indian past, therefore, becomes text-based Sanskritic Hinduism. The actual practice of what we today call Hinduism may have been much more variegated and idiosyncratic, the product of little and local histories that time has rubbed away.

Nor are details of material culture in texts always set up with factual accuracy as their primary aim. The descriptions of vast wealth and splendour of the imperial court and capital in the *Ramayana*, for instance, may have behind them the literary impulse of inciting wonder and awe in the reader. Similarly, it's easier to write the histories of settled societies than those made up of nomads, to trace a broad narrative of unification and consensus rather than the smaller ones of resistance and heterodoxy, to project modern religious and political categories and motivations upon the past rather than face up to its strangeness. 'We should not forget,' says Thapar, 'that there is always a part of history which is forgotten.'

And what of the future of Indian history? The arrival of the nation-state in the 18th century, Thapar reminds us, led everywhere in the world—whether the nations of Europe or the later decolonisation struggles of Asia and Africa—to the gradual reinterpretation of the past through a nationalist frame. Indian anti-colonial nationalism, although it was finally riven by a Hindu-Muslim divide that became the basis of a 'two-nation theory,' was an inclusive ideology that did not see Indianness as anchored in a particular religion or language.

This led, at Independence, to the ambitious construction, in the new nation-state of India, of a new platform for Indian history, one that sought to draw a line around the violence and inequity of the past and endowed all those who lived within the boundaries of India with the same rights and freedoms. The secular and democratic leanings of this new order (as also trends in the wider world of historiography) greatly affected the aims and aspirations of Indian historiography. Indian historians aimed to recover the marginalised histories of women and Dalits, peasants and artisans, traders and travellers—even non-human histories focused on ecology or geography.

Indian history became richer, more textured, more clamorous. But its political implications and reluctance to endorse a grand narrative were vigorously contested by Hindu nationalism, with its emphasis on religion as the main constituent of Indian identity across the millennia, and on Vedic Hinduism as the starting point of Indian history (thus the desire to prove that the Aryans were actually native to India). As Hindutva has gained political strength, so too has it attempted to reclaim Indian history for itself—paradoxically often using concepts and formulations, Thapar reminds us, first proposed by British colonialism.

It would not be excessive to say there is a civil war raging in India today, only it is being fought on the ground of Indian history. What we make of our history today, will be a great influence on the history that we ourselves make.

# 44. Pankaj Mishra on the March

*Butter Chicken in Ludhiana,* by Pankaj Mishra (1995 [2006], Picador)

In 1993, Pankaj Mishra, then in his early 20s, was living in a village called Mashobra in Himachal Pradesh, working on a novel, when he received out of the blue an offer from Penguin India to write a travel book. Mishra took up the offer and, formulating a project around the kind of Indian milieu with which he was best acquainted, and his reading of writers like Thorstein Veblen, set out to across India for a period of six months to chronicle the signs of what he thought was 'a nascent sensibility,' a change in the self-conception and the aspirations of India's burgeoning middle-class. His account of what he saw and heard and sensed on those travels was published to great acclaim in 1995 as *Butter Chicken in Ludhiana: Travels in Small Town India*, and launched Mishra on travels that were to take him around the world.

Eleven years since it was first published, it is clear that *Butter Chicken in Ludhiana* (available in India next week in a splendid new edition published by Picador, with a new afterword by Mishra) stands as a classic of Indian non-fiction. Reading it for the first time, I was struck both by the smoothness of its style and the strength of its argument, often more implied than asserted, from the picture of small-town Indian life it offers. It is a book that can be just as easily read to pass the time as to understand our age. Unlike most travel books, which suffer from more than a touch of the random and the inessential, it forges something cohesive from the writer's widely scattered rovings. Yet throughout, there is a sense of the thrill of being on the road, of not knowing who or what one is going to come across next.

Among the characters who appear on these pages are Mr Sharma, a businessman from Ambala and star of one of the book's funniest sequences, in which Mishra realises that, although he is a lowly writer, he is being sized up as a prospective son-in-law ('*Ab to suna hai ki kitaab-vitaab likhne mein bhi bahut paisa hai*'); Mr Tomar, owner of a haveli in a village in Rajasthan which he has turned into a hotel, who boasts non-stop about his contacts; a Jain teenager from Rajkot who declares the Hindus and the Jains have the same enemy, the Muslims, and declares that they must be finished off; Rajendra, an acquaintance of Mishra's from Allahabad University who wants to improve himself through reading ('he was the only person I knew who had actually read Dasgupta's five-volume study of Indian philosophy') but cannot come to terms with the fact that he is homosexual; Mrs Shukla, escorting her daughter to Bombay because she wants to become a model; Salim, the caretaker of a museum in Murshidabad who speaks of how the city kept its peace after the demolition of the Babri Masjid ('*Bas thoda ajeeb laga kuch dinon tak*, It only felt slightly weird for some days'); and Raghubir Azad, a communist party worker in caste-conflict-ridden Jehanabad, who speaks of how the *Ramayana* and the *Mahabharata* legitimise taking up arms against oppression. They are individuals, but most of us know of other people like them: they also become types.

After a while, it becomes possible to intuit a scale of values by which the various characters are judged. There are those who exhibit affectation, snobbery and high-handedness—such as Mr Sharma's teenaged daughter, who throws a fit because a relative has used her bar of Camay soap, or Mr Tomar with his preposterous blather—and are made the subject of ironical comment. Others exhibit a more serious, even shocking, failing, the absence of any kind of moral compass—such as the young men at the engagement ceremony in Muzaffarnagar, who 'boasted about the bribes they had given to municipal officials and sales-tax inspectors, and spoke with awe and reverence of a certain police inspector who had personally killed seven Muslims in a communal riot,' or the spiffily dressed teenager from Rajkot with murder in his heart, 'oblivious to the morality of his desires and actions.' These were people, writes Mishra, who seemed to have 'translated the notion of laissez faire into both economic and social terms.' Their modernity is a superficial one of dress, social demeanour, and consumption; their thinking is barbarous, lacking any sense of good and evil.

On the other hand there are those, like Rajendra, who are striving to make use of their opportunities and to achieve a genuine self-fashioning—'Unlike his compatriots…he realized his incompleteness as a person and strove to overcome that'—and of whom we are given an extended and sympathetic portrait. Still others have become the victim of peculiar predicaments, such as Rajkumar, the owner of a guest house in Pushkar open only to foreigners, not Indians. Asked why, he begins to detail how Indians are filthy and bothersome. 'I was struck by the way Rajkumar used the word "Indians,"' writes Mishra. 'His foreign guests had "modernized" him, and in the process had made him a man curiously at odds with his immediate environment, a man out of step with his own culture.'

And from the hundreds of impressions of Indian life logged in *Butter Chicken*—the appalling civic conditions of most small towns; the 'aggressive individualism' and ostentation of the newly moneyed classes and their love of kitsch; the cultural impact of satellite television and the adoption of new styles of dress and speech; the hunger for and respect given to wealth, power, and prestige regardless of the route taken to them; the nonchalant, unselfconscious voicing of caste and religious prejudice; the widespread sexual harassment and the ubiquity of pornography—there emerges a double-sided critique of Indian society. On the one hand there is the old feudal, hierarchical India, in which discrimination and injustice are rampant, life is heavily circumscribed by one's caste or sex, and the free expression of personality is suppressed. As Rahul, an acquaintance in Banaras, says of life in many parts of Uttar Pradesh, 'The modern idea of regarding people as individuals with their inalienable rights is still centuries away here. For the man with wealth and power everything in his domain, including land and human beings, is his property.'

Such a world is antithetical to the spirit of modernity and there is every reason for wanting to see it changed. But the supposed liberation that has arrived in its place in many parts is itself curiously distorted. To Mishra, while middle-class Indians show a great desire to embrace the modern, all too often their modernity is only something tacked onto their old lives, such as their participation in consumer culture. It is an ambiguous revolution, which has mostly to do with wants and aspirations and very little to do with thought or ideas, and there is often something grasping and pathetic, if not frankly disturbing, about it. The relevance of this argument has not diminished in the decade since *Butter Chicken* was published. 'No other book defines as clearly, and with such troubled irony, our last decade of change,' writes Amitava Kumar.

One of the book's best portraits is that of Mary Roy, mother of the novelist Arundhati Roy, describing her struggles against the Syrian Christian Church over inheritance rights and her complicated efforts to forge 'an independent modern identity' in which all that is taken as given is reassessed. What faults the book has have to do with a tendency to interpret certain details a touch too strongly, such as attendants in air-conditioned textile shops in sleepy Kottayam 'who, listlessly looking out from amid their brilliantly lit enclosures, gave off a strange forlornness,' or business executives in an airport lounge: 'Here, under the fluorescent lights of the departure lounge, they were set apart, they were an exalted breed.'

But for all that it is a serious work, *Butter Chicken in Ludhiana* is a very funny book. Mishra can be both appalled and amused by what he sees and hears, and the characteristic confusion and comedy of Indian life leaps off these pages. Some of the humour is in the recorded speech of others. Elsewhere it is puzzlement building into incredulity. Leaving Udaipur, Mishra's car comes to a halt before an unusually high speed-breaker, and is immediately surrounded by a crowd 'of suggestion- and advice-givers.' Still more people come out from shops and houses to watch: 'From the expectant faces around us, we could have been stunt-jumping a row of burning buses.' Elsewhere, Mishra finds himself one night in the waiting-room of Banaras station, full of sleeping people:

> I tried to doze off in the manner of the people beside me, but failed. I turned instead to following the progress of three large-sized rats, who fearlessly scurried about the floor, nimbly making their way among the recumbent bodies. Once, they accidentally climbed over a sleeping bag and started burrowing into it, mistaking its fluffiness for something edible, and woke up its occupant.
>
> After a brief struggle inside, a startled-looking white face emerged from under the sleeping-bag.
>
> 'Jesus Christ!' he exclaimed. 'What the fuck was that?'

By contrast, Mishra's prose today has a much more detached, austere tone—an air of gravitas, four parts poise, one part po-facedness—itself delivered with perfect pitch in an autobiographical book-length work in 2004's *An End to Suffering: The Buddha in the World.* There can only be a handful of Indian writers who have written two genuinely great books before the age of 35; Mishra is one of them, and of his two, this is the funny one.

## 45. Malcolm Gladwell and the Problem with Modern Narrative Non-fiction

*What the Dog Saw and Other Adventures,* by Malcolm Gladwell (Hachette, 2009)

'On the afternoon of October 23, 2006, Jeffrey Skilling sat at a table at the front of a federal courtroom in Houston, Texas.'

Not too hard to guess: this is the first sentence of an essay from the *New Yorker*. It features the familiar hook—a moment of dramatic tension, a set of precise visual details (Skilling is not attending his trial, as some writers might have put it, but sits at a table at the front of a federal courtroom), and the selection of a protagonist who is an entry point into the story—practised and perfected by generations of writers for that magazine, and other American long-form magazines like *Esquire* and *The Atlantic Monthly*, at least since the 1960s, when writers such as Tom Wolfe began to raid the techniques of fiction for their reportage. The current incumbent of the position of star *New Yorker* writer—a position held in the past by such luminaries as EB White, AJ Liebling, Joseph Mitchell, and the current editor David Remnick—is Malcolm Gladwell, the smooth-talking mind behind the bestsellers *The Tipping Point*, *Blink*, and *Outliers*, all of which offer provocative theses on modern life.

Gladwell's new book, *What the Dog Saw and Other Adventures*, has no central thesis like the previous ones, but instead brings together the best of his essays—on subjects as various as ovens, hair dye, football quarterbacks, and money markets—published in the *New Yorker* over the last decade. The general philosophy of these pieces seems to be, from what I could take from them, that human behaviour and wants are endlessly variable and complex and cannot be reduced to a system, which is why we require writers like Gladwell to explore its oddities, and on the other hand (and somewhat in contradiction to the first emphasis), that human behaviour is endlessly fascinating and is therefore worth systematising and theorising in all its quirks, particularly if such studies yield counterintuitive or logic-tickling results.

Two favourite Gladwell subjects, popping up repeatedly across these essays, are, one, the variables involved in human choice-making, and two, adroit salesmanship or transactional ability. Gladwell explores human behaviour in the public sphere much more than the private sphere. Some emphasis on commerce or a judgment of economic worth is present in most of his essays, and he uses the phrase 'the new economy' a lot. He seems both an adept guide to, and at the same time himself a child of, the highly consumerist, commoditised world in which we live, showing us how 'the products and the commercial messages with which we surround ourselves are as much a part of the psychological furniture of our lives' as emotions and interpersonal relationships.

All the strengths and novelties of this approach are on view in the best essay in this volume, 'True Colors.' Like all the other essays in the book, it begins with a protagonist—Shirley Polykoff, a copywriter—who managed to make the newly available use-at-home hair dye dramatically popular among American women in the 1950s with her hit line for Clairol, 'Does she or doesn't she?' Polykoff's influence on the minds of middle-class American women was soon rivalled by the L'Oreal ad that said, 'Because I'm worth it.' Gladwell's key point is that the revolution in hair-dye technology and the representations of hair-dye users in the advertising of the time were not trivial matters. 'Between the fifties and the seventies,' he writes, 'women entered the workplace, fought for social emancipation, got the Pill, and changed what they did with their hair. To examine the hair-colour campaigns of the period is to see, quite unexpectedly, all these things as bound up together, the profound with the seemingly trivial.' Very striking.

But at many other points, Gladwell's love of a dramatic story (two essays in the book have as their closing image men breaking into tears, while another ends with an upward spike, with a room full of people cheering for the protagonist) and nonchalant fly-on-the-wall approach towards reporting raise difficult questions that cannot be simply brushed aside. Take, for instance, the thoroughly charming opening essay of his book, 'The Pitchman,' which is about a family of inventors of kitchen gadgets, the Popeils, who sell their own products with such a charming, smooth-talking 'pitch' that consumers lap them up. Here is one of Gladwell's portraits:

> S.J. Popeil was a tinkerer. In the middle of the night, he would wake up and make frantic sketches on a pad he kept on his bedside table. He would disappear into his kitchen for

> hours and make a huge mess, and come out with a faraway look on his face. He loved standing behind his machinists, peering over their shoulders while they were assembling one of his prototypes.

Here we have the classic portrait of dishevelled, unruly genius down to the last detail, such as that adjective 'frantic.' This would be a great opening for a novel—even the character's name seems novelistic.

But here we also have the right to ask: is this true? Possibly. But how does Gladwell know this? After all, only S.J. Popeil is on the scene during his bursts of late-night inspiration! It makes sense, then, for Gladwell to say that this is how Popeil, or perhaps his wife, said he worked. But no—Gladwell here, and at several other points in the book, prefers to practise what the media critic Jack Shafer has called 'mind-meld journalism,' giving the impression that he has uninhibited access to his subject's mind and life every hour of the day.

The effect, in this piece, is actually that of a writer who has become so mesmerised by his subject that he himself begins to pitch for Popeil. To me this is dishonest, corner-cutting reportage, though it makes for a good story. It bestows upon a chosen human being intriguing backstories and flaming passions, airbrushed of contradiction, inertia, mystery, or deception (even as the larger argument may insist that people are vastly complex creatures). This approach hankers after the fiction writer's omniscience, but actually turns it into something of a joke by confusing human beings (who are independent, and often inaccessible even when in front of us) with characters (who are invented, and are mysterious only insofar as the author allows them to be). This trend is now fairly common in non-fiction books of our era; it appears not to be a problem that one can raise any more, as one is not supposed to question why capitalism leaves so many people out of the party. Here, for instance, is a passage from Michael Meyer's recent and otherwise admirable book about the fall of the Berlin Wall, *The Year That Changed The World*. Meyer tells us how the Wall was breached on the night on 9 November, 1989, and then moves into a flashback:

> Earlier that evening, just after 6 p.m., [...] Gunther Schabowski, the portly spokesman for the new East German Politburo, installed just weeks earlier, stopped by the offices of the communist party boss, Egon Krenz, en route to the daily press briefing, a recent innovation designed to demonstrate the regime's new openness.
>
> 'Anything to announce?' Schabowski asked, casually.
>
> Krenz shuffled through the papers on his desk, then passed Schabowski a two-page memo. 'Take this,' he said with a grin. 'It will do us a power of good.'

The writer's reluctance to use a distancing device such as reported speech, even when it is clear that the encounter being described was a private one, turns the incident to something that might have come, for example, out of the screenplay of *The Lives of Others*. The reason he does this is that there is something in the memo that will, unsuspected by Krenz and Schabowski, swiftly bring down the whole regime, so the words 'casually' and 'with a grin' work to set up a dramatic irony in the story. But this reconstruction, even if based on the testimony of one of the two players involved, loses in reader's trust what it may gain in storytelling power. The same problem can be found in Rajiv Chandrasekaran's tale of American bungling in post-Saddam Iraq, *Imperial Life in the Emerald City*, which 'reports' scenes of armed conflict down to what the characters were thinking at the time: 'Yee-haw, thought Fish, who was sitting behind Aguero.'

In a platitudinous, self-congratulatory preface to *What the Dog Saw and Other Adventures* ('Along the way, writing has never ceased to be fun, and I hope that buoyant spirit is evident in these pieces'), Gladwell makes a curious point about 'good writing':

> Nothing frustrates me more than someone who reads something of mine who reads something of mine or anyone else's and says, angrily, 'I don't buy it.' Why are they angry?

> Good writing does not succeed or fail on the strength of its ability to persuade. Not the kind of writing that you'll find in this book, anyway. It succeeds or fails on the strength of its ability to engage you, to make you think, to give you a glimpse into someone else's head—even if in the end you conclude that someone else's head is not a place you'd really like to be.

For a writer with so much skill, this seems an amateur's theory. Even so, what interests me most about this passage is not its hazy binaries or tendentious contentions, but why Gladwell has to qualify 'Good writing does not succeed or fail on the strength of its ability to persuade' with the back-door escape of 'Not the kind of writing that you'll find in this book, anyway' instead of going straight on to 'It succeeds or fails on....'

As with Gladwell's other books, there is no shortage of intriguing hypotheses and surprising insights in *What the Dog Saw and Other Adventures*. But the overall effect of smart-aleckiness and the absence of sustained human encounters swiftly becomes wearisome. One longs to be with a writer interested not just in providing 'a glimpse into someone else's head'—this is not as exclusive a community as Gladwell makes it out to be, although it does seem to be top of the to-do list of the modern-day non-fiction writer—but in reflecting on the forces and pressures and limits that operate on that all-seeing eye.

## 46. Utpal Dutt on Theatre and Film

*On Theatre* and *On Cinema,* by Utpal Dutt (Seagull Books, 2009)

'I believe any discussion on films in semi-colonial or newly independent countries must start from the illiteracy, poverty and cultural starvation of the masses,' wrote the great stalwart of Indian theatre and film Utpal Dutt in an essay in

1979. 'It seems blasphemous to engage in comfortable talk about the aesthetics of cinema in a country where the majority starves.'

What can we say about this clearly Marxist aesthetic? Is it true? Was it more relevant 40 years ago than it is now? Shouldn't art be seen as a site, a force, not automatically answerable to social and economic realities? Are artworks themselves a product of class and power interests, or can they be seen as something more ambiguous and capacious, combating propaganda as often as complicit with it?

The great merit of the two new collections of Dutt's combative essays written from the 1950s to the 90s, *On Theatre* and *On Cinema*, is that he writes from the viewpoint of someone with a definite politics and also as a practitioner in these arts, trawling the artistic seas of his time in search of productions that catch his eye. What is the place of local Indian theatre traditions like *jatra*, *yakshagana*, and *tamasha* in modern Indian plays? Do Indian films make cunning use of religious rhetoric to camouflage the iniquities of Indian social life and keep the masses quiescent? Are Indian actors on stage and screen guilty of overacting? These are some of the still-relevant questions explored in these essays, at once critical and empathetic, written by Dutt in the 60s and the 70s.

Outside of Bengal, most Indians probably remember Dutt today as the goggle-eyed, hectoring patriarch of Hindi comedies like *Golmaal*, in which he memorably asserted a continuum between Indian tradition, manhood, and moustaches. But Dutt's work for commercial Hindi and Bengali was only a small part of his oeuvre, and probably to him the least important. As a teenager in the 1940s, he came across the travelling theatre of the Kendals and received a rigorous training in Shakespearean drama. In his 30s, he wrote a string of plays critical of past and present power structures (he was jailed by the Congress government in Bengal in 1965 for the subversive message of his play *Kallol*). Dutt's range was vast. He acted in and directed *jatras*, and reviewed new plays and films (usually under the

pseudonym Iago) for journals. One month he might be seen in a Satyajit Ray film, the next in a speedily made farce.

Like many intellectuals of his time, Dutt looked—with glasses that were too rose-coloured—not to the West, but to the Soviet Union as the crucible where the future of humanity was being shaped. Following Marx and Lenin, he deplored 'the all-pervasive alienation of men in any society based on private property.' He can be heard on these pages haranguing bourgeois society for commodifying 'all that mankind once considered sacred' and for peddling crude superstitions instead of standing up for independence of thought.

He often has a point. In a speech given in 1991, Dutt excoriates the TV *Ramayana* that brought all Indian life to a standstill on Sunday mornings in the 80s for its crude glitz and covert ideological agenda—'monkeys and bears speaking Sanskritized Hindi, holy men flying over painted clouds'—and connects this to the jingoism and chauvinism that led to the sacking of the Babri Masjid a few years later. The serial, he thunders, is nothing but 'a fairytale written by an alcoholic.' After the Babri Masjid was destroyed, Dutt declares, 'a new god appeared in the Hindu pantheon—the common brick,' with the name of Ram inscribed on it.

If this makes Dutt seem like too much of a scold, then elsewhere on these pages we find himself reviewing one of his own performances under a pseudonym and cheekily declaring: 'Mr Dutt as Othello was rather a pitiable sight, with his voice gone, his breathing laboured and his bulk enormous.' There are excellent appreciations here of the films of Satyajit Ray, Mrinal Sen, and Chaplin, presented with great attention to individual scenes and points of detail. Here is Dutt on Ray's film *Devi*:

> Already in *Pather Panchali*, Ray's protagonists suffer not because gods have willed it but because of poverty created by men. They are evicted from their home by a power that is stronger than gods—a social system that condones exploitation. And this revolt against the concept of gods who crush human beings reaches fruition in *Devi*, where a girl,

> a common housewife, is declared a goddess incarnate and is expected to heal and cure every sick villager, until the boy she loves more than her life is dying and is placed before her so that she can touch and heal him. She dare not play with this boy's life and tries to flee, her sari torn and her mascara running all over her face. One has merely to compare this film with dozens churned out from the cinema-machine of the country, where a dying child, given up for dead by medical science, is placed before the image of a goddess—and, of course, there is a lengthy song glorifying the goddess—be it Santoshi Ma or some such forgotten local deity. Then the stone image is seen to smile, or to drop a flower on the boy's corpse, and lo and behold, what the best doctors could not do, the piece of stone achieves in a second! The corpse opens its eyes, even sits up. This is followed either by another unending song of thanksgiving, or the boy's parents weeping and rolling on the ground to show their gratitude. This kind of brazen superstition is peddled by film after film in this country every year. Are they any less dangerous than drugs? If drugs destroy the bodies of our young men, these films destroy their minds.[...] *Devi* is a revolutionary film in the Indian context. It is a direct attack on the black magic that is passed off as divinity in this country. Instead of the vulgarized Ramayana and Mahabharata, the Indian TV could have telecast *Devi* again and again; then perhaps we would not have had to discuss the outrages of the monkey brigade in Ayodhya.

And here are Dutt's entertaining riffs on the Sanskritisation of Hindustani practised by Doordarshan:

> The present rulers have gone after Hindi with a knife, excising every work of Urdu, Persian or Arabic origin (even though that word may be understood all over India), and replaced it with something concocted from a Sanskrit dictionary. The result is a new broadcast which no one but Benares pundits understand. 'Ab aap hindi mein samachar suniye,' wo bolte hain aajkal. Bolna chahiye, 'ab aap samachar mein hindi suniye.' That would make more sense. For example,

> replacing a word like zaroorat. The word zaroorat has entered every single Indian language from Bengali to Marathi. It is, however, being replaced by something called avshyakta. [...] Anyway, what is the object of setting a bunch of half-educated clerks to massacring a beautiful and simple language such as Hindustani? What is the reason behind this madness? The ruling class, all over the world and throughout history, wishes to create an esoteric language of its own. And the Indian rulers describe this destruction of Hindi as the restoration of an ancient tradition, as if our rishis in their forests spoke like TV newscasters.
>
> Thus their vague insistence on a 'link language'—whatever that might mean for India—not only wilfully obstructs the growth of other languages but destroys Hindi itself. It makes Hindi a barren grammatical exercise, not spoken by anyone in the country. A language grows only by being spoken by millions and by borrowing from other languages—consciously and unconsciously. Far from uniting the country, this idiotic bastardization of Sanskrit is rapidly disuniting it.

Like most practicing artists, Dutt never lost his capacity for wonder, for pure pleasure in an artistic idea truthfully realised or a detail vividly brought to life. His politics can be too rigid and censorious, but his aesthetic sense never allowed itself to be shackled, and nowhere on these pages can he be found supporting the banalities of socialist realism. For he knew very well, as someone who became a character each time he went on stage or faced a film camera, that 'all artistic activity consists in camouflage.'

# 47. Chidananda Das Gupta and the Play of Sensibility

*Seeing Is Believing,* by Chidananda Das Gupta (Penguin, 2008)

'Today, serious cinema is far ahead of serious film criticism.' This remark, taken from an essay written in 1982 by the Indian film critic Chidananda Das Gupta, seems even more true today than it must have been then. Most film reviews in the Indian press offer little more than plot summaries and a few desultory remarks of praise or condemnation. They are published because of the enormous enthusiasm and appetite of Indian viewers for cinema, but they very rarely enhance the experience of a movie for a viewer, which might be thought of as the first prerequisite of good criticism.

It is a pleasant surprise, then, to read a set of essays on Indian cinema as combative, as vigorous, and as cogent as those in Das Gupta's *Seeing is Believing.* In these pieces, published in different books and journals over the last 25 years, we see a powerful analytical mind at work, able to generate searching connections between our movies, our society, our literature, our art, our music, and our religion. But we also realise that we are reading a critic in whose work conceptual and analytical rigour and the desire to build interpretative structures is not used as a substitute (the distinction is one made by Das Gupta himself) for the play of sensibility: the attention to the unique rhythms and personality of each work of art, and to our aesthetic experience of the work.

Das Gupta's attractive title refers to the powerful illusion intrinsic to cinema, more than any other art form: the sense that what we are watching is real. He then takes this thought and runs with it, showing how, although film originated in the West, its transplantation to a pre-industrial society heavily invested in faith and myth instantly made it a very different thing in India. Most of the early Indian feature films were mythological, enrapturing audiences by bringing the gods and goddesses of Hindu myth from the hinterland of the imagination (where they had always resided) to visible, palpable life. Here is Das Gupta's winning recreation of that experience:

> When films began in earnest in India, with Phalke's *Harishchandra* in 1913, suddenly the gods and godlike men of mythology came to life. [...] Hitherto the Hindus had seen the trinity and pantheon in their minds and in images of clay, wood and stone; now they saw them walking, flying in space, throwing flaming discuses, setting offenders aflame with a burning look, making the dead come alive, appearing out of, and vanishing into, nowhere. This is how the gods had dwelt in the mind's recesses, held aloft by a network of myths and legends spawned by the epics and the Puranas. The loves and hates of the gods had been seen as leela, divine play, evoked by the bhakta or devotee in his imagination. These now became reality; here was Raja Harishchandra walking barefoot through the brambles, giving away his son Rohita, his wife Taramati, for the sake of charity; and there, Rama roaming the Dandakaranya forest with Sita. Inside the cinema theatre, the devout took off their shoes, sat with folded hands, and even threw offerings at the screen. [...] As the screen lit up in the vast night in the open air or inside the dark womb of the theatre, before their eyes a primeval dream unfolded in which the gods lived and had their being, emerging from an ancient communal memory secreted within the self.
>
> [...] This was different from seeing [the actors] in the folk theatre. The actors in the folk theatre were too real; too often you knew where they lived, and saw them paint their faces before they entered the arena. In the cinema they were real and shadowy, not gross enough to lose their distance and dignity.

'Too often you knew where they lived, and saw them paint their faces before they entered the arena'—there is a rapture to be felt in lines like these, lines that allow us not just to register but actually to enter the worldview of that early Indian film audience Das Gupta is describing.

Cinema, then, was a product of science but, in this case, science had 'reinforced faith and blurred the distinction between myth and fact.' Although the pure mythological film has made a retreat with the passage of time, Das Gupta argues that the basic accord between cinema and religiosity has not changed. Even where the exterior of what is being depicted is modern, beneath the surface, the present is being mythologised constantly and the currents of traditional belief are being kept alive. Again, Das Gupta is very good on the Hindi film song, and on why the songs are so often better than the films themselves. The Hindi film song, he says:

> is the transcendental element in the language of popular cinema. It expounds philosophies; proposes inductive and deductive syllogisms on the truths of individual life in relation to the social universe; explains hidden meanings; comments, like a chorus, of the worth or consequences of an action, besides providing aural enchantment to the otherwise music-less urban world at its rural grassroots.
>
> [...] The song is like divine speech, filling the firmament, and all vacant space on earth. It flows into the pores of the mind, like balm on wounds inflicted by the daily battles of existence. It represents an experience shared by a vast, varied, divided populace in the cinema theatres, in roadside restaurants for the poor, at fairs, festivals, temple yards, weddings, and all celebrations. [...] Film music blares forth everywhere for everyone, including the unwilling ears of those who are used to high art. This imminence of the film song shared by all lifts it way above the bounds of realism required by particular films and gives it an autonomous, transcendental presence in society.

But Das Gupta does not succumb to the glorification of Bollywood drama, increasingly prevalent in film studies, as the most authentic kind of Indian film. Popular cinema, he argues, must inevitably be populist, because it is made on large budgets and for the delectation of mass audiences. But, for criticism to follow the line of 'what is most popular is best' is to truckle to this populism, and that would be a fatal mistake. Accordingly, a number of Das Gupta's essays are vibrant appreciations of work—socially engaged, psychologically complex and technically restless—produced in parallel and regional cinema: Satyajit Ray, Shyam Benegal, Mrinal Sen, Ritwik Ghatak, Adoor Gopalakrishnan, M.S. Sathyu, G. Aravindan, and Girish Kasaravalli. He shows how there has been, and still is, a strong current of Indian cinema that wishes to challenge societal prejudice and entrenched inequalities, and that promulgates, often without didacticism, a concern for the deprived or the oppressed sections of society whom our expanding middle class would rather turn its eyes from.

One exceptional essay explains how M.G. Ramachandran and N.T. Rama Rao ascended the throne of politics on the back of their on-screen personae in Tamil Nadu and Andhra Pradesh. Here again was an example of 'seeing is believing' on the part of the audience. Another argues that Indian film studies relies too reflexively on trends in Western criticism, and on Western ideas such as catharsis and alienation, instead of drawing from our own rich native traditions. This is one of the richest and most satisfying books of criticism I have ever had the pleasure of reading.

## 48. Sonia Faleiro's Narrative Leela

*Beautiful Thing: Inside the Secret World of Bombay's Dance Bars,* by Sonia Faleiro (Penguin, 2011)

It is much easier to establish what literary genius is in fiction than in non-fiction. To the demanding reader of fiction, genius resides for the most part in the experience of aesthetic pleasure, in being disarmed. We come to a work of fiction sceptical that it can make a world real and meaningful, even essential, for us, and ask to be won over by the writer's vivid and imaginative use of their freedom in the realms of language, story, and characterisation.

But when it comes to narrative non-fiction, the writer is both liberated and constrained by his responsibility towards a world that precedes the book, and is the reason for its being written. This limits expectations of the genre, and makes its purveyors appear more dependent than independent. Indeed, the very techniques and effects that thrill us in fiction, and are now increasingly channelled by modern-day long-form reportage, make us suspicious: we wonder if the writer is making some stuff up. For the work of non-fiction to be good, truthful, solid, we feel, it should essentially be duplicable by another intelligent human being entering the same field. There is no room here for the wilfulness and wizardry of literary genius—truth and invention cannot be simultaneously indulged. Non-fiction writers, it seems, are either industrious worker bees, like David Remnick, or smart alecs spinning a grand theory per book or essay, like Malcolm Gladwell, or else unreliable fabulists, like Ryzsard Kapuscinski. It says something, then, that the narration of *Beautiful Thing*, Sonia Faleiro's book-length portrait of Leela, a teenaged Bombay bar dancer, and her bright but brittle world, is so striking that it invites from us the question of exactly what might constitute genius in non-fiction.

Behind Faleiro's protagonist lies a Bombay institution with a storied history: the dance bar. Now controversially outlawed by the government of Maharashtra, the dance bar was for decades the channel of many of the city's nocturnal pleasures, adding the shimmer and sizzle of glamour, the exuberance and melancholy of Bollywood film songs, and a frisson of romance upon the eternal and often sordid story of men seeking to trade money for sex.

By dancing in front of customers in an environment where the pleasure of actual physical contact was denied to them, a dance bar girl became an object of desire with a power far greater than her importunate suitors, some of whom would have to throw money and gifts at her for months before she agreed to meet them in private. ('They think I dance for them,' says Leela, 'but really, they dance for me.') Although at first sight no more than an ornate screen for prostitution, the dance bar was also an institution in its own right, with its own codes and rituals. Crucially, it was seen by many of the girls who worked there, often after early experiences of abuse in their own homes or in villages where feudal norms prevailed and women were seen as chattel, as a place of refuge, even as a gateway to riches.

Dance bar girls, as revealed by Faleiro's enormously detailed description of the psychological landscape of the trade, were likely to view other classes of sex workers as queens might commoners. When the bars were shut down (we see from the arc of Leela's story), the girls suddenly found themselves independent in the most negative sense of the word, and plunged into a world of abasement, desperation, and fear.

The book's great achievement lies in its breaking down of the walls between its upper-middle class narrator and her bold yet skittish, cynical yet fragile subject, and its invention of a language that accommodates the registers of both these voices without either one coming across as contrived. From the very beginning, Faleiro strives to establish a kind of phonetic naturalism that lets us into the world from which Leela and her colleagues come from, giving us, through their vivid monologues, japes, flights of fancy, and sneers, 'bijniss' for 'business,' 'hotil' for 'hotel,' 'hensum' for 'handsome,' and 'kalass' for 'class.'

This is not mere mannerism. Each time such a word is repeated, we are taken by language from our polished dictionary world into a place foreign to us, and begin to hear in these words layers of meaning specific to the circumstances in which they circulate. Faleiro is not the first non-fiction writer to discover that the truths of a subculture can be opened up only through a detailed attention to its vocabulary and syntax, but she is certainly among the most skilled. It is not just the Indian way of pronouncing a word that she replicates, but also the cadences of Indian speech, with its instinct for persistent repetition (among the gifts Leela desires from customers is 'a new wardrobe, everything within matching-matching') and its tendency to coax agreement for every assertion by adding a '*na?*' at the end.

Although it is ostensibly 'reported,' and therefore not original, in truth the dialogue in Faleiro's book carries a power more earned than inherited, achieving its effects not merely because of the speaking and cursing of its unforgettable characters, but also because of the writer's remarkable ear. To Leela's gifts for metaphor, Faleiro adds her own. A girl is seen with her silken hair 'billowing about like an unpinned dupatta,' while Leela's boyfriend, the balding bar-owner Purshottam Shetty, makes up for his many shortcomings 'by being cooler than a chuski.' These are metaphors rooted in the very world they describe.

Faleiro's book stands alongside Vikram Chandra's novel *Sacred Games* as the most memorable representation of Mumbai's street language in its literature. But it is also moves and shocks through the acuity of its portrayal of the most peculiar kinds of guilt and predation, provocation and neediness, generosity and spite, surreal spectacle and moral reversal.

In one episode, we hear of a bar dancer who has been raped by a man: her own son. We expect her to be unhinged by rage and self-pity. But instead she creeps into a corner and is heard comforting herself: 'At least he didn't hit me. I'm an ugly face in a glamour line and had he damaged me further I would have been thrown out of the dance bar and forced to become a waiter...The humiliation! Merciful God, you saved me.' Elsewhere, a police constable, mocked on the street by a group of hijras, assaults one of them and tears open her blouse, 'freeing fistfuls of paper napkins like doves in a cage.' To the eunuch this is a humiliation that can never be lived down, yet it is the man who is more disturbed: 'Now they would get their revenge, because he was alone, because he stank of fear, and fear was a stench the hijras picked up on immediately because often they stank of it too.' It expands our moral awareness to be told stories such as this.

It is in the context of such encounters that the story of Leela's own life, racked by violence and its memories, 'proudy' and abrasive even in its poverty and need, holding no illusions about the nature of desire or power, lusting for material comfort and the highs of intoxicants, is told by Faleiro, all the way down to the fantastic fatalism and unconscious courage revealed by the protagonist in the book's final act. *Beautiful Thing* is a model for how a work of nonfiction may be both journalistically rigorous and brightly novelistic, and places the author, alongside writers like Basharat Peer, Samanth Subramanian, and Siddhartha Deb, prominently at the vanguard of the revolution currently gusting across the landscape of Indian non-fiction.

## 49. Sasthi Brata's Acid Thoughts

*My God Died Young,* by Sasthi Brata (1968; reissued by Penguin, 2006)

A recurring figure in modern literature is that of the Questioning or Dissatisfied Man—distanced, for this or that reason, from the customs and codes of his own society, but also rendered strangely apathetic, rootless by his rebellion, and almost chronically discontented and splenetic, ill at ease wherever he goes and whatever he does—the very definition, in other words, of an alienated human being. This condition, while never pleasant, is nevertheless a fashionable attitude towards life, which is why it is the task of readers coming across this predicament in literature, whether in autobiography or even fiction (for fiction can be untruthful too), to judge whether it is genuine or merely a pose—fruitful dissatisfaction with fossilised ways of life, or merely the caterwauling of a pretentious human being.

Reading Sasthi Brata's *My God Died Young*, a flaming autobiographical work in English first published in 1968, I can't say I can make up my mind on this point. Rather, I judge it to be six parts solid, worthy, caustic writing to three parts romantic angst and egotistical flailing (consider the very title of his book) to one part pure flab. The best parts are very powerful, but even when Brata is on less solid ground, he sometimes searches out his own egotism and immaturity. 'I wrote this book to try and understand myself,' he says at the beginning (he was not even 30 when he wrote it), and autobiography, he knows, 'demands honesty.' One feels that the two sides of Brata are somehow intertwined, and that we must learn to take the good with the bad. Nearly four decades after it was first published, there is still something for the contemporary reader in Brata's journey towards self-understanding. If his ideas and language have dated slightly, the kinds of pressures and predicaments he describes have not. He still speaks to our times.

Brata was born in 1939, the youngest child of a prosperous Bengali business family. A late and probably unexpected arrival, he 'was not awaited with any sense of excitement' at his birth, and wonders if this has anything to do with his lifelong attitude 'of strained resentment with the world.' A spoilt child, doted upon by his mother, he received a traditional Brahminical upbringing, strewn with constraints, boundaries, and taboos, and an education at a stern Catholic school that imbued in him feelings of guilt at any kind of perceived transgression, such as his awakening sexuality. (He rightly remarks of this type of complacent, writhing, moralising Christianity, still commonly found in Indian convent schools, 'Adolescence is the most impressionable period of life. We were taught values which were obviously perverse at a time when we were defenceless.')

'Thanks to the twin pressures of a Brahmin home and a nonconformist upbringing,' Brata notes, 'most of the time I move around in the steel braces of subconscious inhibitions.' Many Indians, not always middle-class or Brahmin, will be conversant with this feeling. Indeed, one of the themes of

Brata's book is the extent to which our adult lives are in thrall to conceptions and attitudes formed in childhood. Going to Presidency College in Kolkata, and a love of debating, somewhat freed him of these shackles. He studied science, flirted with fashionable Marxist ideas, believed he was a young genius and prophet, fell in love, agonised about religion, and contemplated his place in the world. Later, unhappy in enclosed, stratified India, he moved to the West, and decided to pursue a path as a writer. Everywhere he found that obstacles to his dreams lay not just in the conventions of society and the shape of his personal destiny, but also in something marshy and tortured in his own nature, even more generally human nature.

Brata's confessional language has a powerfully persuasive air. 'I hated my family and since I was a part of them, I hated myself too.' 'My outward actions were frenzied and daring because the inner man was so tame and ordinary.' 'Even the most genuine emotion [I felt] was centripetal, tending towards myself in the centre, with the other person as an incidental circumference. I don't believe I had any real feelings. I sometimes wonder if I do now.' 'I move about in a thick viscous cloud, always looking over my shoulder to see if anyone is watching.' 'I was the shadow of a shadow. It is always hard to build a life on such foundations.'

Many readers will perceive that it is not that some of Brata's feelings, particularly about his pervasive egotism, denote an abnormal man, but rather that most people manage to go through life without realising these things. The effect of Brata's work, even its more extreme formulations, is to point us towards greater self-knowledge. As when he observes, thinking about the failure of his relationship with a girl he loved deeply and in particular about his callous and hurtful behaviour towards her:

> 'Love' is an exposition of personality, essentially against the grain of ordinary experience. To be viable, we have to conceal. Sophistication, manners, tact, in a word all the qualifications of civilized living, insist on our ability to appear different from what we really are. To love someone else, we have to reverse

> the processes of our conditioning. We have to be naked, giving, non self-possessed. This is hard. There must always be a fight. Few people win. At best it is an uneasy truce, with the ego forever ready to stage an unexpected ambush.

Some of Brata's phrases—fusty Britishisms, and curious analogies to English examples rather than native ones of the kind one can still find in, say, a professor of English in Kolkata—are a mark of his time and place and his education. The old midwife who delivered him 'looked as close to the Witches in Macbeth as Shakespeare could have imagined them to be.' 'A great gulf had come between [my father and me] and not even a risen Lazarus could hope to bring us together again.' Even if Lazarus did manage to rise, it is hard to imagine him doing so to reunite a Bengali youth and his father.

But a great many of these pages bear the strong stamp of Brata's personality and experience—it is not just his thoughts that are of interest, but also the force of his language. 'The years of childhood are slow and timid; the transition to youth comes in a sudden rush.' On Kolkata's College Street: 'Bookshops cling like running sores all along its sides; bazaar notes, made-easies, a-pass-in-half-an-hour, sure-predictions, stare at the passer-by from the shelves.'

Brata's restlessness and dissatisfaction are infectious. 'I believe there is a basic contradiction,' he writes of his unwillingness to live in India, 'between the premises of Indian society and the kind in which I wish to live.' 'Count me in!' I hear a thousand progressive intellectuals and four hundred million women saying. Brata is unembarrassed about writing a sentence like, 'How [does] Man achieve dignity other than by asserting the freedom of his will?' No contemporary writer would capitalise that word 'man' unless he was being ironic.

Brata can be pleasurably caustic. 'I am often reminded of the "great Indian heritage" and of "an Indian sensibility". I am aware some people have made professions of exploiting these myths...Such a vision possibly exists. It does not consist in the mere fact of destitution, hunger, famine, and superstition.' Or, of his decision to move West, 'It is the obsequious, cringing facet of Indian personality that I despise. Hosts of explanations are given for this aspect of Indian character. But I have only one life to live. I would rather have an "essay in failure" on my epitaph than die in the comfortable niche of mediocrity.'

*My God Died Young* culminates in a beautifully realised scene in which Brata, having returned to India for a visit, is persuaded by his parents to 'view' a potential bride. Reluctant, but also curious, he submits to all the rituals of the arranged-marriage experience, driving to the would-be bride's home with his parents, listening patiently to her father reeling off a list of her achievements, scrutinising, and being scrutinised by, the gathered women of the girl's family. He asks the shy, veiled girl a couple of questions in front of the entire company, and hears her sing a song at his mother's request. Despite his reservations, he is impressed with, and even entranced by, the girl. At the same time, the curious scene in which he is the chief player arouses in him a strange horror and repulsion, expressed in these beautiful sentences that simultaneously evoke both a burgeoning, thriving life and a kind of moral blindness:

> The girl sat there like a Goddess. And for a moment I felt that no one but a Goddess could have her forbearance, her beauty, the sweet maddening melody of her voice. Restively, my eyes swung round to her, so calm, so removed, so enchantingly graceful like the swift green curves of spring. Then over the rest of those hard deadening faces, severe and resolute, presiding over the closing cries of an auction mart.

*My God Died Young* is a pensive, cranky book—the kind of work that results when the narrator is both impatient with the hypocrisy of the world and despairing of himself. Readers may find in it echoes of Naipaul or Nirad Chaudhuri. Like them, Brata is always asking the question: 'Why do we live in this way and not in any other?'

## 50. Gyan Prakash's Urban Fables

*Mumbai Fables,* by Gyan Prakash (Princeton University Press, 2011)

'Bombay, it has been said, is not a city, but a state of mind,' the journalist and screenwriter Khwaja Ahmed Abbas writes in his autobiography *I Am Not an Island*, one of many Mumbai-obsessed texts that the historian Gyan Prakash draws upon in his book *Mumbai Fables*. 'It is the state of a young man's mind, exciting and excitable, exuberant and effervescent, dynamic and dramatic.'

Abbas's words, smoothly transmuting the city into a mental rather than a physical landscape, demonstrate, further, that a great metropolis is not just a state of mind but also a story—a work in progress in both the physical and the narrative sense. In *Mumbai Fables* Prakash, previously known for his work on Indian labour history and the intersection of colonialism and science, brings his interpretative skills to bear on the many visions of Bombay/Mumbai nurtured and asserted by a colourful cast of characters across the centuries. Colonial governors and cotton kings, opium traders and tabloid barons, muckrakers and trade unionists, poets and politicians, thugs and town planners, all summoned up and guided by the (sometimes too overbearing) presence of the author himself, lend their voices to a series of tableaux stretching from the early colonial regime to the present day.

A set of small, swampy, spottily inhabited islands on the west coast of India that over the course of the 17th and 18th centuries were transformed into a thriving port city and a geographically contiguous landmass by the British, Mumbai is of course a city with a past deeply implicated in colonialism and the asymmetric power relations that it vigorously exercised. For even the most generous observer, this would be a story brimming with iniquity and prejudice. But some indication of

Prakash's overly negative attitude towards Bombay's colonial history becomes visible when he speaks of the city's 'doubly parasitical birth and development,' as land simultaneously colonised by the British and also reclaimed from the sea by the force of modern industrial technology. The founding of the city represents, for Prakash, a double sinning: not just a significant episode in the colonisation of India by the British, but also 'the colonization of nature by culture.'

But isn't this second claim not particular to Bombay, but true of just about any great city in the world? It is hard to see how any city could be founded and then allowed to expand without tampering with nature in some significant way. This line of argument allows Prakash to interpret the story of Bombay somewhat too simply and adversarially as one of 'colonial and capitalist spatialization.' This sets up a persistent strain in the metanarrative of Prakash's book where the word 'capitalism' is reflexively associated with the exploitation of land, workers, and natural resources, and with injustice, misery, and subterfuge. The history of capitalism in Bombay is viewed entirely negatively, without any wonder at the remarkable energies it unleashed and the prosperity it generated.

This approach allows Prakash to point out, entirely fairly, the extent to which Bombay's economy in its early years was dominated by the British-run trade in cotton, which fed off cheap Indian labour, and the profits generated by local opium lords. But Prakash's eyes are closed to the extent to which Mumbai's presiding spirit is essentially an entrepreneurial one, and that its reputation today continues to be that of the one city in India where a man (or, significantly, a woman) may advance not because of his advantages of family or education, but for his capacity for hard work and enterprise.

Not all profit-making is iniquitous, and some kinds of capitalist success may themselves be viewed, as much as labour agitation or radical historiography, as instances of anti-capitalist resistance. Capitalist innovation gets short thrift in Prakash's book, for which reason there is something grumpy and grudging about long sections of his narrative. The narrator of his book seems most enthusiastic when writing about left-wing movements in the city over time, whether the Progressive Writer's Movement of the 1950s or the agitations of the mill workers in the 80s, and here it would sometimes seem that all scepticism is abandoned. ('The Communists worked furiously to keep up the workers' morale, organizing eight hundred public meetings'; 'Sucked into the exciting whirlpool of Communist political and intellectual vision, Raj and Romesh [Thapar] became active in party activities.')

Some of Prakash's most interesting stresses have to do with space (or, as he might put it, 'spatialization'). He paints a lovely scene of the early city around present-day Fort and Colaba, self-consciously designed as a European and colonial neighbourhood, being something of a mystery to Indian natives in the layout of its roads, the look of its buildings, and the strangeness of its mores. Meanwhile, a short walk from the Fort area brought the resident Englishman into the teeming and chaotic native quarter of Kalbadevi and Girgaon—a space just as puzzling to him, and one that served as the ugly underbelly to the ordered city dreamed up by the colonial imagination. Much of the story of Mumbai is not just about the expansion of the city northwards and eastwards into the Indian mainland, but also southwards and westwards, in the form of land reclaimed from the sea by governments functioning as a fig leaf for private interests.

However, in one of the book's many tendentious passages, Prakash attacks an influential group of intellectuals and urban planners in early post-independence India, including the novelist Mulk Raj Anand (founder of the influential architectural magazine *Marg*), the architect Charles Correa, and the urban planner Shirish Patel. These men dreamt of a Mumbai that was more ordered, friendly, and equitable in the form of a satellite city, just east of the main one, called New Bombay or Navi Mumbai. The planners saw the new city as a space that would counterbalance the old city's congested north–south axis, relieve the pressure on its land by making cheap housing available, and supply a zoned set of spaces for habitation, work, and recreation instead of the harum-scarum sprawl of the old city. They also envisaged the state legislature moving base to Navi Mumbai to encourage migration to the new city.

This was a grand vision that, persistently held up by red tape and apathy, has only seen partial realisation over the last half-century, and might now be thought of as a tragic failure. But, attacking this project for wanting to 'engineer an organic urban space to meet the needs of capitalist industrialisation,' Prakash leaches the movement of much of its civic idealism, and presents it instead as yet another imposition upon the masses by those in power. Drawing upon Freud, he argues that 'Politics and society, which the planners had suppressed, returned with the rage of the repressed to sour the modernist dream of postcolonial geography.' Indeed, any kind of planning by governments or urban planners is inevitably described by Prakash with loaded words like 'dream text,' 'fantasy,' or 'utopia.' Sometimes this jeering becomes infantile. ('The grand plan was now a grand mess…')

Surprisingly, even as he criticises the Navi Mumbai plan of the 60s, Prakash is entirely silent on, or perhaps even ignorant of, a recent episode that might much more justifiably thought of as a scandalous capitalist land grab in connivance with the government: the amendment by the Maharashtra Government of clause 58 of the Development Control Regulations in 2001 (whereby the word 'land' was changed to 'open land'). This meant that only a fraction of the defunct mill lands in the centre of the city were returned to the government for public use and for housing projects, and the rest were cleared for sale or development by the mill owners.

Various oppressed entities are persistently, though not always persuasively, seen extracting their revenge in Prakash's narration. For instance, we are told, in the context of avaricious land reclamation in the posh neighbourhood of Marine Drive in south Bombay, that the sea 'had avenged its loss by blasting the surface of Art Deco architecture with unsightly blotches of mildew.' I didn't want to be the one to point this out, but the sea blasts buildings with mildew even on unreclaimed land, or that occupied by the poor. The sea is avenging nothing here, merely being itself.

Moreover, Prakash's prose, often swinging unstably in its registers from the academic to the journalistic and back, is often guilty of practising a kind of colonisation of its own. Since his book is based primarily on archival research and a synthesis of secondary sources, he frequently enlists artworks—paintings, poems, films, and comic books—to buttress his points. Often, as with many academics in the social sciences attempting to interpret artworks, this happens at the cost of denying their specificity, their embodiment in a medium.

Of a painting by the Mumbai artist Sudhir Patwardhan we are told only that, 'In *Riot* (1996) we see communal vitriol at its rawest. The image of society as a collective recedes.' But what happens inside the painting? Doesn't its materiality come before its meanings? This is a very slapdash way of thinking about art. Quoting from 'Mumbai, Mumbai My Dear Slut,' a poem by the fiery Dalit poet Namdeo Dhasal, Prakash argues that Dhasal 'exhorts us to revisit the Island City's past to disclose Mumbai's history as culture's triumph over nature.' I very much doubt Dhasal has this intention. Although it is interesting in patches and harnesses a wealth of unusual material, *Mumbai Fables*, once its own code is cracked, is finally too predictable and too negative to be a persuasive lens on the energy and enthusiasm of the city that it takes for its subject.

## 51. Gallery Gaz: The Chawls of Mumbai

*The Chawls of Mumbai: Galleries of Life,* edited by Neera Adarkar (Imprint One, 2011)

Mumbai would not be the city and the story that it is today without its chawls. These three and four-storey blocks of one and two-room tenements, built all across south and central Mumbai on a massive scale over the 19th and early-20th centuries by both the colonial government and private landlords, stand at the centre of the city's social history. Although each of the great chawl neighbourhoods of Mumbai—Girgaon, Kalbadevi, Worli, Byculla—has its own distinct history and religious and class composition, together they form an architectural and city-specific continuum through which many of the city's traits can be understood. The quiddity of chawls and their longstanding influence 'as a historical actor' on Mumbai's landscape are illuminated through a variety of academic and narrative perspectives in Neera Adarkar's fascinating new anthology *The Chawls of Mumbai.*

The word chawl is a slightly anglicised version of the Marathi *chaal,* which means 'anklet' and by extension came to mean 'corridor' or, to use the Mumbai word, 'gallery.' The very etymology of this architectural form, then, reveals what kind of residential space it was meant to be—one in which the boundary between private and public space was blurred, and communal areas were as significant as private ones. 'It is difficult to view a chawl as an empty built form in isolation, like a bungalow or an apartment building,' writes Adarkar in her excellent introductory essay, 'because a chawl cannot be stripped bare of its occupants. Its existence in the cityscape can be seen as a theatre, imagined only with performers on a stage.'

It was this human crush, fending for itself as best as it could, and devising a variety of creative solutions to problems of food, domesticity, and childcare, that turned Bombay, over the decades, into 'the city of gold.' From the mid-19th century onwards, as the Indian cotton industry boomed, filling up the breach left by the Civil War in America, chawls began to come up in great numbers in the 'Indian quarter' of Mumbai, north of the spacious, landscaped European quarter in Fort. The colonial government and an emerging class of Indian capitalists needed labour; migrant workers thronging the city from the Western Ghats and the Konkan coast needed cheap housing. As Bombay urbanised and industrialised, many chawls were built by private parties on what was formerly farmland.

But after an outbreak of plague in 1898, attributed to unsanitary conditions in the native neighbourhoods, the colonial government stepped in, in its own interest, to build chawls on a large scale. The massive Bombay Development Department (BDD) Chawl in Worli, for instance, a colony of over 100 chawl buildings, was built by the government in what was then cheap, uninhabited land in north Bombay, now turned by the advance of history into Mumbai's centre. (There is a marvellous joke about this phenomenon of moving centres in the recent Marathi film *Harishchandrachi Factory*, in which the struggling Dadasaheb Phalke squanders so much money on his cinemania that his family has to sell their house. The Phalkes are seen receiving the sympathies of their neighbours as they move to some distant place 'out in the wild,' which turns out to be...Dadar.)

From the very beginning, then, the chawls were marked by human plenitude, by an enormously resourceful attitude towards space, and the assumption of openness to continuous negotiation and 'adjustment.' Although (some would say 'because') chawls threw great numbers of people together, they tended to be socially homogenous, each chawl marked by the stamp of a particular religious or caste group and brought alive by shared festivals and mores. Though often remembered now with the rose-coloured glasses of nostalgia, they were often fractious places, from quotidian squabbles over space, water, and access to the communal toilets to murderous communal conflict during times of crisis, as evinced by some of the heartbreaking testimonies collected by Sameera Khan in an essay called 'How The Mumbai Riots [of 1992] Changed Life for Muslims in Chawls.'

Elsewhere, Adarkar observes acutely that the chawl corridor, centre of its social life and the space that effectively turned the building into a kind of neighbourhood, 'brought a spirit of buoyancy to the interface of the chawl and the city, and diffused the boundaries between them.' This 'chawl spirit' has been extensively investigated and celebrated in the city's literature, from the short stories of Sadat Hasan Manto and PL Deshpande's famous Marathi work *Batatyachi Chal* ('The Potato Chawl') to Kiran Nagarkar's *Ravan and Eddie* and Manu Joseph's recent novel *Serious Men*.

Among the pleasures of Adarkar's book is its exceptionally attentive historicisation of the changing status of chawls over time in terms of their religious and gender composition, relative position in the various classes of property available in Bombay, and self-image. After the passing of the Rent Control Act of 1947, which froze existing rents and granted many more rights to tenants than previously, the humble chawl-room suddenly acquired a great cachet as 'property.' Many renters chose to evict other men whom they entertained as sub-tenants and bring in instead their families from the villages, completely altering the social character of the chawls and throwing up a fresh set of problems of adjustment to the needs of women.

The Rent Control Act also spawned the city's indigenous *pagdi* system of property sale, whereby long-time tenants who could not be shaken by landlords could sell their tenancy rights to a third party as long as they passed on a third of the sale price to the landlord. The tenancy structures of chawls eventually became so complex that often developers seeking to buy up the entire property to build it anew threw up their hands in despair. This was because, as Prasad Shetty explains in his essay, of the number of ownership claims registered for every square foot of the chawl, from 'subtenants who had forcibly taken over from original tenants, multiple children of deceased tenants wanting different houses, a divorced wife occupying a room that was in the ex-husband's name, loft occupiers, staircase occupiers, shops within homes, homes inside shops, etc.'

With the closure of the textile mills in the 80s, Bombay became a post-industrial city, and, in succeeding decades, home to the new wealth of a post-liberalisation 'new economy.' Defenceless against the march of history, the chawls became the site first of the despair of joblessness, and then the object of the profit-seeking eyes of developers. Many chawls today stand uncomfortably in the shadow of tall apartment buildings that were only recently themselves chawls. Creaky with decay and disrepair, sometimes crashing down completely in the gusts of monsoon, they still comprise a large portion of the available housing stock in the island city.

From Shetty in his superb essay 'Ganga Building Chronicles,' a history of the fortunes of a chawl building over several generations, to the Dalit poet Namdeo Dhasal in 'My Old Neighbourhoods,' a memoir of his childhood across several chawls in Bombay, the contributors to Adarkar's book do an excellent job of characterising how the chawls made up the motley social fabric of the city and were home to many of its root energies. Chawls have contributed many resonant words to the city's vocabulary, from the word 'gala,' or dormitory, to the concept of the 'gallery gaz,' or a measure as wide as a chawl corridor, in fabric. Somewhere in the story of almost every migrant family in Mumbai—and most people in the city are migrants—lies a chawl. The place of this architectural form in Mumbai's history is extensively mapped in this concert of energies, one of the most warming books ever produced about the city.

# 52. On the Memoirs of General Pervez Musharraf of Pakistan

*In the Line of Fire,* by Pervez Musharraf (Free Press, 2006)

'At the precise instant of India's arrival at independence, I tumbled forth into the world,' says Saleem Sinai in the first chapter of Salman Rushdie's *Midnight's Children,* as he reveals that 'thanks to the occult tyrannies of those blandly saluting clocks I had been mysteriously handcuffed to history, my destinies indissolubly chained to those of my country.' In the prologue to his memoir *In the Line of Fire,* Pakistan's president General Pervez Musharraf, born four years before the creation of the state of Pakistan, sounds very much like a Pakistani Saleem: 'The story of my life coincides almost from the beginning with the story of my country—so the chapters that follow are not only the biography of a man, but of Pakistan as well.'

Saleem Sinai's claim is supposed to be interpreted by the reader as comic. Rushdie wants us to marvel at this fantastical linking of the destinies of man and nation, and Saleem himself always bemoans 'that benighted moment' that robbed him, as it were, of his own independence. But the good General's claim is made in all seriousness. Providence has singled him out—the son of middle-class immigrants, reconciled at one stage to seeing out his career as a high-ranking military officer—for some reason for a special place in history, and, handcuffed to history, it is his duty now to carry out his role, responsibly if reluctantly, of commander of the ship of the Pakistani state.

'My autobiography,' he says solemnly, 'is my contribution to the history of our era.' A simple, plainspeaking, moral man ('truthfulness is a sine qua non of good character' he tells us in a passage on moral development), he will, along the way, also tell us the real truth, obscured until now, about many things—the tussle in which he overthrew Pakistan's erstwhile prime minister Nawaz Sharif, the Kargil War, Pakistan's role in the War on Terror and the hunt for Osama Bin Laden. 'I want the world to learn the truth.' 'It is time to lay bare what has been shrouded in mystery.' Bring it on, General!

If *In the Line of Fire* reveals anything about the president, it is the centrality of the army and the martial way of life to his worldview. 'I was only eighteen when I entered the Pakistan Military Academy in 1961,' he recounts in a chapter about his youth, one of a handful that is low on rhetoric. Indeed, it is somehow symbolic that he has spent all his adult life as a soldier. In his thought, the word 'army' is always associated with positive values: valour and heroism, commitment and sacrifice, integrity and intelligence. The army is a world within the world, a bastion of discipline and order to counterbalance the disorganised sprawl of civilian life and of electoral politics.

When it comes to his beloved army, Musharraf is especially sensitive to insult and especially susceptible to posturing. What stung him most in the aftermath of what he sees as Sharif's ill-advised withdrawal from Kargil in 1999 is the sullying of the army's image by the country's own government: 'I am ashamed to say, our political leadership insinuated that the achievements of our troops amounted to a "debacle." Some people even called the Pakistan Army a "rogue army."'

The truth, he would have us know, is quite the opposite. 'Considered purely in military terms, the Kargil operations were a landmark in the history of the Pakistan Army.' Against all evidence, he doggedly maintains that 'whatever movement has taken place so far in the direction of finding a solution to Kashmir is due considerably to the Kargil conflict.' This is a curious stand coming from a man who has, since becoming president, purported to taking the lead in resolving the Kashmir problem through dialogue.

For someone who considers himself 'a soldier's man,' the General also reveals himself to be an expert juggler with words. Although he agrees that he deposed Nawaz Sharif after the famous hijacking drama of October 12, 1999, he does not agree that it was a coup d'etat. In the General's opinion it was *Sharif* who actually launched 'a coup against the army and myself' by dismissing him as chief of the army while he was away in Sri Lanka and appointing another general in his place. Therefore, what the General did in retaliation was a *countercoup*—'for there can be no other word for it.'

By rehauling the meaning of the word 'coup,' which my *Shorter OED* defines as 'a violent and illegal change of government,' the General carves out a kind of moral legitimacy for himself, even as he unintentionally demonstrates how in Pakistan, a country which has seen four military rulers in its short history, the army's self-image and functions often overlap with those of the state. To depose the chief of the army in such a country can also be a 'coup.'

The General drips with contempt for his two predecessors as the head of Pakistan's government, Benazir Bhutto and Nawaz Sharif—particularly Sharif. For him, the decade between 1988 and 1999, when Benazir and Sharif each spent two terms in power after winning elections, was a period of 'sham democracy.' Nor does he think very highly of Indian democracy, using quote marks always to show what he thinks of 'the largest democracy in the world.' And in one sense his scepticism is quite justified. Where is the hand of the army in the affairs of the Indian state? Indian politicians thrive unchecked by military power, instead trying to oust one another all their lives through elections.

Which reminds us of the basic point that democracy, through elections, confers legitimacy upon leaders, and every leader craves legitimacy. Musharraf had his own tryst with the electorate in the infamous yes-or-no referendum on his rule in 2002, in which he emerged with a staggering 97 per cent yes vote. In a piece on this exercise called 'The April Fool Referendum,' the Pakistani human rights lawyer Asma Jahangir remarked that 'the rigging was so brazen that it will embarrass any foreign government to accept the exercise and its result as a democratic process.' But while Musharraf himself admits that the exercise 'ended in a near catastrophe,' here is his foxy attempt at explaining it (the italics are mine):

> The referendum went smoothly. There was a very high turnout, and the overall count was strongly in my favour. There were some irregularities, though. *I found that* in some places overenthusiastic administrative officials and bureaucrats had allowed people to vote more than once, and had even filled out ballot papers themselves. *I also later found out that* this absolutely unwarranted 'support' was helped along by the opposition in certain areas where they have a hold and where *they stuffed ballot boxes in my favor as to provide supposed evidence for claims of foul play.* The whole exercise ended in a near catastrophe. [...] Finally, in a national broadcast, I had to come clean. I thanked the people for their support but also admitted that some excesses had indeed taken place *without my knowledge or consent.*

In this passage, Musharraf appears more sinned against than sinning, with both his supporters and opponents remarkably conspiring towards the same ends. Meanwhile, the General was oblivious to these happenings, but the chorus of 'I found' is meant to attest that, insofar as he had any agency in the whole case, it was in bringing the wrongdoings to light. Truthfulness, remember, is a sine qua non of good character.

To be fair to the General, life has not been easy since he came to power. He took over a country on the brink of economic collapse. Later, the American government's demands after 9/11 and the resentment of Pakistan's religious hardliners put him between a rock and a hard place. His crackdown on terrorism led to two attempts being made upon his life. Even *Time* magazine declared that he held 'the world's most dangerous job.' Musharraf's account of how he negotiated his way through these troubles shows a commendable understanding of realpolitik. One of his redeeming qualities is that, at least in domestic matters, he has no patience with fundamentalism and religious obscurantism. On the demonisation of Islam around the world as a religion of intolerance, he sensibly observes:

> It is all very well for us to say that Islam is nothing of the sort, that it is in fact a very progressive, moderate and tolerant religion—which indeed it is—but why should the people

> of the world bother to go out of their way and spend their precious time to explore the authentic sources of Islam? They are going to judge Islam by the utterances and actions of Muslims, especially those actions and utterances that affect their lives directly, and not just by the protestations of academics and moderates, no matter how justified.

Six years in power have taught the General to weigh and to aim his words carefully. His book can itself be seen as a work tailored carefully for a Western audience interested in Asian affairs but not expert in the finer details. His book tour in the US in 2006, which featured, among other events, a hit appearance on Jon Stewart's *The Daily Show*, was in stark contrast to his official visit to the US in 2005. That turned out to be a PR disaster after he spoke recklessly on the Mukhtar Mai rape case, suggesting that rape in his country was used as a tool by women to gain riches and to emigrate.

Now, in his book, his thoughts on the case are shoehorned into a chapter full of pieties called 'The Emancipation of Women.' It is a chapter that shows he has learnt that, whether or not he actually walks the walk, a statesman should always talk the talk. He drones:

> Rape, no matter where it happens in the world, is a tragedy and deeply traumatic for the victim. My heart, therefore, goes out to Mukhtaran Mai and any woman to whom such a fate befalls.

'My heart, therefore…'—you're not convincing me, General *saab*. And what is the point of that phrase 'no matter where it happens in the world'—how should that be relevant in any way? We understand when, a little later, the General reveals that no rape case should be allowed to besmirch the good name of the nation:

> Rape and violence against women are universal phenomena, but this does not justify their presence in Pakistan. We need to set our house in order. I only object when Pakistan is singled out and demonized.

When a case of female victimization in Pakistan comes to light, sometimes the first victim is the truth.

*In the Line of Fire* itself often takes liberties with the truth, but in doing so, it is so revelatory of the General's personality that it makes for a far more interesting book than a safer, more cautious account. Autobiography always stands at an angle to historical truth, but in doing so, it lets us in on other valuable truths. And if some excesses have indeed taken place, the General will surely investigate and have them explained in the next edition.

## 53. Jonathan Bate's Shakespeare

*Soul of the Age,* by Jonathan Bate (Penguin, 2009)

In a brief but dazzling short story about the life of Shakespeare called 'Everything and Nothing,' the great Argentine writer Jorge Luis Borges portrays Shakespeare as a man without a personality. 'There was no one in him,' writes Borges, and this explains why Shakespeare could put himself in the shoes of hundreds of myriad-minded characters, imagine them all from within. Thus the paradox: Shakespeare was not fully a human being, and yet 'nobody was ever as many men as that man.' At some point, 'before or after dying,' Shakespeare finds himself before God and makes the demand for a stable, discrete personality, for a 'myself.' God's reply comes: 'Neither am I one self; I dreamed the world as you dreamed your work, my Shakespeare, and among the shapes of my dream are you, who, like me, are many persons—and none.'

In his new biography of Shakespeare, *Soul of the Age*, the Shakespeare scholar Jonathan Bate attempts to take the measure of how a man of such unpromising circumstances—the son of a small businessman, brought up in an insignificant market-town, educated in an ordinary school—managed to expand his mind, his language, and his imaginative and worldly power to become, as the book's title asserts, the soul of the age. Or, to adapt Borges, how did a man who should have been nothing end up encompassing everything?

Bate has worked on two previous books that involve Shakespeare: he is the author of *The Genius of Shakespeare* (1998), which I remember reading with great pleasure in my undergraduate years, and the co-editor of *The RSC Shakespeare* (2007), a new edition of the complete works. Fittingly, *Soul of the Age* is itself founded upon a Shakespearean structure. Bate organises his material around the concept of the 'seven ages of man'—infant, schoolboy, lover, soldier, justice (or householder), and then two levels of old age, the latter being 'a second childishness' so vividly described by the character Jacques in *As You Like It*. Making astute connections between Shakespeare's plays, what is known of his life, and the social beliefs and theatrical practices of his times, Bate comes as close to achieving a sense of Shakespeare's felt presence as any other biographer ever has.

Since he left so few traces of himself, and since so much other evidence has been lost or destroyed, Shakespearean biography has never been a matter of simply collecting and interpreting the sources. Yet there are dozens of other extensive documents left behind by Shakespeare: the plays and poems themselves. Bate quotes approvingly the critic Barbara Everett, who argues, in an essay called 'Reade him, therefore' published in the *Times Literary Supplement* in 2007, that 'if [Shakespeare's] biography is to be found it has to be here, in the plays and poems, but never literally and never provably.' Much of what Bate posits is a result of interpretation, correlation, juxtaposition. But if his method is speculative, the result is a very rich, educated, and revelatory speculation.

For instance, is it not significant that in Shakespeare's earlier works, doctors are usually comic figures, but after the marriage of his daughter, Susanna, to a widely respected doctor called John Hall, the doctors in the plays become 'dignified, sympathetically portrayed medical men'? If this is one direction taken by Bate in his exploration of medicine in the world of Shakespeare's plays, then in another sally he takes note of the wealth of plants, herbs, and flowers named in the plays, demonstrating Shakespeare's deep engagement, as someone who grew up in the country, with 'the herbal economy of rural England.'

This then leads Bate into a meditation on how, although Shakespeare is always identified with the London stage, he always had one foot in his hometown of Stratford-upon-Avon. He always lived in rented lodgings in London, and many of his plays shuttle, just as he himself did, between the worlds of city and country. When the London theatres were closed for periods of a year or more because of the plague ('Plague,' Bate reminds us, 'was the single most powerful force shaping [Shakespeare's] life and those of his contemporaries'), Shakespeare returned home. 'It is unlikely to be a coincidence,' remarks Bate, 'that Shakespeare turned to pastoral romance in the plague years around 1607-10: of all of his plays, *Cymbeline* and *The Winter's Tale* are the ones to have the most distinctive air of having been written back home in Stratford.' Bate dwells on some of the specific descriptions of flowers or plants in Shakespeare, such the mole on Innogen's breast in Cymbeline, 'cinque-spotted, like the crimson drops/ I'th'bottom of a cowslip,' and asks, 'Is there any other English poet, save John Clare, who has such an eye as this?'

Imagine such an approach being replicated with respect to Shakespearean politics and statecraft, Shakespearean language (such as the relationship between Latin, the 'high' language of schooling, and English, which was not the self-confident world language that it is now), Shakespearean cosmology, and Shakespeare's use of both ancient and recent history, and you have some notion of the wealth of ideas and associations in Bate's book. Bate's discussion of love in Shakespeare, particularly as it is explored through the sonnets, is the best I have ever read, and his brilliant analysis of how *King Lear* enacts a critique of conventional rationalistic philosophy on the subject of suffering and asserts instead, via Shakespeare's reading of Erasmus and Montaigne, the value of the path of 'love and folly' in human affairs kept me thinking for several days.

Nor is Bate a bardolater of the kind often to be found arguing that Shakespeare has no rival in any literature. In fact, in one of the best moments of *The Genius of Shakespeare*, he argues that the profusion, range, linguistic depth, and artistic worth of Shakespeare's work were matched in his own lifetime by a contemporary, born two years before him in 1562: the great Spanish playwright Lope de Vega. Lope wrote hundreds of plays and sonnets, and was, like Shakespeare, 'wily in his aspectuality.' Like Shakespeare, Lope's characteristic form 'was a mingle of tragedy and comedy, high and low, the poetic voice accordingly shifting from elegance to coarseness.' Perhaps, Bate suggests, it was the politics of empire and of language that played a role in Shakespeare's preeminence:

> [Lope] answered to every element of my prescription of a world-genius in literature. But Spain went into decline and Lope was not translated. The whole of Shakespeare has been translated into scores of languages; less than ten per cent of Lope's surviving plays has ever been translated into English.
>
> Twentieth-century physics has made the idea of the co-existence of 'alternative universes' easier to comprehend. Picture an alternative world in which Spain triumphed over England. Lope then would have triumphed over Shakespeare and I would be writing a book called The Genius of Vega. What do we learn from our picture? That the apotheosis of Shakespeare was and was not a matter of historical contingency. It was a contingency insofar as it happened to be Shakespeare, not Lope. But it was a necessity because the chosen one had to be a particular kind of genius and could therefore only have been Lope or Shakespeare.

Among the aspects of Shakespeare's nature that emerge most clearly from Bate's book is his prudent business sense. Surveying the dramatists who were Shakespeare's competitors—Marlowe,

Greene, Kyd, Nashe, Dekker—Bate shows that many of them died young, or in penury. In contrast, Shakespeare not only lived frugally, he was also the first playwright of his time to become a joint-stockholder in a theatre company, thereby ensuring his financial stability through a share of gate receipts, and his indispensability as the company's in-house dramatist. Even though he never bought a house in London, he acquired and consolidated a massive property back home in Stratford, as if wishing, after his years of physical and mental roving, to retire as a big fish in a small pond. It is these homely details, as much as the evidence of his subject's genius, that make us warm to Bate's book, and leave us feeling on such intimate terms with Shakespeare that we too can address him, as God does in Borges' story, as 'my Shakespeare.'

## 54. Patrick French's Naipaul

*The World Is What It Is,* by Patrick French (Picador, 2008)

Biographies always have to shuttle between small and large frames, between the humdrum detail and the world-changing intervention. But rarely is the gulf between high and low, petty and profound, as glaring as it is in *The World Is What It Is*, Patrick French's long-awaited biography of V.S. Naipaul. On the one hand, we make an intimate acquaintance with the oddities, perfidies, and infidelities of an exceptionally egotistic and unreasonable man, a man suffered rather than loved, even by those closest to him. On the other, we see that the larger journey of this man from provincial outpost to metropolitan centre, and thereafter eagerly, restlessly, back and forth across the newly decolonised world is the story of the 20th century in miniature: the story of mass migration, of failed nation-states, of changing race relations, of multiple personal histories and affiliations.

French's biography is exemplary on the details of Naipaul's childhood, and later on his troubled—and troubling—conjugal life. One of the best sections of his book is the early one on Trinidad, tracing the Naipaul family story all the way back to the first arrival of indentured Indian labourers in Port of Spain in 1845. As Naipaul has himself recounted, his father Seepersad, the son of an agricultural labourer who taught himself to read and write and became a journalist, spurred his dream of becoming a great writer. But French also shows how Naipaul's projected sense of himself as a Brahmin, a lover of learning with a native sense of entitlement, fastidious about details of food and clothing, is in a way a disguise. Seepersad was probably not a Brahmin.

Brought up in a fractious joint family, the details of which he would later use in his fiction, the young Vidia longed to escape from Trinidad and set about studying for the scholarship to England that would allow him to do so. Naipaul later saw his arrival in England in 1950 as being at the vanguard of 'that great movement of people that was to take place in the second half of the 20th century.' At Oxford, he was to meet his future wife, Pat, who offered support for his literary ambitions and soothed his insecurities about being a brown-skinned man in a predominantly white country.

After Oxford, Naipaul worked grudgingly at a variety of jobs (as a presenter on the BBC programme, *Caribbean Voices*, as a book reviewer, even as a clerk), married Pat, and produced the brilliant early works of fiction (*The Mystic Masseur*, *Miguel Street*, *A House For Mr Biswas*) that won him acclaim in England as a promising writer from the Caribbean. French is particularly acute in his analysis of how, in his late 20s, realising that the vogue for Caribbean fiction in England was dying, Naipaul reinvented himself as 'a displaced, unaffiliated, un-Caribbean writer' and inserted himself into what the Indian publisher Ravi Dayal termed 'the mainstream of history.'

Thus began his travels around the world. A commission from the Trinidad government led him to write a short, critical book about the island; he journeyed to India with Pat in 1962 and produced his unsettling and controversial book *An Area of Darkness*; an offer from a university in Uganda became the springboard for a series of books on Africa. Naipaul's life settled into a pattern. He visited a country, travelled widely with the assistance of local guides, spoke to people, transcribed his notes every evening, came back home, and wrote up a book in a burst of focused work. His books, which almost always stoked controversy, tried to unveil the deep structure and crippling malaises of these civilisations through a combination of keen observation and recorded testimonies.

Meanwhile, Naipaul's relationship with Pat had swiftly degenerated into a scene of relentless egotism and volatility for one, and suffocation and self-abnegation for the other. Sexually unfulfilled, he took to visiting prostitutes. Then, on a trip to Argentina in 1972, he met and instantly fell in love with an Anglo-Argentine woman called Margaret Murray, a mother of three. There began immediately a bruising affair, in both the figurative and the literal sense. Over the next 25 years, Naipaul and Murray loved and lacerated one another without ever coming close to marrying or living together.

Naipaul could not bring himself to leave his wife, the first reader of his manuscripts, yet, pitilessly, he told her about Margaret and often flew out to meet his lover in different parts of the world, leaving her to deal with her grief. French's book is as much a biography of Pat as it is of Sir Vidia. He quotes often from her diaries, which are housed in a vast archive of Naipaul's papers at the University of Tulsa, and closely tracks her attempts at making a life for herself during her husband's absences. In one of the book's most poignant moments, French shows us Pat living by herself in London, researching, of all things, an anthology of love letters at the invitation of a common friend of her and her husband, the historian Antonia Fraser. French's narrative ends in 1996, with a moving description of Pat's death and the scene of a tearful Naipaul and his new wife, Nadira, scattering her ashes in the woods near their country estate.

French beautifully mines and marshals the sources all biographies are made of—entries in diaries and notebooks, letters, recorded interviews, reminiscences of people close to the subject. Sometimes glimpses of a figure—an anecdote, a memory—can tell us more than pages of analysis can. French's narrative is full of such glimpses, which allow us to put together a private picture of Naipaul. (French wisely eschews the kind of moralising commentary and complacent retrospective judgments that mar so many biographies.) Moni Malhotra, an IAS officer who assisted Naipaul with *An Area of Darkness*, recalls that Naipaul 'was very athletic and he used to do a particular movement with his leg, he used to pick it up and bring it up towards his head from the back. It's the kind of posture which you'll see in some sculptures in the Tanjore temples...He loved to do that.' Asked to judge a literary competition while serving as a writer in residence at a university in Uganda, Naipaul, we are told, 'awarded only a third prize.' A harried manager of the Taj Hotel in Bombay writes to his demanding guest: 'Dear Mr Naipaul, thank you for filling in the Guest Comments form and bringing to my notice the flaw in the design of the Tea-pots.' A journalist requesting an interview with the master is rebuked: 'Dear Mr Bellacasa, Nothing in your questions suggests any knowledge of my work. An interview would be a considerable waste of my time and energy.' (That word 'considerable' is the funniest part of that sentence.)

Naipaul himself gave his consent for this project, and revealed freely of himself to French. 'Of all the people I spoke to for this book, he was outwardly the frankest,' writes French of Naipaul. 'He believed that a less than candid biography would be pointless, and his willingness to allow such a book to be published in his lifetime was at once an act of narcissism and humility.' This seems an astute judgment, and French's biography is certainly candid. But for this very reason, long sections of it make for depressing reading. The darkness of Naipaul's attachments (if 'attachments' is the correct word) is not offset, in French's narrative, by the excitement of the work—and there must have been such an excitement on an almost daily basis, given Naipaul's ambition, talent, and dedication to his craft.

For instance, since French was given access to all the Naipaul records and papers at the University of Tulsa archive, he had an opportunity to look at the draft versions of Naipaul's books and tell us by what stages they came to acquire their distinction (writers are very interesting beasts when when revising their work). As Naipaul himself has said, 'The value of a literary archive is that it takes us as close as we can get to the innermost self of the writer who produced the work.' French does not, I think, fully exploit the potential of the material to which he had access. In the same way, French does not tell us enough about how Naipaul came to perfect his pellucid, ringing style—the unmistakable sound of his writing voice. Nor is there very much about Naipaul's reading, or the kinds of things he discussed with other writers. Glimpses of Naipaul's attention to the minutiae of composition appear here and there, as in a letter to Random House's Sonny Mehta in which he complains about the work done on his text by a copy editor: 'I don't want anyone undoing my semi-colons, with all their different shades of pause; or interfering with my "ands", with all their different ways of linking.' But the paucity of such material means that French's biography is finally somewhat unbalanced. The *World Is What It Is* exposes the many skeletons in Naipaul's closet, but it leaves the secrets of his books in the dark. To put it another way, French's book is perhaps too sexual, and not textual enough.

## 55. Patrick French's India

*India: A Portrait,* by Patrick French (Penguin, 2011)

Like the proverbial three blind men before an elephant, unable, because of the vastness of its size and the diverse traits of its parts, to make a reasonable guess about the whole, all books about India 'get' some things about the country and miss others. Each observer distinguishes or incriminates himself in his own way; for the reader, the task lies in making a reckoning of exactly what they see and what they choose to make of it. Advertised as 'an intimate biography of 1.2 billion people' (the adjective alone is worth investigating), Patrick French's *India: A Portrait* sets itself up from the very beginning alongside the most ambitious books written about the country.

Whole cupboards of non-fiction are now published every year about Indian politics, society, culture, religion, philosophy, and business. Indology is a crowded market, buzzing with grand claims. French's own contribution to these maxims is the somewhat nebulous: 'India is a macrocosm, and may be the world's default setting for the future.' But for most part French is sharper than this, and, indeed, he often has a merciless way with cant, whether the jargon-laden calls to war of Maoist revolution or the play-it-safe boilerplate of the Congress Party. Cutting up his book into three major axes of inquiry entitled 'Rashtra,' 'Lakshmi,' and 'Samaj,' French deploys impressively the grasp of history and social context and the love of bright detail that he last displayed in his 2008 biography of VS Naipaul.

The only clunky section of French's text appears right at the beginning. His long essay on Indian politics requires him to make a foundation-building survey of events from the time of independence onwards: nation-formation and constitution-framing, the crisis of succession post-Nehru, the Emergency, the rise of dynastic politics. Here, even French's talent for elegant synthesis and summary, often finished off with brief, probing glosses—Nehru's *The Discovery of India* is 'a fine, slanted and sometimes romantic version of history'—is not enough to reanimate an extensively reported period of national history, the contours and fault lines of which are familiar to even the casual reader on India.

Once it has emerged from the congestion, though, French's narration begins to pick up steam. One of his most diverting studies is that of nepotism in Indian democracy. As a case study he takes the Lok Sabha, home to 545 elected MPs. With the assistance of a team of researchers, he attempts to figure out just how many of them might be considered to be what he called hereditary MPs or 'HMPs'—that is, MPs with a strong family, if not directly filial, connection to politics.

He finds that almost 30 per cent of MPs fall into this category, including two-thirds of the 66 MPs aged 40 or under. Thus, he demonstrates just how much weight a family name carries when it comes to the restocking of Indian democracy with new blood. Sixty three years after its ambitious inauguration, then, Indian democracy remains semi-feudal. 'I am not suggesting that a "hereditary MP" is a bad MP,' French says, concluding tidily, 'merely that this system excludes the overwhelming majority of Indians from participation in politics at a national level.' With a new law mandating that 33 per cent of parliamentary seats be reserved for women about to come into effect in the 2014 general elections, the situation could grow worse as the mothers, wives, and daughters-in-law of India are catapulted into the hustings. 'India's next general election,' warns French, 'was likely to return not a Lok Sabha, a house of the people, but a Vansh Sabha, a house of dynasty.'

A pair of brief but trenchant sketches of Sonia Gandhi and Manmohan Singh sets off a convoy of polished portraits, the strength of which holds the diverse strands of the book together. The double-sided method that French employs is to let his subjects, when they open up to him, speak for long stretches in their own voice, and to gird this with a few paragraphs of telling detail sourced from books, reports, and personal observation.

By throwing together the famous, the modestly well-known, and the anonymous in complex formations, French achieves an effect of intimacy with both the powerful and the powerless that justifies the word 'intimate' in his subtitle.

A Congress functionary in Uttar Pradesh, Yusuf Ansari, talks revealingly about the complexities of local politics and the weaknesses of the Congress Party at grassroots. The Indian telecom baron Sunil Mittal, head of Bharti Airtel, recalls, in a passage that is almost novelistic, wandering about street markets and trade fairs in east Asia in the 80s, looking for a business opportunity, before finally picking on phones as a growth area for the future. A fatalistic, enfeebled low-caste labourer in Karnataka who spent 21 months in chains after failing to pay off a debt to his employer puzzles over his own story after he is freed. Nor far away, in the buzzing metropolis of Bangalore, a construction worker takes French around the pathetic camp thrown together for him and his colleagues by a company erecting premium apartments.

In Kashmir, the lapsed terrorist and political protestor Shakeel Ahmad Bhat (aka the 'Islamic Rage Boy,' who made it to newspapers worldwide in 2007) speaks heartrendingly about outrages visited on his family by police in his childhood, a black-and-white world that he still inhabits despite, or perhaps because of, his troubles. Elsewhere, in the closing sections of a forceful critique of Naxalism, French visits Delhi's infamous Tihar Jail to meet one of the movement's masterminds: the recently arrested Kobad Ghandy. He asks the ideologue how he can continue to believe in Maoism after the arbitrary snuffing out of hundreds of thousands of lives in Mao's China. Ghandy acknowledges there have been mistakes, but valiantly defends the 'philosophy' of the movement. 'When taken to an extreme,' remarks French acidly, 'idealism is little more than a form of prejudice.'

French's ear for the exact registers and locutions of Indian speech, reported without smirks or condescension, elevates his work above most other books of reportage on India, eliding the distance from one's subjects that often appears in the work of other writers and turning his narrative into an impressive act of ventriloquism in the manner of Suketu Mehta's *Maximum City* or Sonia Faleiro's recent *Beautiful Thing*. Late in the book, an army officer is heard saying, as he describes a face-off between two colleagues, 'The 2IC, the second-in-command, started abusing him when he was giving a report, saying your mother, your sister and all.' In such instances, it is not the space granted to the subject as much as the attention to cadences of his voice that humanises him.

Elsewhere, French remarks, inhabiting an Indian idiom instead of merely marking it, 'Of the 38 youngest MPs, 33 had arrived with the help of mummy-daddy.' In a diverting passage on Indian school textbooks, he notes the resonant pan-Indian neologism 'byhearting,' or committing to memory. One begins to feel that working on India has made an Indian of the French. But this idea falls apart when, interviewing one of the administrators of the famed dabbawalas of Mumbai, who declares he won't speak without a fee of ₹5000, French asks for a receipt. Even so, *India: A Portrait* stands alongside the Australian journalist Christopher Kremmer's *Inhaling The Mahatma* and the novelist MG Vassanji's memoir *A Place Within* as the most linguistically rich and morally inquisitive books written about India in recent years.

## 56. How Charles Dickens Became Himself

*Becoming Dickens,* by Robert Douglas-Fairhurst (Harvard University Press, 2011)

That an increase in information does not always produce an increase in knowledge is one of the lessons of our overdriven age. But on a smaller scale, it might also be seen as one of the essential principles—and, when forgotten or ignored, criticisms—of the practice of biography.

The fundamental question of biography, or the art of the interpretation of one human being by another, has always been the question of the selection of detail, of the shape of significance. The massive biographies that take a cradle-to-the-grave approach to their subjects, pouring over the distinction of the person every factoid, reminiscence, contextual detail, and speculative whisper that can be gleaned from labour in the archives and interviews with stakeholders, might be seen as actually dodging this question, content to bask in the reflected light of the subject's name.

A more provocative approach to biography, particularly when applied to over-interpreted subjects, concedes that even a fascinating human being is not evenly interesting, that even in the richest of lives there seem to be periods when every hour is hot with ferment, followed by passages of consolidation, drift, torpor, even regress. If the reason we are attracted to biography is the allure of the drama of human self-fashioning seen from the inside, then these rewards can just as well be gleaned by the choice of a set of simmering years, and not the whole life.

The excitement of this method—that of the partial, but pointed, biography—is that it is defamiliarising, hovering not above its subject but beside it. In place of the person whom we believe we know, intimately, we are given a figure, answering to the same name, seen confronting a decisive problem in a way that will change both self and world. Through the verb in its title, *Becoming Dickens,* Robert Douglas-Fairhurst's study of Charles Dickens in the early years of his career, shows us what it wants to give to the celebrations of 2012, the bicentenary of Charles Dickens. It is a Dickens who, throwing himself into the currents of London in the 1830s, could not even be sure of his next move or source of income, much less that his name would still chime in the minds of millions 200 years after his birth.

Indeed, this Dickens was not even sure of the literary appeal of his own name, reaching out to the reading public, after the fashion of the day, through a pseudonym ('Boz'), and reserving his full name for contracts with publishers and letters to the woman he was wooing. Having served, in his teens and early 20s, as a clerk in London's teeming law courts and a parliamentary reporter for a newspaper, he thought of himself principally as a writer of scenes and sketches, holding on to a chamber in the courts even as he tested the waters of 'the most precarious of pursuits'—that of the professional writer.

Douglas-Fairhurst, a scholar of English literature at Oxford, brings to his book two very different strengths. The first is his knowledge of the literary and social world of 19th-century London, which is his area of academic specialisation. Indeed, with this book, he ties together within his own oeuvre a work about the greatest novelistic chronicler of the British underclass, Dickens, with the greatest journalistic chronicler of that class, the reporter and editor Henry Mayhew. Mayhew's massive four-volume work of reportage, *London Labour and the London Poor* (1861–62), came out in 2010 in a new edition abridged by Douglas-Fairhurst and introduced by him as 'the greatest Victorian novel never written.'

Dickens and Mayhew were both captivated by the clamour and despair of a London that, over the course of the 19th century, saw a demographic boom that took its population from a million to six million. (Mayhew writes in the opening pages of his fascinating study *Criminal Prisons of London* that 'in every thousand of the aggregate composing the immense human family, two at least are Londoners.') In so booming, the city itself became interested in measurement, statistical projection, and patterns of complex cause and effect, and cultivated an enormous appetite for newspapers and, indeed, novels.

Trawling the periodicals in which Dickens published his early, atmospheric pieces, Douglas-Fairhurst returns him to the literary-social frame within which he worked out his own method and the form in which he first published his novels—that of the serialised story, gathering momentum or changing direction over the weeks in dialogue with a feedback loop immediately generated by readers. He shows Dickens 'transforming himself from sketch writer to novelist, and from reporter to editor,' when these were not at all easy or obvious decisions, although they seem so now because ratified by time.

Douglas-Fairhurst's other talent is for a very attentive and sophisticated kind of close reading—for tracing the contours of Dickens' imagination and social vision through the analysis of sentences, phrases, even single words. This is invaluable, because if we are to understand through novels how people are marked by life, we need to pay attention to how characters and situations are marked by the text.

In his childhood, Dickens's father was briefly sent to prison for defaulting on debts, resulting in the young Charles having to work in a blacking factory while his sister continued to go to school. Observing the importance of prisons, real and metaphorical, to Dickens' imagination, Douglas-Fairhurst stops on a sentence in *Little Dorrit*. The protagonist speaks of life with her family in a debtors' prison and of how it has marked them forever, misting up memory of life before the prison and darkening any future that might lie after it: 'Whatever we once were (which I hardly know) we ceased to be long ago, and never can be any more.'

Glossing this remarkable sentence, with its exquisitely balanced clauses (two parts of four words each, then two parts of six, and melding past, present, and future tenses), Douglas-Fairhurst remarks, 'The prison expands to fit the size of the world, and the world contracts to fit the size of the prison.' Indeed, we might say about the work of literary criticism that it shows how a sentence, too, may expand to the size of the world.

Again, writing about the sprawl, even the excess, of narrative energy and colour in Dickens, Douglas-Fairhurst writes: '[T]he centrifugal force of his imagination, which could never resist spawning extra characters and narrative details, is always on the verge of escaping from the centripetal force of his plots.' But this very gracefully expressed idea, which serves in this instance as a compliment to Dickens, might also be applied to Douglas-Fairhurst's own book, and here it becomes a criticism.

The writing is sometimes self-indulgent—never more so

than in the opening pages, when, in setting up the idea of Dickens having many competing paths before him as he was 'becoming Dickens,' Douglas-Fairhurst supplies a portrait of an imaginary London in 1855 borrowed from a novel, *The Difference Engine*, published in 1990 by a pair of science-fiction writers. This is a very strained kind of counter-factualism, and it lays the ground for many later passages when Dickens disappears completely from view and the writing slackens from being centreless.

Douglas-Fairhurst's other unreliable tic is his penchant for supplying dialectical explanations for situations or states of mind, which is sometimes extended to the point of self-parody ('only by trying to lose his train of thought could [Dickens] find it, just as only by leaving his home could he enjoy returning to it'). These faults mean that *Becoming Dickens,* while frequently insightful, falls just short of being essential.

## 57. MG Vassanji's Hindus and Muslims

*A Place Within,* by MG Vassanji (Penguin, 2009)

The novels of MG Vassanji—born in Dar Es Salaam, Tanzania, to Gujarati immigrants in the middle of the 20th century, just before the wave of African decolonisation, and then from mid-life onwards a resident of Canada—are an embodiment of the winding path of history, of migrations that yield strange gains and losses. Vassanji's work often tracks those communities, or practices, made marginal or invisible by the march of time (as in his majestic novel *The In-Between World of Vikram Lall*, set among the Indians trapped between the political binaries of black and white in British-ruled Kenya), or individuals seeking to excavate their history and traditions in order to understand themselves better.

With his previous book, *The Assassin's Song*, Vassanji chose an Indian setting for the first time, giving us the story of the keeper of a Sufi shrine in the wake of the Gujarat violence of 2002. Now, in *A Place Within*, Vassanji considerably extends and deepens his engagement with the country of his ancestors with a memoir of his travels within India over the last two decades. One could say that Vassanji has taken the usual questions that inform his novelistic practice and turned them upon himself to ask: Where do I come from? What meaning does the past of my community hold for me in an increasingly rootless world, and what are my own responsibilities towards that past? This question also has a political valence because, historically, Vassanji's people, the Ismaili Khoja community of Gujarat, were practitioners of an 'odd, syncretistic faith,' combining elements of Hinduism and Islam.

The highlight of *A Place Within* is a long section on Delhi—really the many Delhis of history founded by a series of dynasties, each one replacing, but not quite erasing, the other. Some of Vassanji's legwork will come as a surprise to even those who have lived in that city, like myself, and thought they know it quite well. Vassanji shows how, for the longest time, Delhi was a city moving ever northward, from the Qutb Minar of Qutbuddin Aibak to the Lal Qila and Jama Masjid of Aurangzeb, till after Independence and the inflow of Partition refugees the process was reversed and it has begun to drift southwards again, 'towards the oldest Delhis and beyond.'

Whether quoting from the imperial historians Amir Khusrau, Alberuni, and Zia Barni, journeying to distant, unpromising Tughlakabad, or ferreting for Mirza Ghalib's house in Old Delhi, Vassanji is consistently interesting. Some of his thinking about the role of place in human experience is aimed towards the foreignness of what we easily assume to be familiar. 'It is always instructive,' he writes, 'to remind oneself of the obvious fact: The boundaries and names of many places are only recent in origin and often hide richer, more complex truths than one might imagine; the past then becomes inconvenient and slippery, far less easy to generalise.'

This idea of burrowing beneath the surface of the world's present face, along with a related desire for the redrawing or replenishing of the self, might be of thought of as the fundamental impulses of travel writing, and both are present in Vassanji's work. 'I have always felt a sense of wonderful elation while travelling in India,' he writes. 'It has helped that I remain, and indeed feel, communally anonymous and ambiguous, identifiable only by that cipher of my very Gujarati last name.' Elsewhere he writes, 'It's only oneself one ever discovers.'

Especially noteworthy is Vassanji's refusal to shirk the difficult questions of history: the fact that the Indian past is not just one of a fabled tolerance that might serve as a beacon for present-day discontents and that is codified in the idealism of our constitution, but also of considerable hatred and violence. 'No one who reads accounts of the early Muslim historians of India would fail to feel uneasy at the bigotry and the arrogance they reveal among the ruling classes and in the behaviour of the sultans,' he writes. 'They remind us, let's be honest, of Muslim fanatics of today. [...] Surely we must acknowledge this past, which casts a shadow upon our lives even today, when a politician can invoke it to create discord and mayhem in the nation. Surely we must ask if we can turn away from those aspects of it that disturb us while allowing others to move us. We must come to terms with it.' On the subject of the riots following the destruction of the Babri Masjid that broke out in India while he was visiting, he writes, 'I could not accept India's embrace and turn away from the violence. It must in some way be a part of me.'

While Delhi is a city that celebrates its great history, Vassanji finds no such consciousness in Ahmedabad, a city older than present-day Old Delhi, but one that seems 'uneasy with time and history.' Vassanji's search in Gujarat for the shrines and settlements of his ancestors, the Khojas, and for the icons and religious songs (or *ginans*) taught to him in the small Khoja redoubt of his African childhood, yields a section as moving and as beautiful as any of the great narratives of spiritual seeking in our literature. This, even though the author acknowledges that he is 'a rationalized being who is acquainted with spiritual longing but cannot yield to it,' cannot cajole and implore and supplicate before God as so many do. 'At any dargah, a shrine of this kind,' he writes, 'and even at a temple before a priest, I cannot but help but allow in me a solemn feeling, some respect and humility, for I stand alongside others in a symbolic place that in some manner reflects human existence and frailty, or smallness and exaltedness, and our striving for understanding.'

Roving beyond the usual roll-call of tourist destinations, Vassanji discovers at many religious sites, even in communally sensitive Gujarat, 'a certain laissez faire in matters of the spirit' that seems to be on the retreat. If he resists the labels 'Hindu' and 'Muslim,' he writes, it is not because they don't have an element of truth, but rather because they are 'too exacting, too excluding,' and they mask the extent to which the past is a foreign country. But how can one avoid these terms when they are such an essential part of our conceptual vocabulary? Vassanji chooses to remain a dissenter and explains the various implications of his position:

> I have already said that I find the labels 'Hindu' and 'Muslim' discomforting, because they are so exclusive. [...] I refuse to use them this way, perhaps naively and definitely against a tide; but I am not alone. I use the distinction of 'Hindu' and 'Muslim' only in context, and especially when it has been used by people for themselves or others, as in the Gujarat violence.
>
> So deep is the suspicion when one talks of conflict, that one has to state over and over that to describe the murder of a Muslim here is not to deny, let alone justify, the murder of a Hindu elsewhere, that a fanatic group does not represent an entire people, and there is no entire people, Hindu or Muslim anyway. Attempts to create them, of course, have always been there.

At the same time, Vassanji casts an astringent eye on both the excesses of Hindu chauvinism and the problematic tendency of a section of Indian Muslims to adopt 'a primary identity defined by faith, in a unity (the "umma") that transcends political, cultural, and ethnic boundaries.'

Narrated in the distinctive cadences of a novelist in possession of a secure and cogent style, and animated by a love of both language and place and a powerful appetite for the mystery and fugacity of the past, this book about coming home to India cannot but make a richer person of every Indian reader.

## 58. VS Naipaul's Library

*A Writer's People,* by VS Naipaul (Picador, 2007)

What is it that makes a writer's essays on other writers so interesting? Several reasons present themselves. One is *awareness*. Although they may not have a explicit method or theory of literature, writers enjoy a comparative advantage over literary critics because of their immersion in practicalities, their understanding that works of literature are made up of words and sentences before they are made up of ideas or themes. A second reason is *urgency*. Writers are what might be called proselytising readers. They typically have stronger likes and dislikes than the common reader, and the arguments they make in favour of or against books are weighted at a pitch we are accustomed to hearing only on big questions, like 'Does God exist?' or 'How can I save on tax?'. And this brings us to a third reason: *personality*. A writer's criticism is often a revelation of their own aesthetic, and all the more interesting for being so. We enjoy what a writer has to say about other writers because of the pressure of their own ideas.

Certainly the emphases of VS Naipaul's latest and perhaps last book, *A Writer's People: Ways of Looking and Feeling*, emerge directly from his autobiography and from his own efforts as a writer to present the verities of the world. In a series of shrewd, detailed, and rewarding essays on writers as different in time and method as Gandhi, Flaubert, Virgil, Nirad Chaudhuri, Derek Walcott, and his own father Seepersad, Naipaul teases out the ways in which their writing expresses an original vision of the world, 'sees' more and reveals more than conventional writing does.

Indeed, the verb 'see' is the word most central to Naipaul's understanding of literature, of the source of the power latent in writers. It can be found as early as 1964, in his assessment of Gandhi in *An Area of Darkness*: 'He looked at India as no Indian was able to; his vision was direct, and this directness was, and is, revolutionary. [...] He sees the Indian callousness, the Indian refusal to see.' It emerges in his admiring remarks about a trio of 19th-century French writers of fiction—Flaubert, Balzac, and Maupassant—made in a famous interview with Farrukh Dhondy in 2001: 'This imaginative writing enabled people to possess their societies. That's the most extraordinary gift that these writers gave people—the ability to see their societies.' The centrality of this verb 'see' in Naipaul's idea of a writer's work is echoed in a slightly different, more paradoxical, way by Proust, who also imagines the writer as a kind of optical instrument that clarifies both self and society: 'Every reader, as he reads, is actually the reader of himself. The writer's work is only a kind of optical instrument he provides the reader so he can discern what he might never have seen in himself without this book. The reader's recognition in himself of what the book says is the proof of the book's truth.'

True sight in literature, then, breaks past the veil of reality and of received thought. Naipaul's test of great literature through the book is not so much prose style (though naturally he has his preferences there) but something larger, more numinous: a quality he calls 'vision.' For him, how well a writer 'sees' is what makes his work forceful, ageless, truthful. Those who see clearly bring to their work some original perception of the world, do not merely imitate established forms, treasure

precision, avoid rhetoric. Bad writers are verbose and tend to over-explain; even worse, they are often intellectually dishonest.

For instance, Naipaul finds both good and bad things in Flaubert. He praises the style of *Madame Bovary*. Even though Flaubert's reputation is that of an ambitious, even self-flagellating stylist, the language of his great novel is 'plain and clean and brief.' Indeed, the continuous pleasure and surprises of its details are in stark contrast, to his mind, to the straining and languor of Flaubert's historical novel *Salammbô*. There, the novelist's determination to parade the fruits of his research 'sets up a barrier between the reader and what is being described.' The writing rings false because it is too detached, overstated, theatrical.

Similarly, Naipaul bestows warm praise—a Naipaulian warmth, still a bit cold by the general standard, but exceptional from Naipaul—on Gandhi. The *Autobiography* of Gandhi is 'direct and wonderfully simple'; the book is a masterpiece. Even Gandhi's petitions to the authorities were 'concrete and precise, without rhetoric.' But it is important to note, he reminds us, that Gandhi the writer is inseparable from Gandhi the man, the man who learnt from his labours to see. The young Gandhi, like the young Naipaul, left the settled moral universe and easy satisfactions of his provincial environment to voyage to England and seek a place in the world. Naipaul admires his diligence, his assiduous self-fashioning. Gandhi's travels, 'first to England and then to South Africa, made him see that he had everything to learn. It was the basis of his great achievement.' Naipaul compares Gandhi to the Buddha: 'Both these men make wounding journeys.' The reader may hear here the shadow of an allusion to Naipaul's own wounding journey from 'the periphery to the centre.'

As ever, Naipaul's sentences are tightly coiled and muscular: they seem to be revealing something even when Naipaul is merely summarising. His recapitulation of the movement of a poem by Virgil—one that 'celebrate[s] the physical world in an almost religious way…making us see and touch and feel at every point'—is as delectable as the poem itself.

The counterintuitive idea that a writer may gift his readers their own societies, the very world they live in and experience all the time, explains why Naipaul sees many societies, including present-day Indian society, as existing in a kind of limbo—because their writers are not good enough. In all of *A Writer's People* he is never more acerbic than in a short coda about the state of literature in India. 'India has no autonomous intellectual life,' he huffs. 'India is hard and materialist. The most important judgements of an Indian book continue to be imported… literary criticism is still hardly known as an art.' All the qualities that Naipaul considers necessary in an evolved civilisation, such as 'identity and strength and intellectual growth,' are to his mind still nascent in India.

We have heard these complaints from Naipaul before; if all he did here was repeat himself, his book would have been tiresome. Thankfully, *A Writer's People* is more appreciation than obloquy. The beautiful opening chapter, with its magisterial sentences wandering between school, family, society, slowly opens a window on the provincial and suffocating world of 'the small place I grew up in,' Trinidad in the 1940s. The buying of books was seen as a luxury, a fancy: 'Though as a writer I was to depend on people buying my new book, that idea of book-buying as an extravagance stayed with me for many years.' It was in this world, yet to arrive at a proper understanding of itself, that a young poet called Derek Walcott announced himself. For a while, says Naipaul, 'I was full of Walcott,' but later he grew to perceive an element of distortion, of tricks used to generate sympathy, in Walcott's verse.

Here, as elsewhere in the book, autobiography and literary observation advance hand in hand. A chapter on Anthony Powell is inlaid with memories of life in England in the 50s and the years spent making a living from book reviews and work at the BBC. Naturally, I especially enjoyed a section in which Naipaul recalls the years he supported himself by reviewing books. The concerns of this passage are things like word counts, the ways of literary editors, factions and petty rivalries, the pleasure and the dread of seeing oneself in print. All very mundane, except to the writer who must accept being bound by them before he is free to see.

## 59. EE Cummings's Tumbfalling Prose

*Eimi*, by EE Cummings (Norton, 2007)

In Michael Schmidt's enthralling survey of the length and breadth of English poetry, *Lives of the Poets*, the writer of such famous poems as 'Buffalo Bill's/defunct,' 'since feeling is first,' and 'somewhere i have never travelled' is given this amusing introduction: 'Edward Estlin Cummings was born with capital letters in 1894, in Cambridge, Massachusetts.' But even if he was born with capital letters and had to stay that way all his life, in his own poems Cummings (this was the most prominent of all his rejections of typographic convention) always used the first-person pronoun in the lower case. As he joked in a letter to his mother in his 30s, 'I am a small eye poet.'

Two of those small i's can be found embedded in the title *Eimi*, one of two large and rambling prose works Cummings wrote in his youth, now reissued after nearly 50 years. *Eimi* is an account, in diary form, of a five-week journey made by Cummings to the Soviet Union (in the wake of other American writers such as Dos Passos and Dreiser) in the spring of 1931. There is of course no word like 'eimi' in the English language, but Cummings liked to get syllables to ring and resonate, and his title permits all kinds of interpretations: exuberant ('Hey, me!'), quizzical ('Eh—me?'), or even an echo of 'enemy,' which is what the Soviet regime no doubt classified him as after he was done with his mordant survey of that country.

At the time of Cummings's journey to Russia, America was still struggling with the aftermath of the Great Depression.

Conversely, Russia's new Communist regime had the best reputation and the best press it ever enjoyed. It had the admiration and support of intellectuals of a socialist or utopian bent the world over, and its vision of an all-powerful state leading society towards a radical classlessness (an echoing word that might have come straight from the Cummingsian lexicon) and a planned economy supplying the needs of every citizen seemed like a powerful rebuke to the reactionary practices of the West.

Cummings, however, was an implacable opponent of collectivism. If anything, his poetry expresses an exuberant individualism that borders on the anarchic. But the political critique of *Eimi* is made implicitly, through the use of different registers of language. The narrative enacts a linguistic clash between the whimsical, free-spirited tone of the 'i' or 'me' and the joyless theories and formulations of the Soviet state, parroted by its sympathisers and members of the Russian intelligentsia.

In the early chapters of *Eimi,* the narrator arrives in Moscow and checks in at the Hotel Metropole, where he meets a fellow American now settled in Russia who, in a mock-heroic allusion to the Divine Comedy, is given the appellation 'Virgil.' In reality 'Virgil' was Henry Wadsworth Longfellow Dana, grandson of the famous American poet and an ardent admirer of the Soviet experiment. 'Mymymymymy,' gushes the starry-eyed Virgil, 'How I envy you. Seeing Moscow for the first time….'

Virgil takes Cummings around the city: on their wanderings they take in various sights and scenes, watch proletarian plays (Dana was a theatre professor), ingest uniformly bad food in restaurants, and attempt to call on Maxim Gorky, 'the world's foremost proletarian of letters.' They meet intellectuals who live in various states of ideological servitude, and who call up the 'comfortable minds' of Cummings's poem 'the Cambridge ladies who live in furnished souls.' These 'unmen,' as Cummings piquantly calls them, address the poet as 'Comrade Kemminkz' and justify 'from soup to nuts the ways of Marx to man.'

None of this is reported in a conventional manner. In

prose as much as in poetry, Cummings's lines are a vehicle for typographical leaps of daring, experiments with and distortions of, syntax. Even at its most controlled, it is distinctively a poet's prose, looking to forge a new sound from language. Nouns, verbs, and adjectives are always forming cliques instead of lining up in the accepted fashion: on a street the narrator notices 'listless dinky runningnose children'; switching rooms in the hotel, 'I pluck yank jerk and twitch possessions here there and nowhere.' Words are broken up by dashes and semi-colons, and neologisms explode on every page, such as a man who, beautifully, 'siftdrifts' towards the narrator at a party (that is, both drifting amongst people and sorting through them for interesting ones at the same time), or a group of people who emerge from a tram 'tumbfalling.'

Cummings' poetic reputation has waned from the high of his last years, when he used to leave his readings, rockstarlike, by a 'secretbackentrance.' Yet he still has his admirers, and his words turn up in all kinds of unusual places (most recently in Nikita Lalwani's Booker-shortlisted novel *Gifted*, which quotes the line 'nobody, not even the rain, has such small hands'). The republication of *Eimi* revives a fascinating part of the oeuvre of a poet perhaps more talked about today than read.

## 60. Kafka Against Kafka

*Dearest Father*, by Franz Kafka, translated by Hannah and Richard Stokes (Oneworld, 2009)

The correspondence of writers and artists is often a neglected part of their oeuvre, thought to be of interest only to scholars and specialists. But in truth, the letters of a writer or thinker can often supply a more lucid illustration of their life and work, and the relationship between the two, than most biographies can. Sometimes, the letters themselves can approach the depth, complexity, and tension of great art. *Dearest Father*—the text of a letter written by Franz Kafka to his father Hermann in 1919, a few years before Franz's death—is one such work.

It is already a commonplace that Kafka is one of the most complicated, tortured, and inscrutable spirits of world literature. In *Dearest Father,* we find the man himself attempting to provide a full account—almost a self-defence—of how he came to be so. In Franz's view, from the early days of his childhood onwards, it was his father's arrogance, abrasiveness, and contempt that stymied his progress at every turn. His long letter might be imaged as a set of concentric circles, evoking the particularities of Kafka's relationship with his father, then the general nature of childhood and parenthood, and finally human nature itself.

One of the letter's attractions is the way in which the son's sufferings are not only described in great detail, but actually become manifest through the very style of Kafka's prose, through the contortions of his sentences. 'Dearest Father,' the letter begins, 'You asked me recently why I claim to be afraid of you. I did not know, as usual, how to answer, partly for the very reason that I am afraid of you...' We learn that Kafka always stutters and fumbles when trying to hold his own against his father, which is why he has chosen to express his thoughts in writing.

Moving from one incident to another, one feeling to another, the 36-year-old son—sickly, self-conscious, and indecisive, in stark contrast to his vigorous, self-assured, and authoritarian father—explains how the older man's behaviour 'damaged me on the inside.' Although Hermann rarely ever beat his children, his constant threats of corporal punishment reduced the child Franz to a state of submission and abjectness. Later, the older man sought to fashion the younger after his own image by force, not realising that he was cut from totally different cloth.

Whenever Franz took some initiative, his father's contempt was absolute; when Franz made friends, his father made disparaging comments about them ('He who sleeps with dogs wakes up with fleas'). Finally, and most disastrously of all, when the son sought his independence and escape by deciding to marry, Hermann reduced him to a wreck by implying that he had foolishly succumbed to the wiles of a low woman.

'I was no real match for you, you soon disposed of me; all that then remained was escape, bitterness, grief, inner struggle,' writes Kafka. The general tone of *Dearest Father* is one of a helpless flailing in the face of a remote and unshakable power that is the exact existential condition of the protagonists of Kafka's novels, such as Josef K. in *The Castle*. Indeed, at one point Kafka confesses: 'My writing was about you, all I did there was to lament what I could not lament on your shoulder.'

But if we are left convinced about the atrocities half-consciously perpetrated by Hermann, we see no less clearly the extreme fragility and anxiety of Franz, a condition that turns all the colours of the world into grey. In closing, Kafka suggests to his father that although the problems between them are too many and too basic to be eradicated, his attempt to make a pattern of meaning out of them 'might comfort us both a little and make it easier for us to live and to die.' So we naturally want to know how the letter was received by Hermann.

But the most striking fact about the letter was that it was never sent. Perhaps the same fear and guilt exhibited by Kafka in the letter prevented him from sending it. He left the typewritten letter behind in a bundle of manuscripts at the time of his death, asking his friend Max Brod to burn them all. So, it is the reader today who has become the letter's real recipient—and it is up to us to bring about, in our imaginations, a belated rapprochement between father and son.

## 61. The Year of Reading Adam Smith

*Adam Smith: His Life, Thought and Legacy*, edited by Ryan Patrick Hanley (Princeton University Press, 2016)

The flight lounge was in Kuala Lumpur, the crisps were jackfruit, and my travel companion was Scottish and had been dead for over 200 years. I was on a trip to Vietnam. My cut-price ticket allowed for no checked-in luggage. The small bag lying by my feet was all I had.

Even pared to the bare essentials, though, there was room in my luggage for Adam Smith's *The Wealth of Nations*. This is one of the foundational books of the modern world. Every right-leaning person keeps quoting stuff about butchers, bakers, and free markets at you from this book, but no one actually seems to have ever read it in its entirety. Journeys are a good space for intellectual challenges. While in the skies and then abroad, I wanted to break the Smith barrier.

Taking books on vacation with no chance of any substitutes is tricky business, but the gamble proved to be a good one. High up in the peace of the clouds, down in the clamour of airport lounges, in the little cafés of Ho Chi Minh City offering jasmine tea and coffee percolated in phins, recumbent at night in the silence of a cheap hotel room, I read Smith's magnum opus with pleasure—and a steadily escalating admiration for his intellectual ability, stealthy empathy, and rhetorical flair. Two weeks later, one journey ended, but another was just beginning: one of the great literary love affairs of my life.

The first thing that strikes the reader about Smith is that he is so much more than even his admirers make him out to be. Often, his arguments can't be reduced to a precis: as with the great novelists, you have to immerse yourself completely in his long, delicately weighted sentences and paragraphs to catch the full drift of his meaning. Then, when you hear other people interpreting and paraphrasing Smith, you always find yourself saying, 'Yes, but….' He is like that charismatic friend that everyone in a group fights over, everyone thinking 'I know him best.' What is so engaging about Smith is not so much his matter as his manner. He is a writer of great clarity and courtesy. Brilliantly and convincingly, he first recapitulates the arguments of his opponents—cheap point-scoring is not his thing—before just as dexterously undermining and refuting them. Once you pick up the sound of his voice, you hear it in your head all day long like a tune. Further, Smith comes across as exceptionally well-adjusted. He is a realist who never seems to lapse into cynicism or dogma, a worldly man who insists, nevertheless, that life demands from us some grand ideal and commitment, even sacrifice. He seeks the continuous advance not just of markets but also morals; not just knowledge, but self-knowledge. When you read him, you feel that, somewhat like Gandhi, he seems to know you even better than you know yourself, to believe in you more than you do yourself.

And last—and this is something no scholar of Smith ever tells you—the great Scotsman can often be laugh-aloud funny, as piquant as an Indian grandmother observing modern life from a charpai. Has anybody ever managed to match the truth and tartness of Smith's characterisation of love as 'the passion [that] appears to everybody, but the man who feels it, entirely disproportioned to the value of the object'? There is a discussion of value here, as befits someone known for his attention to costs and measures. But one also senses a distinct sympathy, even admiration, for the deluded.

That cracking sentence appears not in *The Wealth of Nations*, but in *The Theory of Moral Sentiments*. I believe you must read both these books, or none at all. *The Theory of Moral Sentiments*, Smith's other masterwork and one that describes the peculiarities and potential of man as a social and ethical creature, was long given short shrift by economists, who built their representations of Smithian thought—and applications of it to present-day economic debates—entirely upon the argument of *The Wealth of Nations*. *Moral Sentiments* was written when

Smith was just 36 (he published *The Wealth of Nations* when he was 53), and Smith remained so engaged with its argument that he revised and expanded it through his lifetime, publishing a final edition just before his death in 1790. One might even say, as a riddle, that Smith's first book was also his last; for diversion in between, he shot off *The Wealth of Nations*.

Yet it is the book in the middle that immediately caught the imagination of the world—and not without reason. *The Wealth of Nations* is still the core of Smith's intellectual achievement, a touchstone in the human effort to understand how our material lives cohere and interlink on the macro level. And it is especially worth reading today, when capitalism—Smith himself never actually used this word—is under attack from many sides. Partly this is because it seems to have been taken over (as Smith himself feared) by elites who want more to capture than to produce wealth. But also, a combination of rising inequality, static real wages, and an explosion of human desires linked to mass media and consumer culture have made both white-collar and blue-collar workers in the developed world unbalanced and resentful. In fact, the journey from poverty to (relative) prosperity described in *The Wealth of Nations* is a story Indians today can appreciate better than most Europeans, for it is the great Indian story of the last 25 years.

The core of *The Wealth of Nations* is devoted to Smith's magnificently comprehensive description and original and frequently counter-intuitive defence of what he called 'commercial society.' This was the newly emerging 18th century world order in which the eternal human need 'to truck, barter and exchange' (Smith loves aggregating verbs) was taking a new form, very different from the top-heavy economic order of the feudal world, with its lords and vassals.

Smith, at heart an egalitarian if not exactly a democrat, greatly approved of this transition and gave it the intellectual steel frame it needed. With a wealth of rigorous and ringing detail, he showed that simple price signals in a market could deliver justice, and stimulate an economic energy that no regent or government could fashion or force. If economic actors were allowed to work in their self-interest, the 'invisible hand' of the market would likely allocate goods and prices in a way that could serve the interests of all. A liberal new economic order would provide rich rewards for the exercise of the virtues and habits that Smith admired the most: prudence, thrift, and industry. (Smith is actually not a big one for spending money and—readers of *The Theory of Moral Sentiments* will find—is even sceptical of the idea that great wealth is conducive to happiness.)

But there is more to Smith's theory than just a defence of the profit motive as an engine of growth. As the Smith scholar Ryan Patrick Hanley neatly puts it, Smith saw that 'commerce substitutes interdependence for direct dependence and makes possible the freedom of the previously oppressed.' In commercial society, the shape of material life begins for the first time to lean towards economic independence and political freedom even for the meanest labourer. The gates of commercial society open out, eventually, onto the garden of freedom (a difficult, challenging freedom) and democracy.

Sadly, though, over the course of 200 years after his death, for a wealth of reasons, Smith was co-opted as the father of pure capitalism, insisting, apparently, on the primacy and inevitability of self-interest in all human dealings, and on the need for governments to allow the market mechanism to determine how resources in a society are allocated (and by extension, how social problems are resolved). Smith's famous sentence about butchers, bakers, and brewers working not out of a sense of benevolence for others but from a regard to their self-interest was taken as the touchstone of his thought.

But no one who reads *The Wealth of Nations* can fail to see that this is a very distorted—one might even say self-interested—view of Smith. Amartya Sen, who has done as much as any other modern scholar to draw attention to the complexities of Smith's world view and rescue him from the clutches of free-market fundamentalists, gets Smith's view of the powers and limits of the market exactly right in his contribution to a new book of essays on his life and work. 'It would be hard to carve out from Smith's works,' writes Sen, 'any theory of the sufficiency of the market economy (as opposed to the necessity of markets). He sought substantial supplementation of the market mechanism, though he would not endorse any proposal to supplant it.'

Even the invisible hand of market forces needs visible hands to supplement its work in a just society. One of the surprises of *The Wealth of Nations*, I found, is how often Smith sides with the interests of labourers against those of merchants and manufacturers, and proposes and delineates a system of moral reasoning that will frame and discipline the very markets whose virtues he extols.

When I was done with *The Wealth of Nations*, I moved on to *The Theory of Moral Sentiments*. I had by now become convinced of Smith's great qualities not just as an intellectual guide, but as a travel companion. Every time I packed a suitcase, which was often, he was the first thing I threw into it after my toothbrush and notebook. Whenever my days became disordered, whenever I woke up with a hangover, or drooped with a sense of inertia, I had only to read two or three pages of his even, tranquil prose to set the world in order again. ('Happiness,' he states quite simply at one point, 'consists in tranquility and enjoyment.') Smith was 36 when he published this precociously wise book—the same age that I was now when I was reading it. It took me many more months to read than *The Wealth of Nations*, for I read it as slowly as possible, realising that when I was done, there would not be much more of Smith left to read.

Trade and economic activity barely appear in *Moral Sentiments*. Rather, Smith is found here contemplating another kind of economy: the economy of our emotions and the moral exchanges of our lives in society. For Smith, man is fundamentally a social being, embedded in multiple networks that answer not just his material needs but his need to be loved and respected. Or, as the Smith scholar David Schmidtz puts it, 'a human life is a social life.'

Yet this does not take away from the inescapable truth, Smith observes, that we are violently, spontaneously, self-centred. We feel our own pleasure and pain, our own joy and sorrow, much more deeply than that of others. A failed investment, an unrequited love, even a sprained ankle (or, if you are a writer, a herniated disc in the spine) gives us much more grief and engages us more deeply than a war in which thousands lose their lives. Our instinctive reaction to any new development is to think, 'What does this mean for me?' If possible, we would always privilege our own self-interest over that of others—until we come to realise that others must feel exactly the same way about themselves.

Where do we go from here? It follows that to form a truthful understanding of reality, we need to be able, habitually, to see ourselves as 'an impartial spectator' would. 'The natural misrepresentations of self-love,' writes Smith, 'can be corrected only by the eye of the impartial spectator.'

Here we arrive at one of Smith's greatest concepts, perhaps even more central to his thought system than that of the invisible hand (which phrase, after all, appears only twice in his work). The impartial spectator is something more than just a conscience; it is an emotional rudder that keeps us balanced. By listening to the whispers of this invisible companion, we work out just how complex and peculiar and fallible we are; true selfhood requires continuous self-command.

Our moral sentiments are full of strange biases. Many of Smith's insights—for instance, that pain leaves a much more lasting impression on us than pleasure—have today become the staples of behavioural economics. To take another example, he observes that we are instinctively much more sympathetic to the woes of the rich than those of the poor, and mourn the overthrow of a king, although most of his material privileges remain unaffected, much more than the tragedy of someone going hungry. What we need to do, then, is to acquaint ourselves with the general terrain of our moral nature, and then use self-knowledge to compensate for our weaknesses and oversights.

Virtue, for Smith, inheres not so much in what we believe, but in how—and how much—we act. And here Smith issues a clarion call, a sentence one never forgets once one has read it, 'Man was made for action,' he writes, 'and to promote by the exertion of his faculties such changes in the external circumstances both of himself and of others, as may seem most favourable to the happiness of all.' Man's actions must be guided both by the invisible hand of the market, showing him opportunities for work and profit, and by the ethical promptings and expanding social imagination of the impartial spectator, 'the great inmate, the great demi-god within the breast.' The market can be man's friend. But he diminishes himself when he makes it his god.

It seems clear, when one has finished reading Smith, that it will not do to call him an economist. He is certainly one—maybe even the father of economics as we understand the discipline today—but he is so much more than that, and this very word is, like one of those human biases he describes, an unreliable road into his thought. He is also a moral philosopher, a historian, a literary critic, a student of linguistics. Even his economics might more properly be called 'humanomics'—this is the phrase used by the economic historian Deirdre McCloskey.

One morning in February 2017, I sat in my balcony in New Delhi, drinking coffee, and put my mark on the last page of *The Theory of Moral Sentiments*. It was over. A whole year had passed with Smith by my side. He had said his piece and gone. I felt enormous gratitude for everything he had given me. But perhaps, across a gulf of two centuries, I had been able to add to his own stock of capital as well. After all, doesn't he say in *The Theory of Moral Sentiments* that 'the chief part of human happiness arises from the consciousness of being beloved?

## 62. Finding Liberation with the Lotus Sutra

*The Lotus Sutra: A Biography,* by Donald S. Lopez Jr (Princeton University Press, 2016)

Every morning at thousands of Buddhist shrines in Japan—and at the Nichiren Temple in Queens, N.Y., the Rissho Kosei-Kai Center of Los Angeles, and the Daiseion-Ji temple in the small town of Wipperfürth, Germany—there rises the chant '*Nam myoho renge kyo.*' These six syllables don't sound so lyrical in translation—'Glory to the wonderful Dharma of the Lotus Flower Sutra'—but for those who utter them, they proclaim the enduring mystery, wisdom, and salvific power of one of the most important and ancient books of Buddhist teachings, the *Lotus Sutra*.

The lotus, which roots in mud, rises up through water, and raises its beautiful petals towards the sky, is the most ubiquitous of Buddhist motifs, an image of the ascent from the morass of worldly desires and suffering to beauty, peace, and virtue. 'Sutra' comes from the Sanskrit word 'sutta' or 'thread,' meaning a set of thoughts or aphorisms on a given subject. Since there is no written record of Buddhist doctrine from the time of the Buddha, the canon of Buddhist literature brims with hundreds of such sutras, which purport to reveal his true teaching.

The *Lotus Sutra* has a special place in the Buddhist canon. A lively, if often confounding, grab bag of parables and proclamations told in both prose and verse, it is rich in narrative pleasure and contains more braggadocio than a Donald Trump speech. ('The Buddha is the king,' we read at one point, 'this sutra is his wife.') Indeed, many scholars trace its self-promotional tone back to the era of its composition, when it had to establish itself within a crowded market of religious texts and sects in India. The nature of the *Lotus Sutra*'s enduring influence is taken up by the scholar of Buddhism Donald S. Lopez Jr in the latest in Princeton University Press's excellent series on 'the lives of great religious books.'

As with so many religious works from antiquity, the *Sutra* has a history shrouded in uncertainty. Even its authorship is a mystery. By the time it was composed in Sanskrit, early in the first millennium, the Buddha had been dead for 500 years. His striking message, at once austere and compassionate, offered a vision of liberation resolutely free of mythological content. The Buddha's eerily convincing diagnosis of the nature of human suffering and the way to transcend it had achieved a wide currency in India and had extended to China and Sri Lanka. But Buddhism had begun to break up into sects over divergent interpretations of the teaching.

The major schism was between the Hinayana and the Mahayana. The Hinayana school stressed the importance of monastic life as the only real path to liberation. Mahayana Buddhism, though, was much more worldly even in its quest for transcendence. Its hero was not the 'arhat,' or the being who has attained nirvana, but the 'bodhisattva,' the enlightened person who perceives the truth but stays behind in the world to help others across to the far shore of peace.

The *Lotus Sutra* is a classic (and cacophonous) Mahayana text. The book unfolds as a series of dialogues between the Buddha and his followers, many of them men of great spiritual prowess themselves. The text slowly and artfully builds to a revelation: that of the *saddharma* or true dharma. The Buddha reveals to his interlocutors that the 'threefold path' that he teaches in other texts—a somewhat arcane theory of different streams of learning and discipleship that open out paths to liberation—is actually something of a deception.

In truth, there is only a single Way. But 'this Dharma is indescribable/Words must fall silent.' (A very lucid account of the possible nature of this vision, which the Buddha says cannot be formulated in language, can be found in Heinrich Zimmer's 1952 book *Philosophies of India*.) The Buddha is so far gone, he explains, that had he taught such a difficult doctrine, he would have made himself clear to precisely nobody. Instead, he used the path of 'skillful means' to set people off on the path to transcendence, preaching to each person according to his estimate of their capacity for enlightenment.

With this masterstroke, the *Lotus Sutra* makes the goal of liberation at once more mysterious and more practicable (and, conveniently, knocks out other sutras competing for the attention of the faithful). The ultimate goal, so elusive, seems almost unattainable, but this makes every teacher a student and every student part of a great, throbbing chain of learning. Indeed, following the Buddha, any teacher must think seriously not just about knowledge, but about the right way to transmit it. In this way, the *Lotus Sutra* makes itself indispensable not just as a teaching, but as a tool of pedagogy. As Lopez writes: 'Perhaps the central teaching of the *Lotus Sutra* is to teach the *Lotus Sutra*.'

The allure of Buddhism eventually faded in the land of its birth, where Hinduism was too vivid and well-established to give way to this more introspective ideology. But the *Lotus Sutra* and other key texts gradually took root in others lands and languages. To the raft of entertaining characters found in the text itself—peasants and princes, initiates and religious masters, the Buddha as both truth-teller and deceiver—Lopez's book adds a cast of historical figures across two millennia united only by their passion for the book. These include figures as disparate as the 13th-century Japanese monk Nichiren, whose fire-and-brimstone message declaring all other Buddhist texts but the *Lotus Sutra* to be heretical earned him a long incarceration on a lonely island, and Gustave Flaubert.

The author focuses on two especially interesting lotus men, both of them translators. The first, the Buddhist monk Kumarajiva, lived in eastern India in the 4th century, and had the misfortune of being taken hostage by an invading Chinese general. Over long years as a prisoner, he picked up enough Chinese to translate the *Lotus Sutra* for the benefit of the Chinese emperor, already a devout Buddhist. Thus, the *Sutra* took root in China, and spread slowly through the Far East.

Just as fascinating is the story of how the book arrived

in the West. The Sutra was among a large cache of Buddhist manuscripts sent early in the 19th century to the French Sanskritist Eugène Burnouf by Brian Hodgson, an enterprising young officer of the British East India Company. Burnouf immediately set to translating it, noting, among other things, the book's 'discursive and very Socratic method of exposition.' His French version, published posthumously in 1852, made its way across the Atlantic, where it was picked up and circulated in translation by Ralph Waldo Emerson and the Transcendentalists, who regularly published scriptures from Asia in their magazine, the *Dial*.

Lopez's book shows us that translators are the unsung heroes of religious, as much as literary, history. Here, he has serviced the text with yet another sort of translation—this one to a general audience. The *Lotus Sutra* is a rejection, observes Lopez, of the kind of nirvana 'that is a solitary and passive state of eternal peace.' Rather, we are all travellers on a long road, even the enlightened ones among us; we cannot see through to the end right from the start, and must begin with small acts of compassion and caring. The inspiring message of the *Lotus Sutra* is that buddhahood is immanent in all of us.

# CONCLUSION

## The Classical Novel, on A Fall Morning in Iowa[11]

The IWP writer Chandrahas Choudhury was in a state of great distress as he walked with long strides from the Iowa House Hotel up towards the Old Capitol Building on the morning of Friday, the 9th of October 2010. He did not see—or if he saw, he did not register—the red and yellow leaves of fall that now rustled beneath his feet, and that only lately had been green leaves above him; nor, mired in his inner discontents, did he respond to the overtures of all the attractive girls winking at him from behind their sunglasses. The only two things in his sights were his destination—the Iowa City Public Library, where he was due to speak in a few minutes—and his dismay.

Because it was private and unspoken, his distress and the reasons for it could be picked up by nothing but fiction, which has a way of looking inside human minds that human beings themselves can never achieve, and this is its value in the world. To keep it short: Choudhury was distressed because he was unprepared. Or rather, he had prepared a lecture, but he had prepared wrongly, and so to the world it would seem that he had been slacking off and had not prepared at all. Only fiction

---

[11] And to conclude, a literary-critical short story. This is the text of a lecture I presented in the fall of 2010 at the Iowa City Public Library, on the question of the persistence of the classical realist novel as a template for fiction. Because it was written to be spoken before a particular audience, including some of the writers mentioned in the story, there are some local references and in-jokes. 'IWP' stands for the International Writing Program at the University of Iowa, one of the world's oldest writing residencies, bringing some three dozen writers from different countries to Iowa every fall.

(which excels at sympathy) would understand that he actually had prepared, only he had prepared wrongly.

What was his error? Choudhury had unfortunately long been misconstruing the nature of his invitation to speak at the panel. Instead of applying himself to the subject of the persistence of the classical novel in modern times, he had instead for weeks now, with the habitual carelessness and the susceptibility to exotic suggestion that was at the root of his nature, been writing up his thoughts on the abiding relevance of the classical *navel*. This was less absurd than it might seem. For thousands of years it has been believed in Indian yogic thought that the navel is the centre of the consciousness, and it is therefore central to any Indian poetics of fiction. Choudhury had imagined that the presiding powers of the IWP, with their usual exquisite delicacy and their characteristic attention to the local contexts of writers from different parts of the world, had been wanting illumination from his proudly Indian self on this hitherto obscure subject of the navel and its relation to fictional realisations of consciousness. But he'd been wrong. It was the novel they wanted to hear about, and he'd only realised this two hours ago.

In a panic, Choudhury had gone to all his friends at the IWP, hoping they might be of some help to him. This was because, on principle, he never wrote more than a thousand words a day, and now, with so much tension in the air, he couldn't possibly manage more than four hundred words—an introductory paragraph, perhaps, and a swift conclusion. But if his friends (all smart people) would be so good as to contribute to his project a paragraph each off the top of their heads, each one taking the argument of the previous one a step further, then he might have something.

However, his friends, in the usual manner of life, disappointed him deeply. The Israeli writer Touche Gafla offered no help other than playing Kate Bush's 'Babooshka' for Choudhury as a way of unlocking his creative energies; the answer to all the problems presented to Touche lay in some obscure rock song or another. The Mauritian Farhad

Khoyratty, a university professor by profession, said that, after a decade of dealing with truant students, he had no sympathy for ludicrous excuses about navels (which, with his characteristic cross-cultural agility, he said were also a kind of orange with their origins in Brazil). The Pakistani writer HM Naqvi was unable to help, because this was not the slender window of lucid time when he was both not asleep and not at a bar (it strikes the narrator that there are three negatives in this particular sentence, while there are four in the opening sentence of that latest and much-lauded exemplar on the classical realist novel, Jonathan Franzen's *Freedom*, and that if only one other 'not' could be found from somewhere, this would be a sentence not unworthy of America's greatest living writer of classical prose). And Choudhury found himself quite unable to approach the Icelander Solvi Sigurdsson, because it had been Solvi's birthday the day before and he hadn't given him a present. As for Pola Oloixarac...well, ever since Pola had started attending those belly-dancing classes with the other IWP girls, she wasn't the same person. If at all there was a subject on which she might now conceivably be of some help, it was that of the (now unwanted) navel.

So there was Choudhury, on his own, walking to the Iowa Public Library without a lecture in the bank, feeling like a character from one of his own stories, typically a person who is in deep trouble, and is feeling the pressure of time on his pulse. Indeed, the same pressures that proved so satisfying in fiction, and gave him the greatest pleasure to construct, proved now, when transferred to real life, to be agonising beyond belief. He resolved to be kinder to his characters from this point on, but then saw instantly that he was making one of those terrible conceptual fallacies that are always being pointed out by theorists of fiction: that of confusing characters in a novel with real people.

He also saw, though, that if there was any stream of literature—and we're talking here of fiction, poetry, drama, essays, and various avant-garde movements that have still to work out their identities—if there was any stream of literature that allowed for this kind of envisioning of a character as a living, breathing individual, as real and as present as one's family or girlfriend or cat, then it was the realist novel. It was also the realist novel that, for the first time in the history of literature, dared to imagine, at extraordinary length and in vivid detail, a protagonist who was typical and not exceptional, and yet highly individualised, presented in his or her everydayness. In other words, the distinction of the classical novel form was precisely that it allowed the reader, through the magic of the extended and elaborate illusion that it was able to spin from mere words and narrative sleight of hand and a wealth of sensory detail, to imagine that he or she was watching a life (or even living an alternate one) and not reading a book. The persistence of the form and its many conventions as a perennial template for fiction was connected to the fact that here, finally, was a form that allowed you to forget the very question of form. The sprawl of the classical novel was like a kind of comfortable armchair, or pint of AmberBock beer, that broke down the self-conciousness—the awareness that this was a book—that both writers and readers had previously brought with them, like a second skin, to the experience of literature.

Indeed, it seemed to Choudhury (as he nimbly avoided a frisbee that sailed out at him from somewhere) that one of the greatest and most durable satisfactions of the classical novel was the way in which it dramatised the passing of time. How the novel loved to play with time! Whole years could be made to pass with a single precise sentence, or the events of a single day could be made to fill up an entire book. Hundreds of things could be done with tense structures, cuts, and flashbacks, and at particularly delicious or fulfilling moments the reader, too, could stop time by closing the book for a few minutes. The realist novel gave both writer and reader the power to control time, which was denied to them by life.

Choudhury was by now consumed by realist-novel-love: it seemed to him that Dickens was walking alongside him, that it was Willa Cather just ahead, withdrawing some cash from the ATM, that Naguib Mahfouz was smoking a cigarette on the patio of the restaurant he was passing, and it was Irene

Nemirovsky who gave him a brief nod, from behind her sunglasses, as she passed. It seemed to him—oh, if only he had some paper at hand, to record these zinging thoughts that were now raining upon him like Iowan autumn leaves!—that the most characteristic experience of human consciousness was that of the workings of memory. The realist novel, through the deployment of repetition, echoes, leitmotifs, and contrast, allowed the reader to powerfully experience memory within the field of the literary work, suggesting a connection between an incident on page 20 to another on page 200, and thereby stoking, without a pressuring hand, emotions just as strong as those from one's own life.

In its attention to inwardness, to the patient tracking of the leaps and bends and flows in the thoughts of characters (thought Choudhury, lost in himself at a traffic signal), the realist novel schooled the reader in life. It taught him or her that that which is the most silent may yet be the most dramatic, and created in him or her a yearning for a greater engagement with the back-story of the world—or, if the world proved disappointing and somehow unnovelistic, then once again with novels. And further: although the realist novel strove to be a comprehensive representation of life, in the most capable hands it somehow proved to be an even stronger and more potent presence than the reality from which it mined its details, because, for one, it could eliminate the inessential, which life couldn't, and two, it could be inflected with the storyteller's personality and tone, and become not just the world but a way of looking at the world. After reading a good novel, the reader was always looking—for a little while at least, while he or she remained within the force field of the work—to heighten their own life to the same level of significance and meaning. The realist novel both bowed to life, and raised its music up a couple of notches.

Choudhury stopped for a moment outside the Public Library and contemplated turning the other way into Bread Garden Supermarket instead, where he could hide himself amidst all the shelves of soup and the rows of microwave meals, the racks of vegetables and the salad bar (and also perhaps get himself some lunch). He felt the sun warm upon his face, and looked up at a blue sky in which he could see precisely one cloud. He saw that his deeply dire situation was once again something that only the novel could adequately record: a state of contingency, of being alive at a particular moment in time, and feeling a particular set of pressures and sensations. The realist novel was both chronicle and snapshot, coiling its nimble fingers equally ably both around an era and upon a moment.

But what of it? All these thoughts were useless, useless. He saw that if only he had half an hour to sit down and write up the reflections of just the last five minutes (how silverquick was thought!), he would have, even at such short notice, made a success of his lecture. (Choudhury was given too often to thinking a little too well of himself.) But alas, there was no time. He was done for.

Choudhury was innocent of the fact that, all this time (and as you and I know), a story was hanging above him like a small cloud. (The first requirement of characters in fiction, of course, is that they never realise they are characters in fiction.) And the story was recording his thoughts anyway, in all their rambles and tangles, occasionally editing a word or eliminating a redundancy, because it wanted to be a better story than Choudhury was a thinker.

And Choudhury didn't know that, in the digital age, the story could take care of itself, and reproduce itself, and circulate itself—it needed no mailman, no agent, no publisher. Even as he walked into the hall where he believed he would soon be undone, the story was writing itself out rapidly on the blank pages of a handout, and when Choudhury glumly picked up the sheets to look at what the others had prepared, he was astonished to find that—astonished to find that!—*really* astonished to find that!—despite having done no writing at all, he was a presence in them and not an absence. Really amazed. Blinking in confusion, and eating two kinds of pizza, one slice above the other to save time, Choudhury took a few moments to register the amazing good luck of this day and, indeed, of his life.

He had, once again, been saved by a story.

# Acknowledgements

Many of the essays published in the book first appeared in a shorter form in newspapers and magazines: *Mint Lounge*, the *Wall Street Journal*, the *National* of Abu Dhabi, the *Observer*, the *Indian Express*, *Himal Southasian*, the *Scotsman*, *Scotland on Sunday*, *Open*, *Pratilipi*, and *Democratiya*. I thank the editors of the books pages of these periodicals for their custom, and for the many other small pleasures of literary life described in the introduction.

A shorter version of 'The Indian Novel As An Agent of History' was first published in India In Transition, a website run by the Center for the Advanced Study of India, University of Pennsylvania.

You already have to
read.' The relationsh
of books and thei
is not a functional o
the more casual, unco
never understands it
having some relationsh
that have come befo
germination of knowle
is actually already